ENCOUNTERS BY DESIGN
Strategies for Spatial Stories
by Atelier Markgraph

FRAME

CONTENTS

THE ATELIER IS A SPACE OF POSSIBILITIES. ALL OUR WORK IS ABOUT CONNECTING.

by Stefan Weil

In the beginning there was the idea to publish a new book. Our approach to this new book was to manifest our conceptual thoughts, professions and projects from the perspective of the visitors, of the benefits for the invited and public audiences. Since we are living in the age of experiences, this might be relevant.

Indeed, there were some discussions about a book as the right medium, the right statement, regarding digital and environmental issues. A book is a visual, haptic and tangible experience, a book is an established medium to distribute knowledge, so it has a relation to the things we develop in our studio, story-based spatial experiences. A book is also something that stays. I don't want to judge between a library and a datacentre; both are relevant in their functions and meanings. The idea of a book is still valid and will continue.

We believe that everything we do, has a growing relevance in how we are doing this. In its depth and precision in finding the right solutions, from the very first scribbles to the supervision and quality management to its completion. And in many cases, in taking care. Our work reflects our society, social issues, private and public spots, urban interventions, in most cases the staging of knowledge. Therefore we need a publisher with a global relevance, with the right contribution to the right spots out there.

With its nearly 200th issue as a printed magazine, FRAME has been my 'Bible' from day one. With FRAME Daily, the FRAME Awards and the FRAME ThinkTanks the publisher has also expanded its role in the digital and experience worlds. During our first meetings with Robert Thiemann, the founder of FRAME and his team we realised that there was a common

understanding in our philosophy, our roles and our thoughts.
And so we decided to work together to create a book in autumn of 2021, published by the great minds of FRAME.

The challenge from day one was to allow others to direct us, even the directors. To leave enough space for the other perspectives, for new points of view. New contexts, new values, new prospects. To leave enough room for the invited strategic and creative thoughts from abroad.

A great chance to discover and share new images and meanings in our work.

To create a concept for the distribution of our mission and our mindset into new territories, new audiences and new fields of interest.

This isn't just a new release from FRAME. It's the starting point of an ongoing collaboration between two companies that are learning from each other and can't wait to learn more.

THE GOAL IS TO STAY CURIOUS AND CHANNEL INDIVIDUAL PASSIONS INTO COLLECTIVE EXCELLENCE. WE THRIVE ON THE DESIRE TO SHAPE A POSITIVE FUTURE.

by Lars Uwe Bleher

Since my first encounter with Markgraph, I have loved the ambidextrous nature of the Atelier's approach of engaging in cultural activities and applied, commercial projects. Only recently I was asked by a museum director how we actually manage to achieve relevance in both fields. On the one hand, the two realms are perhaps not so far apart as one might think. On the other hand, our studio thrives on the holistic view of the world and on the fact that team members are allowed and encouraged to act in both spheres.

Over the years, we have had the privilege of dealing with an incredibly wide array of tasks which, at first glance, do not appear to have much in common. How does a TV broadcasting studio relate to a light rail station? Where is the overlap between a 3D atmospheric spatial identity for a global brand and an exhibition on the polychromy of ancient Greek and Roman sculpture? This variety of topics offer us insightful connections. By reflecting on our work and bringing it together, Erika and François-Luc have opened up new perspectives that will serve as a source of inspiration and a springboard for future endeavours.

Stefan, Tom and I did not invent the basic idea of the Atelier, our founders did. But we take great pride in reinventing and cultivating this approach, according to our individual focuses.

The four original founders remain an inspiration for us – Meinhard Hutschenreuther with his keen eye for detail and witty humour, Rolf Engel with his cosmopolitan, open and generous nature, coupled with the finesse of an ambassador, Roland Lambrette with his energy and irrepressible will to achieve the best, and finally Christoph Meyer, perhaps the most generalist of these four generalists, who in stressful situations is reminiscent of Quentin Tarantino's character 'Wolf' in Pulp Fiction.

As the current creative heads of the studio, we always ask ourselves whether the set task offers a good use of the studio's creative potential. We are not artists, but design and communication solution providers. In dialogue with our clients and future users, our teams look for new, unexpected and yet relevant contributions: an insightful perspective on a subject matter through a digital layer, a spatial translation communicating a philosophical theory, a novel approach to accomplishing a task.

We are architects of atmospheres, world builders, visual translators of complex issues, storytellers, knowledge providers. For our clients, we are a creative workshop, a problem solver and, at times, a challenging but crucial partner. 'Let Markgraph think about it...' That was probably the greatest compliment I have received as a representative of the studio. What could be a nicer job than to think about something for someone else, often times identifying a problem and then being trusted with the task of solving that problem?

We seek appropriateness and connectedness with contemporary culture, but try to stay away from superficial trends. In the studio, we want to cultivate a mindfulness and attentiveness that brings people from different schools of thought together and behind one idea, despite the hectic pace of everyday agency life. That is what we are trying to achieve as a collective. It takes so much more effort and energy to make something just a little better than the standard. We don't strive for that little bit better. We strive for excellence in the tasks we are entrusted with and create excitement with meaning, purpose and depth.

One of my teachers, Thom Mayne, founding partner of Morphosis Architects, describes the beginning of a project as 'blue sky thinking.' This openness in the creative process also characterises our studio. For me, the greatest joy lies in the beginning phase of finding the format – what are we actually doing here?

I was fortunate to start my career when dynamic environments were emerging and becoming possible through kinetic and software-driven spaces. In the coming years, these types of holistic experiences will become even more important for brands and institutions to communicate effectively. Every few years, format and typology evolutions lead to revolution and reinvention. It is up to the readers to decide which of our projects might belong to this category.

I am indebted to the influence of my mentors. On the most personal level, my father's impact is still the most relevant. He supports and encourages me 100 per cent and exemplifies how curiosity, excellent craftsmanship and a precise eye lead up to an unerring sense for quality and meaningful innovation. Through my parents, I have had the privilege to attend two very inspiring architectural institutions and was blessed with bi-continental education. The University of Stuttgart was an open field of the most diverse offerings of design activity at all scales. The University of Oregon, even then, was an architecture faculty focused on people, humanity and sustainability – non-competitive but still rigorous.

When I started my career, a visit to an exhibition about Ray and Charles Eames strengthened my resolve to approach my future field of work with an open mind. Teamwork, diversity, a non-dogmatic approach, openness to new formats; all these and other attributes from the Eames office can hopefully be found at Markgraph.

Today, I am beholden to answering the questions of my own students. It delights me when talents find their way to us during their studies or after graduation and enrich our studio with new impulses and influences.

What brings these people to our office? What is exciting and attractive about working with other disciplines on projects? Do people see it as an extension of their own expertise? Are they expanding beyond the traditional definitions of their role? Still searching for their place in the professional world or are they fleeing from the too-narrow creative corridors in previous jobs?

What connects many is the search for the new and a curiosity about what is to come, as well as the desire to help shape the future. Innovation is not to be misunderstood as technology, but rather as a mindset that covers the entire spectrum of our field of activity.

For many people, success means being able to do what they love to do. Architects like to design, solve spatial problems and realise projects. However, it can also be seen as having access to people who inspire you, challenge you and help you grow. The Atelier has provided me with all of these elements of success in abundance. We are more than a company. We are an organism, an agile construct, a greater idea – at times even a romantic ideal – fulfilling Markgraph's DNA of staying curious and channelling individual passions into collective excellence.

'IT'S KIND OF FUN TO DO THE IMPOSSIBLE.' Walt Disney

by Tom Schubert

One of the phrases that project managers hear at the beginning of a project is that they shouldn't start with the scissors in their heads too early. Creative people need freedom, have to be able to explore and take the wrong path in order to find the right one in the end.

Accompanying the creative process, enclosing it at the right moment, shaping it, giving it direction and marrying it with the planning and implementation-relevant process is an art.

High-flying ideas have to be continuously checked for feasibility, costs and time during the course of the project. Every new idea has the potential to jeopardise the rest of the process. The finely balanced network of budget, quality and deadlines is always subject to the stress test of customer contact and is also thoroughly scrutinised by our own colleagues.

At the beginning of the project everything is unclear. The briefing, the process, the result, the costs, the schedule, the technical challenges, the promised features that have never been realised before, the interfaces, the pitfalls. Actually everything is terrible.

But at some point, light comes into the darkness, something materialises out of the fog, the project becomes more tangible and therefore more manageable.

Realising a project at Markgraph usually means having a rough idea of the goal, without already knowing how to get there. For a long time, there is no certainty about what the final result is going to be. What you are sure about is the unconditional belief in the abilities of the team and the knowledge that working together we can solve even the most difficult tasks.

Many of our projects involve a level of complexity previously unseen. I don't mean to say that we only innovate or constantly reinvent the world, but the complexity never lies in a single feature, in one idea, in one design or in one technical innovation. The combination of all influencing factors, the clever merging of what is partially known and partially unknown is what makes it so special. It often requires courage, a willingness to tread new paths, to dare new processes, and to try new approaches. Doing so often leads to gains in knowledge that were never foreseeable at the beginning of the project.

When a project has survived the very first creative phase and is slowly entering safer waters, the real problems and challenges in the planning process begin. The complete planning of all trades must be coordinated, the interdependencies resolved and the legal and approval-related conditions must be met. At the same time, the creative process continues, content is created, designs are approved and changed, technical features are examined in the test setup and, in case of doubt, everything is turned inside out and changed – all in the interests of the project's success.

The moment of the opening, be it an exhibition, a fair, an installation or a permament exhibition, then becomes the focal point towards which one has been working. All the pain, the anger, the stress are forgotten. Melancholy sets in, relief, exhaustion. A wild potpourri of emotions. Then there's the post production hole and only when you've swam through that, the project is really complete.

In the course of my time at Markgraph, I have been able to support many different projects for many different clients. Each time the tasks and challenges were different, I learned something new in each project and over the years I have never been bored. Our work requires resilience, commitment, empathy, curiosity and humility.

Project work can also be compared to working on a 15th-century sailing ship. Somewhere up there must be India, calm seas alternate with storms alternate with calm, you have to constantly shovel water out of the bilge and nobody looks really healthy.

But in the end strawberry ice cream and kingdoms beckon...

INTRODUCTION

by François-Luc Giraldeau and Noor Al Qayem

When was the last time you walked into a space that struck you to your core, a space that elicited in you a deep emotional reaction? What was going through your mind? What stood out to you? Was it anything specific? A formal anomaly, perhaps? Or an experiential eccentricity that to this day, you still cannot explicitly comment upon?

Atelier Markgraph, a Frankfurt-based spatial communication studio, has identified an elusive niche that lies at the periphery of the design discipline, in which the team is clearly poised to succeed. Over the last four decades, AM – as we've affectionately started calling the studio – has brought to the fore a renewed creative agenda leading to new thinking, new strategies and new tools for innovation and discovery.

Multi-hyphenate in its ethos, Atelier Markgraph is composed of protean and digitally literate thinkers who scan the horizons for what lies ahead; emerging futures. AM is a terrifyingly democratic practice defined by its idiosyncrasies and enigmatic quirks. The studio operates as an investigative enterprise working in the gaps of the all-too-often limiting spectrum of the domain of experiential-oriented design, spatial branding and identity development.

Mostly focusing its attention on technologically mediated narratives, the German outfit sets out to enhance senses of immersion within a familiar world. Atelier Markgraph also strives to communicate novel perspectives by bringing out key layers of sensory engagements for exceptional spatial encounters. The audience's dynamic journey is thus set against this backdrop of creative energy and romantic zeal.

Encounters are casual and/or unexpected convergences that happen all around us; their presence is as prolific and impactful as the decisions we make. We make over 30,000 decisions on a daily basis; we make them with assertive intention; in other words, we make them count. Then there are the encounters we face every day. Whether we are struck by the beauty of the sky, the need for reassurance in a broken world, the whisper of a fond memory or the fair touch of a kind word; we afford these just as much cognizance, both consciously and subconsciously.

AM understands that powerful stories lie at the heart of any compelling reciprocal actions between humans or between humans and objects in space. Expressing a brand's spirit is thus about delivering narratives that give shape to both significant and personal moments, if only for a fleeting, pixelated second.

Supported by case studies from the Atelier's extensive portfolio, the following pages are structured around different types of encounters, from their conception through to their realisation, implementation and reception. Encounters can be interfacial, they can also be poetic, patterned, friendly, mobile, tectonic and even process-based in their expression. This book consists of a collection of thought-provoking essays offering across seven chapters candid yet practical insights into their design and the many ways they shape our experiences, our stories and the spaces we converge in. The projects featured in this volume are classified on the basis of their most evocative conceptual features, properties and the types of encounters they seek to make possible in relation to their context; the spirit and substance of their association are thus non-traditional in their very form.

We've devised new, non-hierarchical 'families' of projects which reflect intangible features, such as parameters, traits, qualities, effects, ontological attributes, etc. The unexpected nature of these novel groupings is designed to highlight Atelier Markgraph's eagerness to leverage encounters to create vividly immersive and engaging holistic experiences where the real and the virtual become inextricably intertwined. This cluster-like organisation also calls attention to AM's genuine desire to craft spatial stories that are not only rooted in the contemporary moment but that are growing within it. In doing so, we prompt and expose questions relating to rich, 'indirect' properties, as opposed to traditional, 'direct' ones. The aim was to formulate and then verbalise key aspects of the studio's projects that lie beyond mere material typologies. Not only do these aspirations leave us grasping to recognise the Atelier's projects as cultural programmers in an ever-changing world, but they also allow us to fully embrace how their observable features, both the constitutive (intrinsic) and external (perceived) ones, are tethered and inherently inspiring. Ultimately, this monograph enables us (as in you, me and everyone else) to engage with AM's work, both from within and looking back, from inside and out.

In 'Thresholds', attention is given to the interface condition and the ways it organises objects and subjects into specific, edge-defined encounters. Canon architecture tropes such as screens or windows are redefined and re-examined. In 'Spectres', different projects emerge as ghostly case studies that evoke fleeting, poetic or transparent settings for meaningful encounters. The chapter's premise is that to meet can also correspond to meeting immaterially. In 'Patterns', swarms and repeated objects situate individuals within new constellations, enabling better ways of meeting. In 'Convivialities', the socialised nature of human encounters is put forward and celebrated, with many friendly, solidary situations. In 'Migrations', movement and dynamism inform the design of projects where encounters become fluid and forward; contemporarily open-ended and vigorous. In 'Plasticities', subjects meet sculptural bodies and environments which adorn or deform spaces in intricate manners. Finally, in 'Metabolisms', encounters are situated in a universe of pulses, cycles and machine-like transformations; users are involved in experiences of growth and immersive absorption within them.

Not unlike the editorial direction of this title, the case studies at the heart of this endeavour are experimental in their very essence. Their experimental status is however not solely defined by the use of emerging technologies, nor is it characterised by short-lived effects; it pertains as much to the idea of embracing marginality and counteracting the 'rules' of design order as to the engagement with digital advances. The Atelier is evidently adept at diverse disciplines and is committed to the merging of various exploratory methodologies, social constructs and interactions. The culturally responsive environments which result from their integrative proficiency target a wide audience and actively contribute to our understanding of complex processes which deal with a great diversity of materials, components, as well as with various cultural factors and systems.

AM has its finger on the pulse of trends as it cultivates an interest in culturally relevant topics, but has also a strong commercial acumen combined with a track record for partnering with forward-looking corporations. However, the studio's output finds its relevance through being the product of an instigator of change, progress and innovation. Atelier Markgraph pairs both material and immaterial design elements to orchestrate something truly scarce nowadays; a pleasing harmony. The team is asking questions that are often under-investigated.
How do we meet? How can a space tell a story? Who gets to be involved in

the narrative? How should we structure encounters? What does it mean to interact with a space; with an interface? The answers to these questions are ever-evolving, but one thing is true: Atelier Markgraph knows something about how to tell a story. This is theirs.

THRESH

i

as encou

OLDS

nterfaces

ters

EMOTIONS UNITED

Imagined in the context of the 2006 World Cup, *SkyArena* is a near hour-long light and media show transforming a 'financialised' skyline into a breathtakingly oversized canvas for the sport of football. **PAGE 53**

2006

ANI-MATED VISION

The IAA's 'Big Picture' is an installation of near urban scale, with massive screens which form a fun patchwork of moving images and, as such, evoke the show's theme of future mobility. **PAGE 44**

2019

2016

SIGNS OF TIMES

***Alles Neu!*, a retrospective exhibition at the Museum of Applied Arts in Frankfurt, features typefaces which constitute actual interfaces, classical and contemporary, between readers and the universe of words, with scenography work emphasising the significance of typography as a design interface.** **PAGE 40**

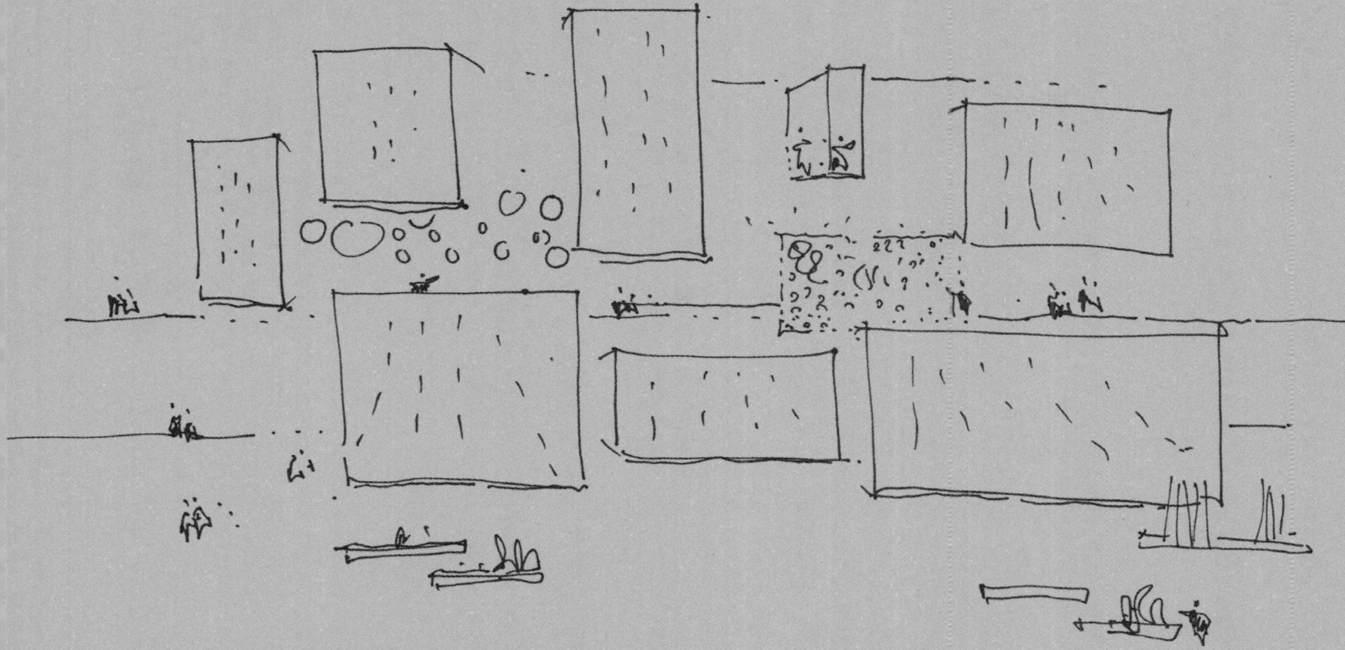

ABSTRACTED LANDSCAPES

The Ötztal tourist information centre creates new proximities through threshold encounters, with various experiential and interactive installations immersing visitors in the strikingly scenic qualities of the site's valley. PAGE 32

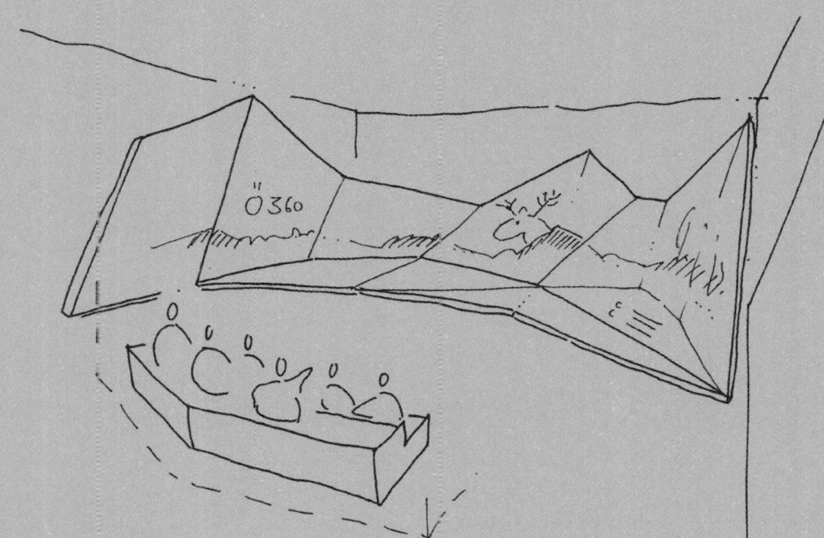

2021

2022

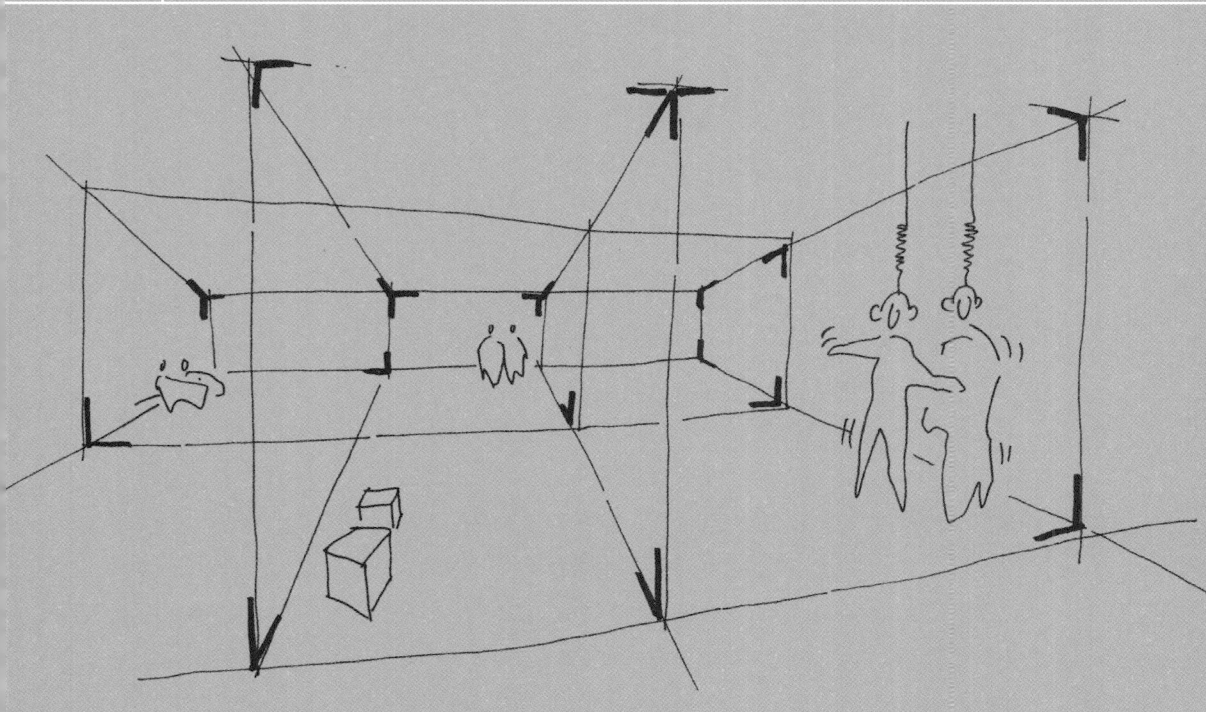

SPATIAL EQUALISER

The synthesised world of electronica is translated in Frankfurt's Museum of Modern Electronic Music (*MOMEM*), which features flowy signage, generous ramifying lights and dancing digital content, with panes of glass doubling as screens between museum and city space. PAGE 20

Shaping and building new environments implies doing so through intermediary means: interfaces correspond to the essential condition of space-making. Interfaces arbitrate; they make the built world that we inhabit, its limits, its walls, its intersections. They materialise information, knowledge. They share, hide, reveal. The formal scope of thresholds and interfaces can be conceptualised as a range of possible mediated experiences, where one encounters a space, an object, an individual, a city.

EDGE-DEFINED ENCOUNTERS ARE MANIFOLD; OUR AGE IS DEFINED BY THE OMNIPRESENCE OF SCREENS AND WINDOWS, OF SHARED SURFACES, MEMBRANES AND SHINY BORDERS.

This muddles a nuanced evaluation of interface projects – and interfaced encounters. In light of their omnipresence and habitual qualities, how are we to make sense of their features and effects? Our primary focus is to distinguish and qualify the characteristics which participate in situating the project within a family of thresholds; of margins, contours and appendages; of frames and slick planes. Varying in sizes and formats, the works presented in this chapter do in fact make up a family; they exist as many examples of the rules and diversity that organise interfaced encounters. And if the medium is the message, this family of projects speaks of eyes and bodies presented with possibilities and meaning in imaginative, edgy ways.

Spatial thresholds are places where two systems, subjects or organisations meet and interact; the assembly and provision of such thresholds is a craft which naturally informs the very meanings of encounters. As devices, they allow for the communication of independent systems, of diverse groups. Thresholds are promises of interactions; in the case of Frankfurt's new Museum of Modern Electronic Music (henceforth *MOMEM*), new interactions are created at the heart of the city. A brainchild of Atelier Markgraph and close collaborators – and pioneers of electronic music

Sparkasse
MOMEM
Museum
Of
Modern
Electronic
Music
MOMEM

Circular or rectangular, spinning or floating: 'alternative' museum displays by Atelier Markgraph show the dissemination of transitory images into open-air space. These eye-catching urban interfaces provoke and order the meeting and interaction of two parties: the art work (music, painting, photography and so on) and the general public of the city of Frankfurt. Spaces of spectacle have become essential in people's occupation of civic architecture; in our societies of entertainment and leisure, such spaces participate, to some extent, in formalising one's access – or right – to the city.

001 A series of stairs lead down to the museum's level, where one can also access transport facilities and other services. This leads to a high volume of pedestrian traffic.
002 The vibrant teal blue colour, found on the façade and overall signage in the project, leaks outside the building's boundaries and animates the ground of the multilevel plaza.
003 The continuous line forming the boundary of the closed space of *MOMEM* holds a double function: its glassy, ornate walls bring some natural light to the entrance during the day (out-in), and leak out lighting and projections towards the public plaza during the evening (in-out).

– Talla and Alex Azary, the *MOMEM* occupies a central yet challenging location; nestled among the tightly packed urban fabric in a sunken passage. Its façade, signage and emitting sounds interface with the flow of descending and ascending pedestrians. Canon architecture tropes have a natural affinity with the art they showcase; the synthesised world of electronica is translated in the museum's generous ramifying lights and dancing digital content. Large panes of glass double as screens, projecting these lights and digital dances onto the partially underground square. Glowing green-blue beams, animated videos and billboards, trancey music are many of the distinct elements that mediate the intramural environment of *MOMEM* with the outer civic life of Frankfurt. The project captures something of electronic music and screen media's unique ontology, inasmuch as it overtly sways, oscillates, updates its content. It catches unsuspecting bystanders' attention through its various fluctuating interfaces.

Traditionally, museums were opaque, sturdy strongholds of art, objects and other valuable samples that made up the cultural and natural world of men. Their stone or brick walls, high and thick; their entrance, elevated and grand; their convenient placement at the end of an axis: these features spoke of an architecture that cut off its content from the mundane outdoors, thus signalling intents of preservation and exclusiveness. Times have changed, and

MUSEAL INSTITUTIONS ARE NOW GRIPPED WITH THE DESIRE TO 'DEMATERIALISE' THEIR WALLS, ENGAGING A WIDE AUDIENCE THROUGH A MULTIFORM ARRAY OF MEANS.

MOMEM is an interesting actor in that lineage – indeed, its key content isn't material per se. This encourages design attitudes in which exhibited pieces are presented beyond the walls of the museum. Electronic music's performative power is to be experienced by many; so are the visual and haptic elements that participate in realising this performative power.

002

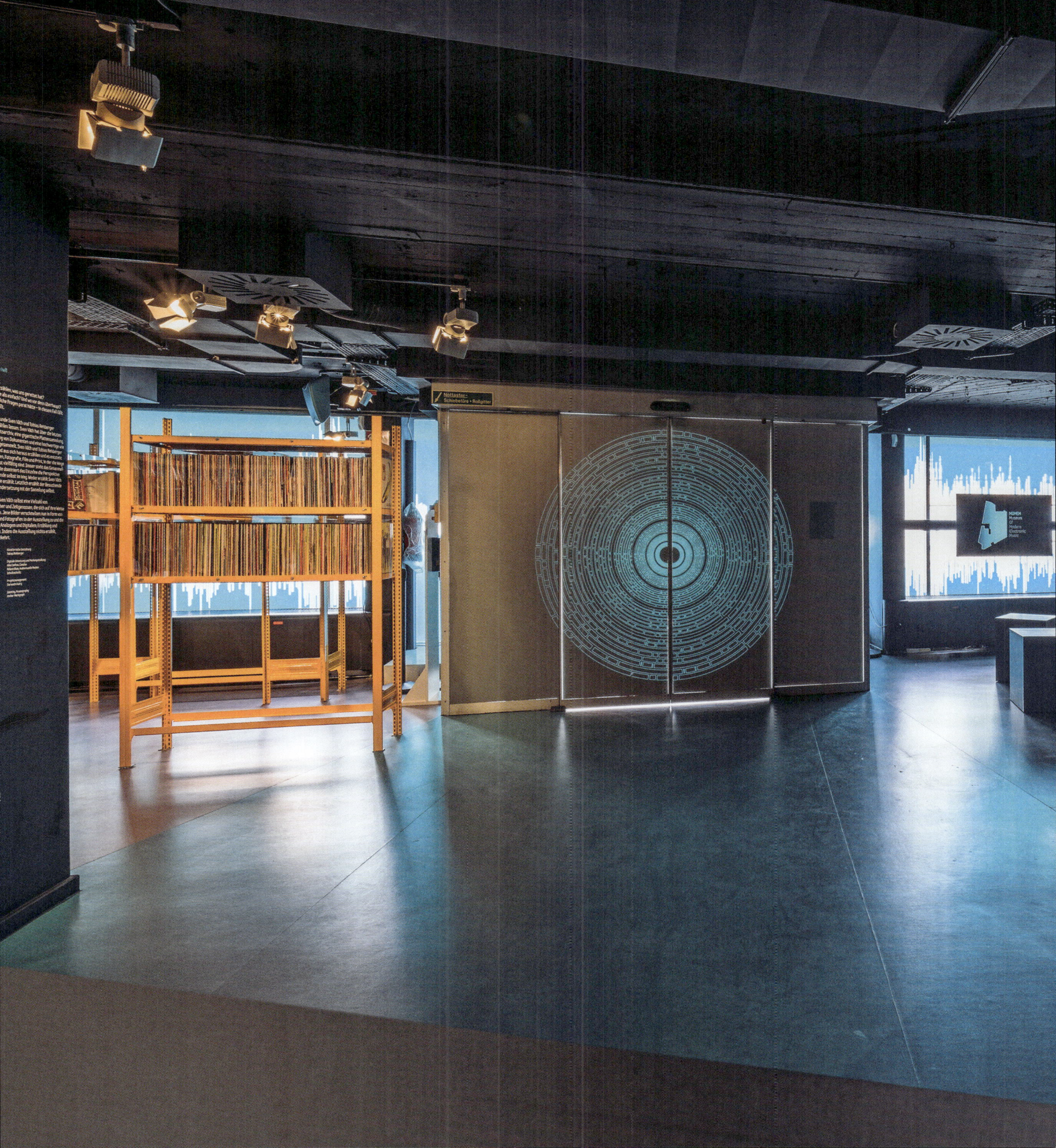
Nottaster:
Schiebetüre + Rollgitter

AG
ONY

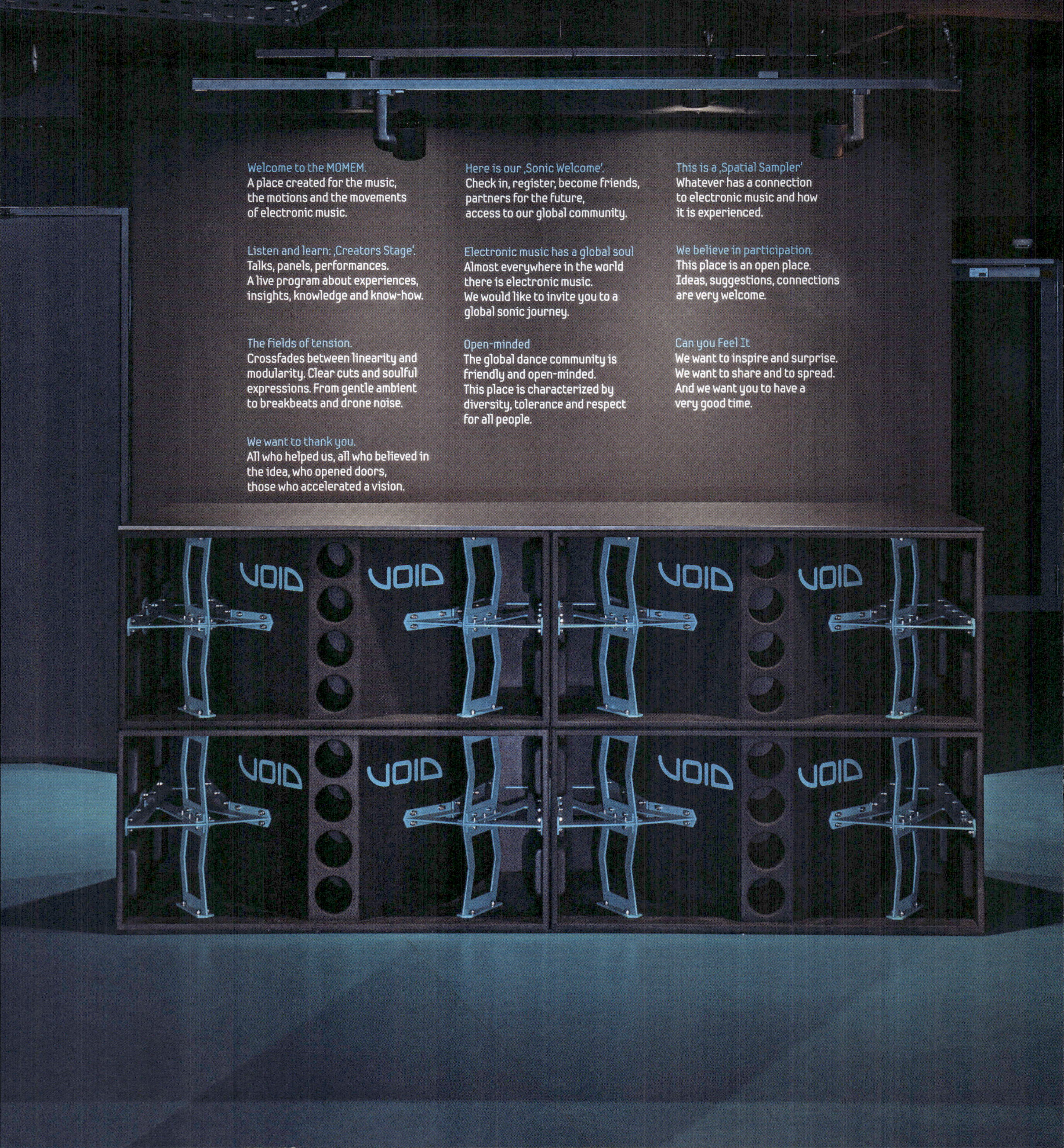
Welcome to the MOMEM.
A place created for the music,
the motions and the movements
of electronic music.
Listen and learn: ‚Creators Stage'.
Talks, panels, performances.
A live program about experiences,
insights, knowledge and know-how.
The fields of tension.
Crossfades between linearity and
modularity. Clear cuts and soulful
expressions. From gentle ambient
to breakbeats and drone noise.
We want to thank you.
All who helped us, all who believed in
the idea, who opened doors,
those who accelerated a vision.
Here is our ‚Sonic Welcome'.
Check in, register, become friends,
partners for the future,
access to our global community.
Electronic music has a global soul
Almost everywhere in the world
there is electronic music.
We would like to invite you to a
global sonic journey.
Open-minded
The global dance community is
friendly and open-minded.
This place is characterized by
diversity, tolerance and respect
for all people.
This is a ‚Spatial Sampler'
Whatever has a connection
to electronic music and how
it is experienced.
We believe in participation.
This place is an open place.
Ideas, suggestions, connections
are very welcome.
Can you Feel It
We want to inspire and surprise.
We want to share and to spread.
And we want you to have a
very good time.
VOID

004 The interior lighting effects, which can be programmed along different tints, intensities and rhythms, make for a markedly graphic experience of space; one which is patterned and dynamic.
005 Many rooms' layout, wall texts and furnishings are arranged in ways which facilitate public usage and information sharing: this reflects the *MOMEM* creators' insight that experiences linked to electronic music can be qualified through a variety of formats.
006 Sound earphones and VR headsets are strategically placed throughout *MOMEM*'s galleries. Visitors can enter 'music bubbles' at will, sampling the songs and mixes which most appeal to them.
007 Animated light effects increase in the evening, where the museum's vitrines become a main source of life. Moving content and colours make for a lively ensemble, on both sides of the vitrines.
008 Many parties and musical events are programmed throughout the *MOMEM*'s yearlong season; local and international artists are featured in the heart of the city, benefitting from a generous public exposure.

So, the ribbon-like façade of *MOMEM* is conceived as a literal screen. It is a generously informative interface that populates the sunken plaza with multimedia, day and night. This guiding principle for the conception and realisation of the museum finds a special relevance given its aforementioned placement: an undesirable, dated space of passage becomes an eye-catching urban destination. Its glassy surfaces alive with bodies, beats and light beams, the *MOMEM* creates a round-the-clock spectacle where threshold encounters are revealed in their best and highest form.

Atelier Markgraph's animation of the *MOMEM*'s public-facing glazed façade arises as a design approach, specific to the project's location and program. Likewise, it is one that the office has refined for decades through different edge-oriented iterations. Bold Markgraph works such as *Ship of Ideas*, presented in Frankfurt in 2003, as well as *ART/WHEEL* also presented in Frankfurt in 2005, suggest a lineage of interfaces where museum walls do in fact 'dematerialise' to spill their contents into the urban space. In the former project, a block of brightly lit media screens and other LED displays was placed on a barge, gliding slowly up and down the Main, offering illuminated vistas of the city's various museum collections. In the latter, a Ferris wheel doubled as an impressive projecting canvas, playfully exhibiting paintings and drawings that otherwise hung in enclosed Frankfurt galleries. *Ship of Ideas*, *ART/WHEEL*, *MOMEM*: three formats for one simple yet impactful idea about the power of interface encounters. Audiences for the wide world of art and music can be accidental, augmented, diverse. Audiences that participate in forming the socio-cultural imaginations of people and cities need to be challenged, stimulated; called upon. By crafting evocative, architectural screen objects, Markgraph confirms its desire to include and share with the multitudes, global and local. It also shows its flair for a humanist use of technology. Certainly, screens and flashy pixels can alienate individuals from the reality of things; from life, from one another. However, these screens and pixels can also be used toward the democratisation of artefacts which were historically enjoyed by too few.

The Ötztal tourist information centre (*Ötztal 360*) reclaims this goal of creating new proximities through threshold encounters. Located in the alpine village of Sölden in the Austrian Tyrol, the centre welcomes its visitors with many mediated experiences. Layers of expansive glass panes and screens direct the eye toward the tourism services, as well as

006

MOMEM
Museum
Of
Modern
Electronic
Music

007

008

Dont You Want Me
Sky and Sand
Ritual of Life
L'esperanza
Music Sounds Better With You

Phuture Will Survive And Phuture Will Stay Alive
Good Life
Good Life
Good Life
Ohm Sweet Ohm

The Spice Must Flow
New Life
Strings Of Life
I Feel Love

MOMEM
Museum
Of
Modern
Electronic
Music

Frankfurt
Hauptwache

‚Reduktion / Loop / Energie!.'

Roman Flügel

009

ÖTZ
TAL
ÖTZTAL.
HEARTBEAT OF
THE ALPS.
Be inspired
Werde inspiriert

010

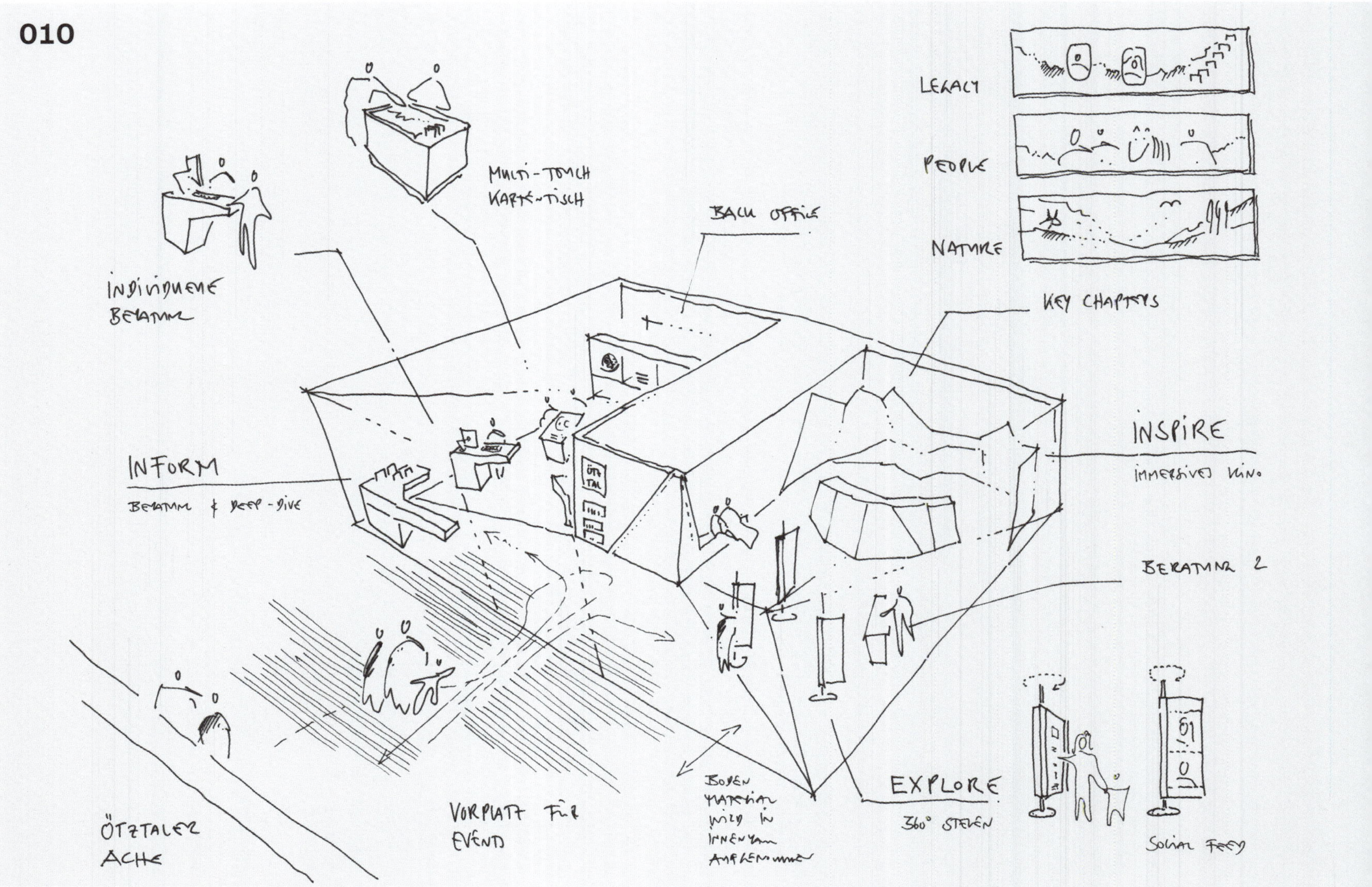
LEGACY
PEOPLE
NATURE
KEY CHAPTERS
MULTI-TOUCH KARTEN-TISCH
BACK OFFICE
INDIVIDUELLE BERATUNG
INFORM
BERATUNG & DEEP-DIVE
INSPIRE
IMMERSIVES KINO
BERATUNG 2
EXPLORE
360° STELEN
SOCIAL FEED
ÖTZTALER ACHE
VORPLATZ FÜR EVENT

009 The centre sits on a key site in Sölden, nested within the mountains and neighbouring buildings, and pleasantly faces the Venter Ache creek. A restrained wood palette crowns the glassy ribbon of the front façade.

010 Through hand-sketching and a series of mock-up surfaces and props, the Markgraph team 'self-tested' visitors' encounter with the project's many interfaces, therefore ensuring an optimal sequential understanding of their spatial design. In plan, this sequence ultimately splits in two zones: left (service area) and right ('experiences').

011 The sculptural screen is modelled as a multifaceted sheet; a prism that dramatically stretches towards its audience, capturing something of the breadth and variety of Ötztal's landscapes.

012 The formal language of the centre's interiors is rooted in movement: flashing images, sharp diagonals, rotating panels and folded screens evoke the power and vitality associated with mountain sports.

013 In the evenings, the building spills light and colour onto the street, then performing its 'architectural attractor' role especially well.

the locations that these services celebrate. The first approach resembles that of *MOMEM*, with its lifted, 'dissolving' ground floor walls, opening up the centre's core to passersby. Past this initial threshold, another approach is required – individuals are now faced with a fragmented, digital restitution of neighbouring mountain landscapes. Various experiential and interactive installations immerse visitors in a world of wind and snow and slopes and sun: integrated light and acoustic ceiling panels make for a sophisticated haptic atmosphere, while slender mobile interfaces perform complete 360-degree revolutions to better capture the strikingly scenic qualities of the Ötztal valley. Shimmering topographic maps playfully pop out of tables. Detailed photographs and seamless 3D models are displayed. Finally, an imposing three-dimensional film panorama unfolds onto long, polygonal surfaces. A versatile high-tech interface recalling entertainment cinema and VR ecosystems, wraps around users' bodies to resuscitate the Alps – their geologies, textures, magnitudes, histories and explorers. The history of interface architectures is strewn with diverse dioramas; replicas of a scene, giant and miniature models and multilayer showcases which all link back to Markgraph's Ötztal tourist information centre in ludic ways. Recreating something of the mountain phenomenology is an appreciable task that, through a collection of dioramic, luminous thresholds, Atelier Markgraph resolves attractively.

AN INTERFACE CONDITION ORGANISES OBJECTS AND SUBJECTS INTO SPECIFIC, CONTOUR-DEFINED ENCOUNTERS:

in the case of the 2016 *Alles Neu!* retrospective exhibition at the Museum of Applied Arts in Frankfurt, typefaces constitute actual interfaces between readers and the universe of words. Concurrently classical and contemporary, Atelier Markgraph's scenography work emphasises the significance of typography as a design interface. More specifically, the Atelier's approach to *Alles Neu!* ensures a clear connection between standard font families and their associated user experiences. Abundant references to the famed history of modernist German typefaces demonstrate the specificity of such experiences: architect Ferdinand Kramer and designer Paul Renner's Futura Bold, which Markgraph features throughout the rooms, is utilised

ÖTZTAL – VIELFALT ERLEBEN
WURZELN UND FLÜGEL
RAUSGEHN. AUSPOWERN. RUNTERKOMMEN.
AUSZEIT
ZUHAUSE IM ÖTZTAL

012

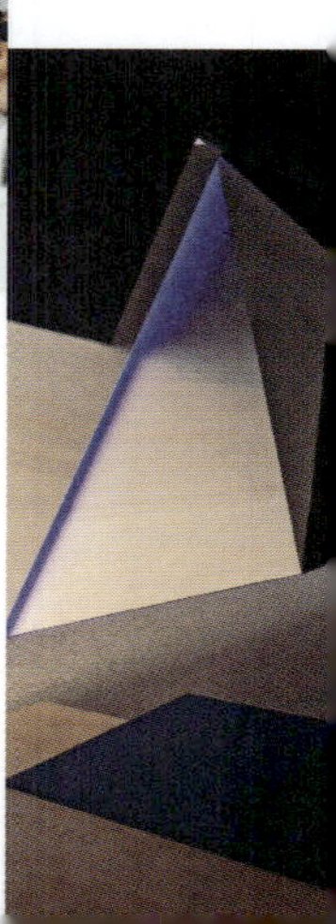

SÖLDEN
GURGL
ÖTZTAL. HEARTBEAT OF THE ALPS.
HÄNGEBRÜCKE LÄNGENFELD
ÖTZTAL. GENUSS IN HOCHFORM.

014 An expressive portal to be sure; the façade of the Museum of Applied Arts is adorned with small letters showing the variety of typographies which the exhibition celebrates. A fun 'font collection' now populates a bit of the city space too.
015 Markgraph doesn't shy away from playing with the juxtaposition of alphabet letters, texts and images; through this juxtaposition, visitors experience the rich worlds which link to a specific typographic style.
016 A ludic series of pictograms was designed and integrated in the signage of the exhibition, providing museum-goers of all ages with inclusive clues about the history of typography.

as the exemplary instance of an interface catering to people's needs. Principles and concerns particular to the font are highlighted: the function-oriented Futura Bold was created by Kramer and Renner in 1926 to accompany the socially ambitious New Frankfurt affordable housing project. Different visuals and spatial cues of *Alles Neu!* follow this lineage; they are situated in a spirit of pragmatism and even distribution, of firsthand simplicity and hope. Large-format zooms on isolated works operate as new windows looking onto a precise visual imagery. Flying letters, black and white alphabets, fine pictograms, silver glyphs: Atelier Markgraph's team mobilises an array of meaningful interfaces, like many portals revealing the intricate grammar and influence of Futura and other long-established typefaces. Doing so with a pedagogical meticulousness, making evident poet Octavio Paz's professed words: to be truly modern, we must first reconcile ourselves with our traditions.

MATERIAL CULTURES OF SCREEN MEDIA ARE UNDERGOING RAPID CHANGES: TRADITIONS AND STANDARDS EMERGE HASTILY AS NEW APPARATUS DEVELOP, MAKING FOR A MULTIFORM IMAGINATION OF HUMAN-MACHINE INTERFACES.

Screens produce and distribute stimuli; from the surface to the observing eye, a flux passes and informs. Now, what happens when this observing eye is presented with more than one flux? How does it make sense of two fluxes, of three, of a hundred fluxes? Large walls of screens have come to symbolise a laden zeitgeist aesthetics of sorts. Like the flashy billboards of Tokyo, London or New York, the *Big Picture* featured at Frankfurt's 2019 Internationale Automobil-Ausstellung (IAA) – among the world's largest mobility show – overloads the visitor's eye with a dozen hefty monitors.

014

015

Egoi

schultzschultz
AMAZIN
GLY FEW
DISCOTH
EQUES
PROVIDE
JUKEBO
XES
bauhaus
idee
form
zweck
zeit
99

EDGE-DEFINED E
ARE MANIFOLD

NCOUNTERS

018

017 Fragments of architecture and landscape are at times resuscitated on the multiple screens: like the remarkable pieces of an imperfect puzzle, they make for attention-engaging vistas.

018 As illustrated, the high-spanning installation unfolds on many levels, allowing for ambitious light plays and multiple vantage points. Visitors can explore both the front and back stages, thus embodying the celebrated mobility.

Protruding screens, receding screens; softly animated screens, strobing screens; monochrome screens, hue-saturated screens work to form a staggering patchwork of moving images which evoke the show's theme of future mobility. Conceptualised by Markgraph in partnership with architects jangled nerves as the grand finale of an experiential trail for Mercedes-Benz, the *Big Picture* is an installation of urban scale, with its massive screens appropriately referred to as façades. A building's façade functions as the discursive interface of architecture: it is fundamental to the formation of spatial meaning and style. The 2019 IAA project understands this discursive power of the façade, which it multiplies through a screen accumulation intended to be embraced in one total gaze. A straightforward, engaging and lushly arranged idea, Atelier Markgraph's *Big Picture* forces the viewer into an act of mad contemplation, where stimuli can only be made sense of by deliberate focus and choice.

EMPOWERED OBSERVERS ARE NOW ACTIVE PARTICIPANTS IN THE ACT OF LOOKING; IN THE ACT OF CREATING MEANING. FLUX DOES PASS AND INFORM, BUT IT DOES SO IN A CRITICAL MANNER.

An environment which thoroughly operates in the realm of glowing interfaces, Markgraph's *Big Picture* design for the Internationale Automobil-Ausstellung finds its place in a lineage that goes way back to the Atelier's roots. The aforementioned *Ship of Ideas* and *ART|WHEEL* showed augmented visions of art in the urban space. With the impactful *SkyArena*, visions of sportsmanship and athletic feats were projected onto Frankfurt's tallest buildings in an everlasting celebration of football and its importance for the city, for Germany, for Europe and for the world. Imagined in the context of the 2006 World Cup, *SkyArena* was a near hour-long light and media show which transformed a 'financialised' skyline into a

019 The overall effect is monumental: dimmed lights erase the screens' support structure, with the eerie effect of gigantic, floating blocks of light. Pieces of a sunset sky, of an underwater landscape: they dominate viewers with their spectacular size and brilliance.

020 Bodies, screens, car lights and LED screens come together to form a true visual spectacle. Atelier Markgraph has a long history of crafting spectacle for Mercedes-Benz at the IAA; the important collaboration began in 1989, and extends to this day.

020
pioneer-
ing the
future

021 The ghosts of football legends are brought back to life, their bodies made flesh by the tall architecture of finance; their athletic grace captured by the slow movement of the light projections.
022 A sublime, out-of-this-world vision: the tall towers of Frankfurt are fleetingly dematerialised by light, thus becoming pure interfaces.
023 More than a million people flooded the streets, bridges and waterbanks of Frankfurt: a true moment of urban togetherness, countless bodies united by their love of the game.
024 Objects, faces and symbols are enlarged to a formidable degree, conveying a range of motions and emotions. Part of the show featured, in live time, a performance from the German-American singer Cassandra Steen.
025 Documentation of *SkyArena's* installation shows how canvases were placed inside buildings' structural grid, preserving their unique pattern expressions.

breathtakingly oversized canvas for the sport of football. Blade Runner-like visions of animated skyscrapers made for an emotional, extravagant display; 500 photographs transformed buildings into superspaces of celebration, friendship and entertainment. Potentially one of Atelier Markgraph's most iconic works, this projection show is pure interface spectacle. It is the concretised dream of a generation of architects who aspired to make their constructions 'speak' through figurative and textual elements. Here the figures have the faces of Pele and Beckenbauer; the texts suggest that one never walks alone. There is true joy in *SkyArena*'s occupation of the city space. There is also a satisfying level of sophistication in Markgraph's execution of the project, with its insistence on installing projection surfaces within the structural grid of the towers' façades. The final effect is delightful; every window simultaneously preserved and transformed into a pixel; football's vibrant imagery thinly sliced along the lines of the architecture that hosts it.

The works by Atelier Markgraph presented above make up a comprehensive family, one that is defined by evocative notions of margins, limits and shared surfaces; of windows, intersections and contours; of translucencies, appendages and new vistas. In their large-scaled presentation, they make the case for generous and multiple points of view. They enlarge audiences and invite them into festive, mediated moments.

THRESHOLDS ARE AS GOOD AS THEY ARE GENEROUS. ANYONE WHO HOPES TO ENGAGE IN THE GOOD *MISE EN PLACE* OF INTERFACES BETTER REMEMBER IT.

022

Schweizer-National

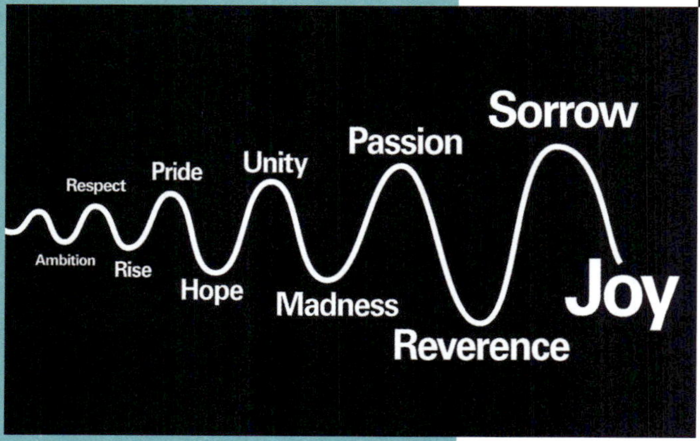
Sorrow
Passion
Unity
Pride
Respect
Ambition
Rise
Hope
Madness
Reverence
Joy

023

024

fleeting,

encou

PECTRES

poetic

nters

SOUND OF SQUARES

The compact, mobile *Sound of Squares* pavilion acts as a beaconing architectural object, its vivid red walls deployed in stark contrast to its various temporary sites. Music arises as a perceptible presence that resonates and lingers with visitors, turning the city into a public concert. PAGE 83

2007

2019

HOUSE OF PLAY

A vitaminised pop-up installation, *House of Play* shows contrast with architectural pasts, its glitzy panels, furniture, fixtures and accessories deployed joyously within two iconographic historical buildings in Germany and Austria. PAGE 90

CULTURAL IMPULSE

The Mercedes-Benz installation at Odeonsplatz in Munich is organised as a simple built volume dominated by an iridescent, ghost-like work of art: a floating sculpture by American artist Janet Echelman transforms the public square into an ethereal spectacle, with colourful threads floating like a cloud over an assemblage of sturdy wooden decks. PAGE 62

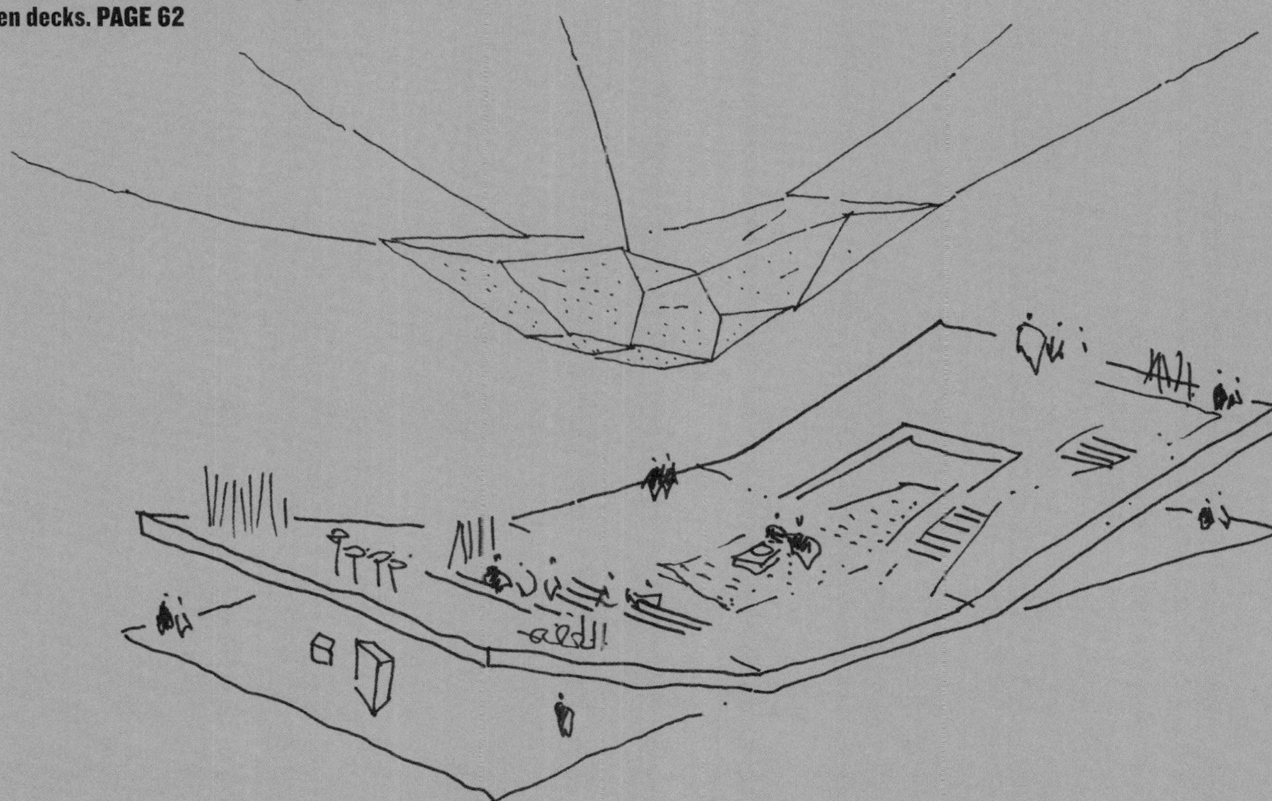

2021

REVENGE

2022

Revenge. History and Fantasy, a one-of-a-kind exhibition designed for the Jewish Museum of Frankfurt, features the controversial notion of 'revenge' in a Jewish context, flipping narratives of victimhood and requital on their head with immersive gallery set-ups, and thus showcasing the past in experiential, haunted ways. PAGE 74

001

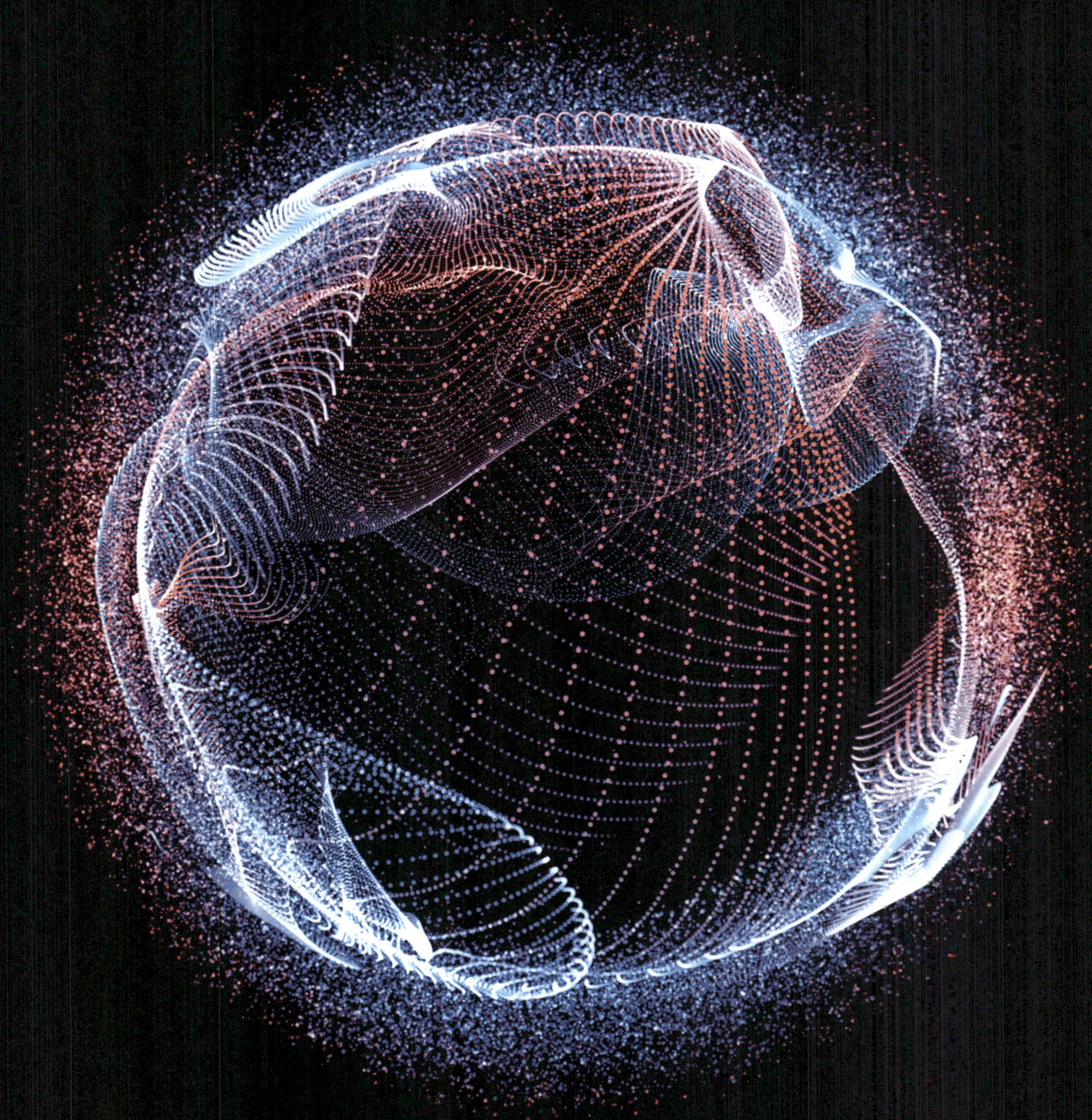

001 As part of Mercedes-Benz's brand presence at the IAA MOBILITY 2021, Atelier Markgraph curated a concert programme featuring international electronic music acts. This festival was promoted under the title Artificial Soul; the key visual, which was animated online and used in print on flyers, conveys digitality and emotion.

002 Bird's-eye views of urban installations are no one's experience of the project; yet they show the scale, ambition and elegance of the IAA MOBILITY 2021, with its eerie, colourful net in a state of suspension among old historical walls.

The creation of space and architecture starts with the arrangement of solid things. Bricks, stones; reinforced pillars and wooden beams; glass panels and hardened cement make for a built world that organises and orients humankind. Yet recent architecture cultures have been marked by a distinct shift: the importance of this material language for the creation of adequate environments has been supplemented with so-called immaterial objects – virtual, atmospheric, emotional; spectres of sorts. How does one define 'immaterial' in that context? What is the space of immaterial presence? What are the possible qualities of spectral interventions? Can ephemerality and shimmer really participate in the desirable composition of buildings and cities? The family of projects that are gathered in this chapter arise as possible case studies of immaterial interventions: here, Atelier Markgraph's works operate in the universe of ghosts, nostalgias and myths. These works appear to viewers in an instant, poetically fleeting, elusive and arresting. Architectural historian Anthony Vidler spoke well of the uncanny as a metaphor for a certain unsettling modern condition. In times when digital narratives ubiquitously participate in everyday experiences, uncanny dispositions ought to be closely surveyed; normatively assessed.

TO MEET AN UNCANNY OTHER IMPLIES VARIED LEVELS OF INDETERMINACY AND WONDER – STRANGE ENCOUNTERS OF THE SPECTRAL KIND REALLY ARE INDETERMINATE AND WONDERFUL.

For a fleeting moment, they create a connection between the viewer and the thing viewed. While the latter cannot offer the solid materiality which characterises most daily infrastructure, it can inspire meaningful meditations about the true matter of the world.

As visible incorporeal spirits, spectres are associated with marked perceptual, emotive or sensory impressions. They are fleeting; of changeable appearance, always reconfiguring and devoid of borders. They must be approached watchfully, treading lightly, as if a too sudden move would lead to their vaporisation.

002

003 The lower pavilion unfolds in a visually stark contrast with the cloud and surrounding architectural elements, making for an evocative experience of products and (urban) space.
004 A low plinth that sits centrally at the Odeonsplatz, the pavilion is articulated as a sober, slick ensemble of horizontal and vertical lines. Above these unswerving slabs and columns one discovers the Echelman piece, in all of its organic, delicate qualities, as well as the historical buildings which border the site.
005 In the evening, sophisticated light projections animate the eerie volume with new colours and life, presenting inhabitants and visitors with Southern Germany's own urban aurora borealis.
006 The marked juxtaposition of dematerialised architecture and the contemporary objects featured at IAA MOBILITY 2021 makes for a clear concept and a playful sight.
007 The formal qualities of Janet Echelman's art piece echo the intricate aesthetics of digital illustrations: there is something decidedly virtual-looking about the net lighting up the city's dark sky.

This peculiar feeling of evanescence is one experienced by the visitors of the 2021 Internationale Automobil-Ausstellung (IAA MOBILITY) Mercedes-Benz installation at Odeonsplatz, in the inner city of Munich. The simple built volume conceived by architects jangled nerves is dominated by an iridescent, ghost-like work of art. A floating sculpture by American artist Janet Echelman, *Earthtime 1.26 Munich* transforms the public square into an ethereal spectacle, one that pedestrians and other city drifters progressively encounter. The immaterial nature of the suspended piece contrasts with the planar logic of the construction below. A delicate web of colourful threads floats like a cloud over an assemblage of sturdy wooden decks, lush green patches and glass sheets; the ensemble strikes a fine expressive balance. As it elevates and gracefully displays the *Earthtime 1.26 Munich* meshwork for all to see, the Odeonsplatz installation succeeds as an inclusive cultural contribution to Munich. The venue's spatial qualities are enhanced by the translucent spectre of Echelman's sculpture, which attractively sets the mood. This is made even more evident at nighttime, when the thousands of cables flicker and glow in the choreographed lighting, offering a truly otherworldly sight; a gorgeous ectoplasm in the city's dark sky. White lines then fuse like a soft skeleton, creating a shimmering irregular grid, on which a finer, pulsating lattice sways. In addition to its smart use of brand as a creator of culture, there is much beauty to be found in the planning partners' approach to the challenge of imagining a new urban attractor within a significant historical site. The elegance of the existing architectural ensemble at Odeonsplatz is enhanced through its glistening encounter with the IAA pavilion, offering poetic past-meets-future vistas.

Markgraph's conception and construction of new, scintillating landmark venues make for a decades-long endeavour. It can be argued that the 2021 Munich installation is the sister project of an earlier design: a special exhibition at the 2002 Light+Building Frankfurt trade fair. The installation *Constructing Atmospheres* also featured a hovering ghost – a cloud, animated with soft lighting, dancing fog and glittering droplets; a true meteorological event inside the wide Galleria of Messe Frankfurt. Generated several times a day from layers of air at varying degrees of humidity and temperature, the floating formation reached an appreciable several hundred cubic metres in size. Like the visitors at Odeonsplatz, individuals are allured as they discover this amorphous apparition, encouraged further in the fair premises, until they meet its milky core. Their encounter with the raised spectre of the *Experimental Cloud* is elusive, its shape transforming as the visitor moves in the room below.

003

004

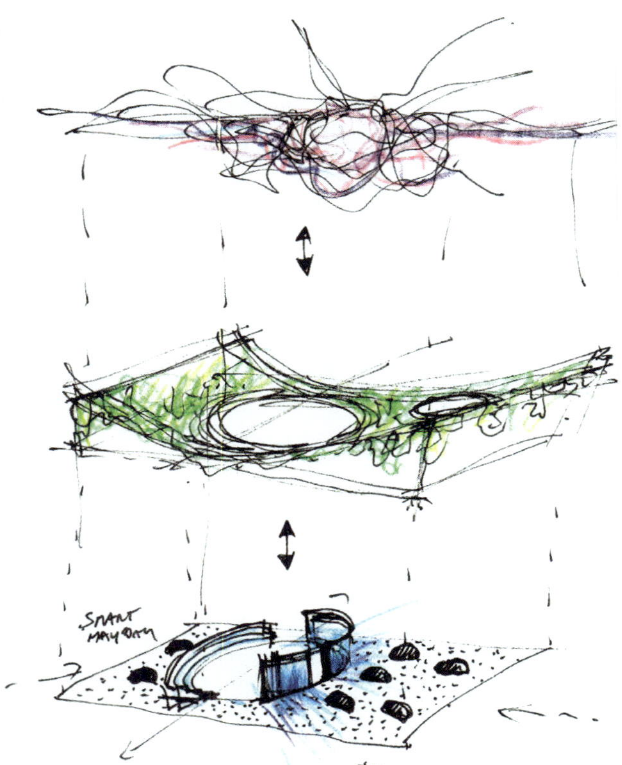

006

007

AS VISIB
SPIRITS
ASSOCIATE
PERCEPTU
SENSO

LE INCORPOREAL
, SPECTRES ARE
D WITH MARKED
AL, EMOTIVE OR
Y IMPRESSIONS

VERFLUCHT SE
DIES LIEST, SEU
UND SICH SEIN
TAGEWERK ZUV
VERFLUCHT SE
TRÄNEN VERGK
UM UNS TRAUE
SAGT: GENUG.
DAS IST ES, WA
VON EUCH FOR

THIS REPRESENTS A CUSTOMISED EXPERIENCE OF ARCHITECTURE WHICH IS DISTINCTIVELY MYSTERIOUS AND VAGUE, ATMOSPHERIC AND DYNAMIC:

the immaterial matter of smokes, webs and mists softens the space with its evocative indeterminacy. It renders itself unique, too, as it is constantly rediscovered by individual, mobile pairs of eyes. Markgraph's conceptual visions for Odeonsplatz and *Constructing Atmospheres* evoke other provocative designs: think of Frei Otto's fragile soap bubble models (1963), Yves Klein's smoky *Fire Fountain* (1961), Olafur Eliasson's hazy *Weather Project* (2003), or Diller Scofidio + Renfro's cloud-like Blur Building (2002). These projects form an interesting family. They present the viewers with true experiential environments; they conjure visions of virtuality, atmosphere, simulation, responsiveness, radiance; of awe-inspiring phenomenology. In their multiform oscillation between materiality and immateriality, they formalise an aesthetic of felt spaces – one that causes a lingering impression.

Revenge. History and Fantasy resuscitates a different kind of ghost. Designed in 2022 for the Jewish Museum of Frankfurt, the exhibition is the first which features the controversial notion of 'revenge' in a Jewish context, flipping common, misdirected narratives of victimhood and requital on their head. In the museum's galleries, Atelier Markgraph showcases the past in experiential, haunted ways: visitors are immersed in ruthless scenes of retaliation, rampage and rage. In doing so, they can experience and comprehend wide-ranging strategies of Jewish self-assertion in the face of violence. Besides the presented material, there exists a phantom exhibition; one which is constructed by the walking viewer. Nostalgia is operationalised in unforeseen means. Brutal biblical stories and dooming rabbinical writings, bloody legends and anti-Semitic myths – as centuries-old spectres, these slivers of past times are revealed to the contemporary viewer once again, and this time through chill-inducing spatial strategies.

008 The immersive world imagined by Markgraph unfolds through the sober installation of various, impactful mediums. Moving images, shimmers and attention-grabbing noises participate in a specific experience of emotion and history.

009 Atelier Markgraph's approach to the exhibition's design involves a play with darkness in the rooms' space, which appropriately ties back to its featured themes.

010 The exhibition strikes a fine balance between immersive installation and object display. Visitors are at turns plunged into sensual spaces; they are also invited to dwell in the contemplation of smaller, intricate items.

011 As witnesses of a sacred, often forgone history, delicate objects are showcased with care and a calculated preciosity; disjointed pieces of information also appear in unexpected places, making for spirit-like visions.

012 There is a ghost-like quality to visual layerings of translucent materials, a quality which is reinforced by the black and white treatments of texts and print surfaces. Such colourless moments aptly evoke photographic mediums of the past.

FAKE NEWS

009

010

Nakam!
Rache! Rache!
Rache!
LEBT WOHL, LASSET ES EUCH RECHT GUT GEHEN UND WENN IHR KÖNNT, DANN NEHMT EINST RACHE.
W OCZACH PROSIMY O ZEMSTĘ, O ZEMSTĘ,

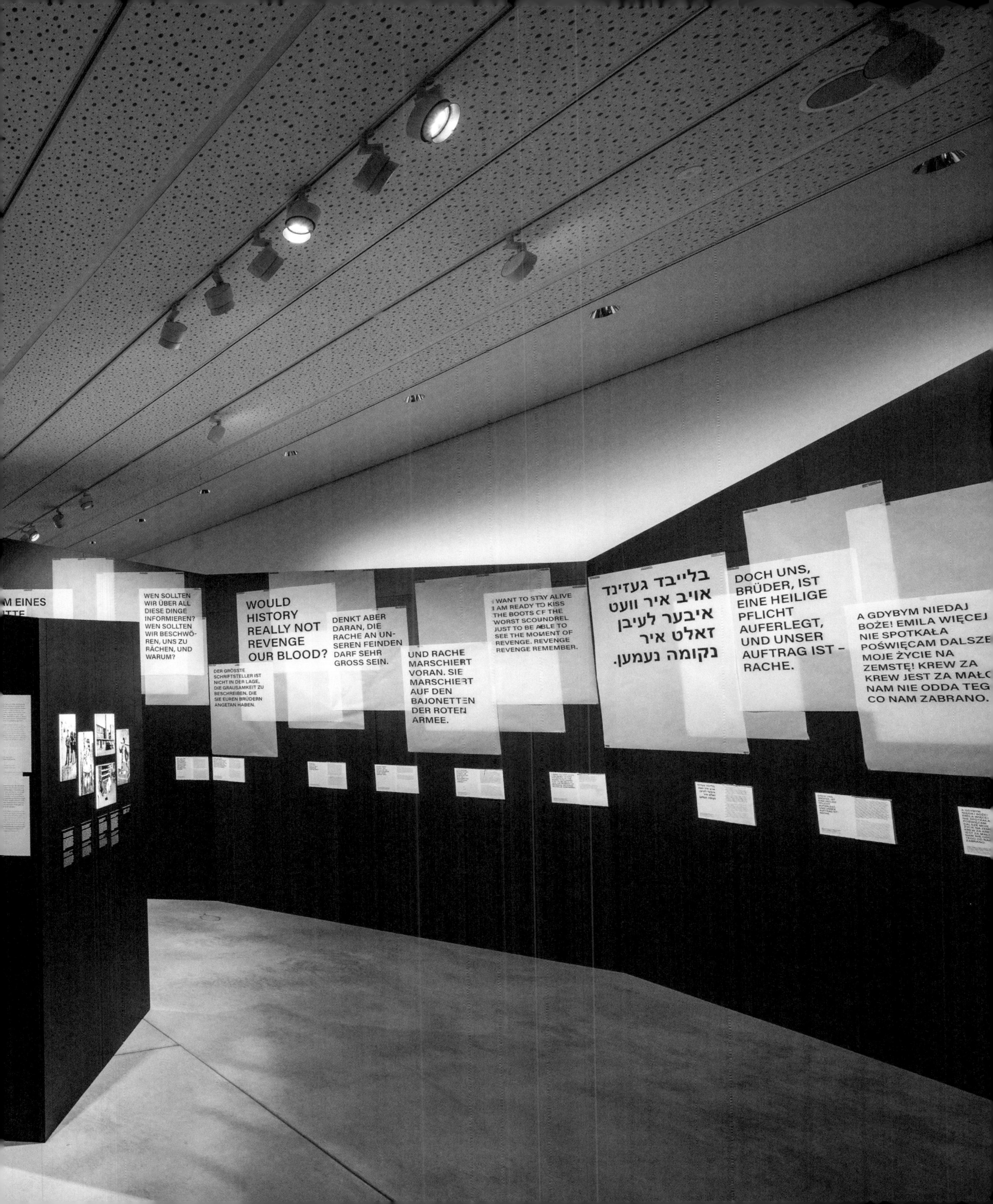
WEN SOLLTEN WIR ÜBER ALL DIESE DINGE INFORMIEREN? WEN SOLLTEN WIR BESCHWÖ-REN, UNS ZU RÄCHEN, UND WARUM?
WOULD HISTORY REALLY NOT REVENGE OUR BLOOD?
DER GRÖSSTE SCHRIFTSTELLER IST NICHT IN DER LAGE, DIE GRAUSAMKEIT ZU BESCHREIBEN, DIE SIE EUREN BRÜDERN ANGETAN HABEN.
DENKT ABER DARAN, DIE RACHE AN UN-SEREN FEINDEN DARF SEHR GROSS SEIN.
UND RACHE MARSCHIERT VORAN. SIE MARSCHIERT AUF DEN BAJONETTEN DER ROTEN ARMEE.
I WANT TO STAY ALIVE I AM READY TO KISS THE BOOTS OF THE WORST SCOUNDREL JUST TO BE ABLE TO SEE THE MOMENT OF REVENGE. REVENGE REVENGE REMEMBER.
בלייבד געדינד אויב איר וועט איבער לעיבן זאלט איר נקומה נעמען.
DOCH UNS, BRÜDER, IST EINE HEILIGE PFLICHT AUFERLEGT, UND UNSER AUFTRAG IST – RACHE.
A GDYBYM NIEDAJ BOŻE! EMILA WIĘCEJ NIE SPOTKAŁA POŚWIĘCAM DALSZE MOJE ŻYCIE NA ZEMSTĘ! KREW ZA KREW JEST ZA MAŁO NAM NIE ODDA TEGO CO NAM ZABRANO.

013 Inviting urban furniture functions as a bridge between the city space and the pavilion's insides. Seats' high visibility and light weight encourage dynamism and engagement from users: visitors can influence ambient soundscapes by sitting down.

014 The stark red colour and markedly industrial look of the *Sound of Squares* pavilion contrast the immateriality of its content: here, architecture solidifies and celebrates the 'bodiless' sounds of Mannheim.

015 The pavilion sits proudly among the high towers of Alexanderplatz, in Berlin Mitte. Other cities which have hosted *Sound of Squares* include Munich, Cologne and, of course, Mannheim. Interestingly, Quadratestadt (which translates to 'squares city') is the literal nickname of the city of Mannheim, with its historic city centre articulated around grid-like housing blocks.

A spectre is an apparition: an unusual or unexpected sight; the invisible becoming visible. With its sombre, dynamic volumes, Markgraph's visual and formal storytelling taps into the uncanny imagination of apparitions, breathing new life into the encountered figures of old Jewish nemeses, Talmudists, robbers, pirates and varied avenging outlaws. In other words, the Atelier's team acts as purposeful 'mediums,' mediating communication between spirits of the dead and living human beings. Historical documents, Hebrew writings, ceremonial objects, paintings, graphic artefacts, photographs, comics and films make for an eerie collection of relics. Hybrid constructions with projections and sharp mobile lights add to the exhibition's overall impression of vitality and hauntedness. Jewish vengeance is celebrated and rendered unforgettable, and like the most potent of spirits, *Revenge. History and Fantasy* leaves a persisting trace.

LEAVING A TRACE IMPLIES THAT A DISAPPEARED OR VANISHED 'THING' STILL HAS A PERCEPTIBLE PRESENCE OF SORTS. AS A PHENOMENON, IT IS NATURALLY ASSOCIATED WITH NOISE AND MUSIC:

think of the resonating echo of thunder or the lingering tones of a concluded symphony. Such reverberations are moving ghosts, often charged with deep meaning and emotion. With its *Sound of Squares* project (2007), Atelier Markgraph harvests this affecting potential of noise and music in a clever, technology-oriented spirit. Realised in collaboration with Stadtmarketing Mannheim as a celebration of the city's 400-year anniversary, *Sound of Squares* consists of a compact, mobile pavilion to be deployed throughout public squares in Germany. Within its walls, visitors find an impressive matrix of 10,000 colourful cubes – sound bites in solid, saturated greens, pinks and yellows. Each sample (or record) cube is associated with an audio clip from Mannheim's metropolitan soundscape, which can be played and

016 The graphic identity developed for the multiple sound files reminds at turns of flashy periodic tables, flavoursome candy packaging or vintage electronic consoles. A neat colour system gives information about the different sound categories; users can rapidly learn to play these musical instruments.

017 Visitors listen to and compose their tunes at the very edge of the transparent pavilion wall, therefore animating its façade with their bodies and movement.

SETZ DICH!

KLANG LABOR

JUBILÄUMSSONG
MEINEWELT
MUSIKER BEKENNEN SICH ZU MANNHEIM. SIE MACHEN IHRER HEIMAT ZUM 400. GEBURTSTAG EIN EINZIGARTIGES MUSIKALISCHES GESCHENK: MEINEWELT – DER JUBILÄUMSSONG.
MEINEWELT GEHT VON MANNHEIM AUS AUF TOURNEE NACH BERLIN, KÖLN UND MÜNCHEN. DORT BEARBEITEN DIE SONGPATEN HENNING WEHLAND, HANS NIESWANDT UND UWE OCHSENKNECHT DEN JUBILÄUMSSONG.
ENTWERFEN SIE IHRE EIGENE VERSION DES SONGS MEINEWELT. ARRANGIEREN, INTERPRETIEREN UND KOMPONIEREN SIE HIER IM KLANGLABOR UND NEHMEN SIE EIN STÜCK VON MANNHEIM
„There's not a problem that I can't fix – 'cause I can do it in the mix!"

Atelier Markgraph's design approach to *Sound of Squares* reminds of their seminal project *LAB.01* (1999- 2000). In both works, the architectural effect is notable: the slick, sturdy elements of the pavilions resuscitate a Constructivist-like vision of civic spaces, rivalling the style and strength of their rooted neighbours. Featured narratives on culture or technology find their way toward a larger public in a series of activities, presentations and concerts, ensuring a continuity between the inner world of the pavilions and their resonating presence in the city.

shoes

G DER
RATE
2
TOUR
MANNHEIM
BERLIN
KÖLN
MÜNCHEN
K
BAHNHOF POTSDAMER PLATZ
DB
Disney's
DIE SCHÖN UND DAS BIEST
2
7
8

04
P6

016

MACHEN
MIXEN
O4
N7
F3
U5
J5
R5
L3
G4
U2

1 Landmark cubes
2 Containe

G WIE GE
U WIE MANNHEIMER U
K WIE KULI

ting cubes
20 Audio forest cubes
10.000 Sample cubes

HÖREN

MAGNUM
House of PLAY

mixed on the pavilion's large motherboard. This is Markgraph's simple, playful concept: individuals from all ages and backgrounds transform into music composers, encountering and resurrecting the soul of Mannheim by taking its manifold sounds apart; by reassembling them in novel, rhythmic manners. The city turns into a concert. In this peculiar universe of urban grid, squares and cubes, music arises as a perceptible presence that resonates and lingers – that leaves an impactful trace, and does so by reaching out to an extensive target group: again, no technical proficiency is required of its users. The project generously shares its tools and tips for the mixing of place-related sounds; for developing one's perceptual creativity. It also candidly activates the public portion of its location, enlivening it with haunting field recordings and new, mysterious melodies.

Sound of Squares was designed as a beaconing architectural object, its vivid red walls deployed in stark contrast to the various historical squares where it temporarily sat. Such a contrast evokes another spectral, architectural condition: that of old building styles, and their complex encounters with contemporary interventions. The past catches up with the present in forceful, ghostly visions; viewers oscillate between the two periods. Numerous Markgraph projects, including the 2019 *House of Play*, are conceptualised around the meeting of historical and modern languages of architecture. A vitaminised pop-up installation, *House of Play* was deployed on two iconographic sites in Germany and Austria – the grand Elisabeth Church (1835) in Berlin, and the equally grand Palmenhaus (1826) in Vienna. Here, the Atelier's concept is one of contrast, not of integration. The design principles underlying the making of *House of Play* demonstrate a clear attitude of demarcation toward the architectural past. Panels and furniture, lighting fixtures and accessories, vinyl carpets and screens: within the masonry walls of churches or greenhouses no doubt exists as to what is old and what is new. Textured stones and bricks clash with polished podiums and glitzy balloons – a visual mood which, incidentally, recalls Atelier Markgraph's joyful exhibition design for *Glam!* at Frankfurt's SCHIRN KUNSTHALLE (2013). Large, sweeping spaces of arches and domes meet the hyper-fragmented world of tinsels, bubbles and booths. Individuals busy themselves with contemporary fittings, yet they explore the installation accompanied by the phantoms of passed days: their eyes repetitively fall upon fragments of the host historical building. These repetitive apparitions are intensified by the contrasting nature of *House of Play*; the Elisabeth

018 In a bold spirit, contemporary objects and signage are placed in direct proximity to classical elements, such as columns, sills, arches and mouldings. They reinforce the desired visual differentiation between old and new.
019 Shiny gold textures are present throughout the project, strengthening impressions of energy, glamour, enchantment, play and splendour in the space.
020 Elisabeth Church's wide, rounded apse acts as the elegant backdrop of lively activities and celebrations. Such activities and celebrations also appeal to a younger public – one which is, unfortunately, too often excluded from corporate or patrimonial events.
021 The perfect figure of the circle becomes a marker of 'the modern,' its platonic precision contrasted with the many imperfections of old walls and openings.
022 A purpose-built recreational landscape of sort, *House of Play* ensures that visitors find many opportunities for play in the installation's space.

SHINE GOLDEN!
MAGNUM
NEVER STOP PLAYING

#never stop PLAYING
SNACK IT!
MAGNUM
SPREAD THE LOVE

Church and the Palmenhaus reappraised, perhaps treasured once more. Interestingly, one of the most spirited current debates in German architecture conservation relates to the desirable use of vacant churches. As patrimonial buildings, their historical value has been validated, but questions remain: how should their present-day value be expressed? How should they be occupied? By whom? Heritage is a mighty spectre indeed. Markgraph's 2019 installation answers some of these concerns by setting up a lively, inviting cohabitation. Old meets new – and they have a lot to say to one another.

The beautiful, ubiquitous term zeitgeist captures the essence of a given artistic or architectural culture; zeitgeist is, quite literally, the ghost of its time – an invisible agent, a force dominating the characteristics of an era. It links the subjective viewer to the world of immaterial forces and feelings, of soft lights, shapes and sounds. Though well rooted in their location, the six projects introduced in this chapter capture something of their epoch's zeitgeist through their evocative articulation. They give us different clues about the general moral, intellectual and cultural climate of the period and place; of their context.

SURELY, THESE PROJECTS ARE MULTI-FACETED: CONTEMPORARY, NOSTALGIC; PHYSICAL, VIRTUAL; EXPERIENCED, MEMORIZED; OPAQUE, TRANSPARENT.

They also exist as phantasms, as echoes – they operationalise a form of resuscitation. What, then, is the mode of operation of a spectral architecture? How can it be experimentally fashioned, and, most importantly, how can it be oriented toward worthy ends? These are complex interrogations. Through a notable range of formats, Atelier Markgraph demonstrates its ability to stage good, ghostly encounters. Designs like the Odeonsplatz pavilion, the *Revenge. History and Fantasy* exhibition, or the *Sound of Squares* installation are luminous, eerie, poetic – they are fashioned in successfully experimental and intrinsically worthy ways.

020

021

022

PATTER

(subjec

field er

NS

t-in-the)

counters

ART FOR CHILDREN

Atelier Markgraph's design and realisation of the *MINISCHIRN* play course for kids at Frankfurt's KUNSTHALLE SCHIRN builds from visual motifs and colours which are arranged sequentially, in a *parcourse* which stimulates little bodies and minds. **PAGE 112**

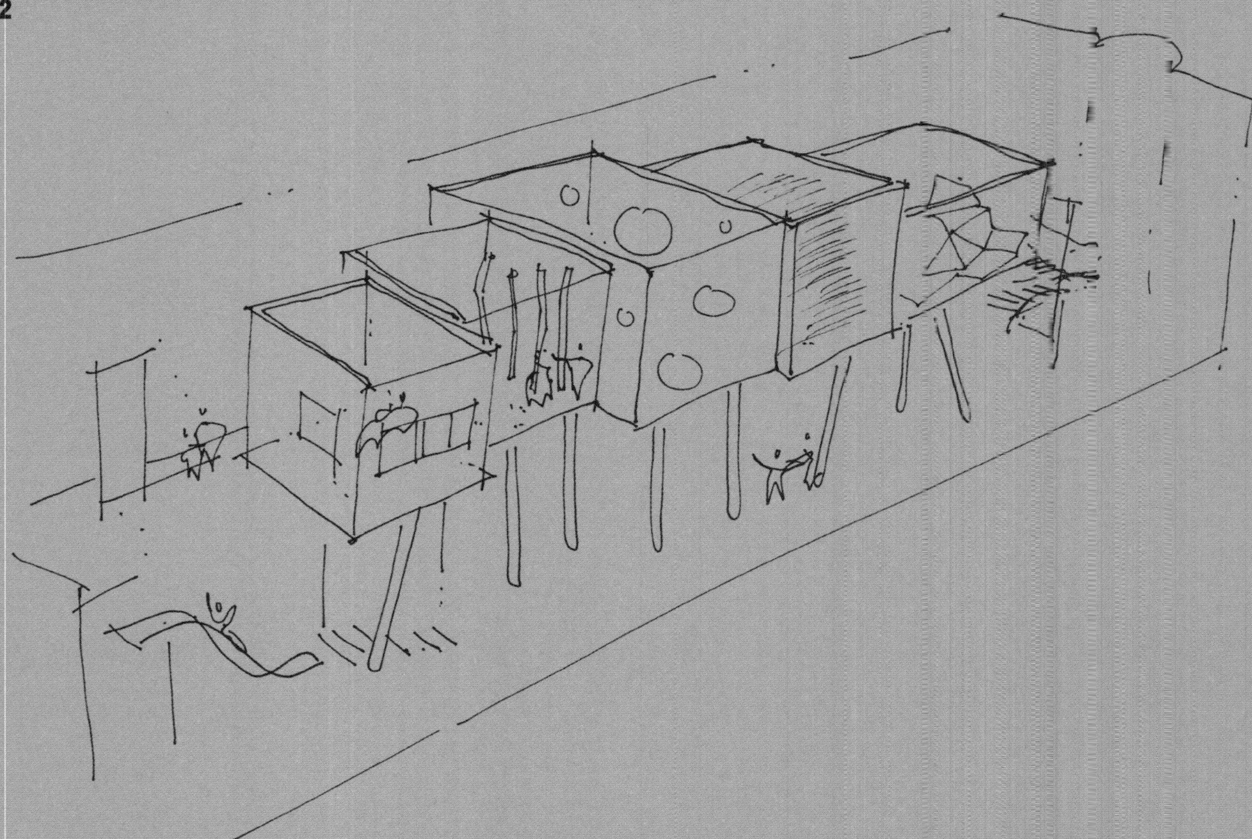

2014

2017

DYNAMIC CURVE

The ZDF television broadcast studio shows LED modules, multiplied and arranged in a dynamic motif which nicely recalls the waving of scarves by football supporters: a visual phenomenon shifts from the stadium to the media set, through a forceful repetition of screens. **PAGE 102**

SWARM INTELLIGENCE

The Sparkasse-Gruppe installation at the 2018 Finanz Informatik convention enlivens the serious landscape of IT and economics with the bold, spirited addition of hundreds of crimson squares and stripes which form an attention-grabbing, dynamic swarm; a playful, modular cloud. PAGE 120

2018

KINETIC PIXELS

The *EQ Teaser* installation, a parametric canvas developed for Mercedes-Benz, features 756 individual LED pins programmed to respond to visitors' motions and impulses: these pins are treated like pixels, advancing and receding to create dynamic depictions of silhouettes and gestures. PAGE 137

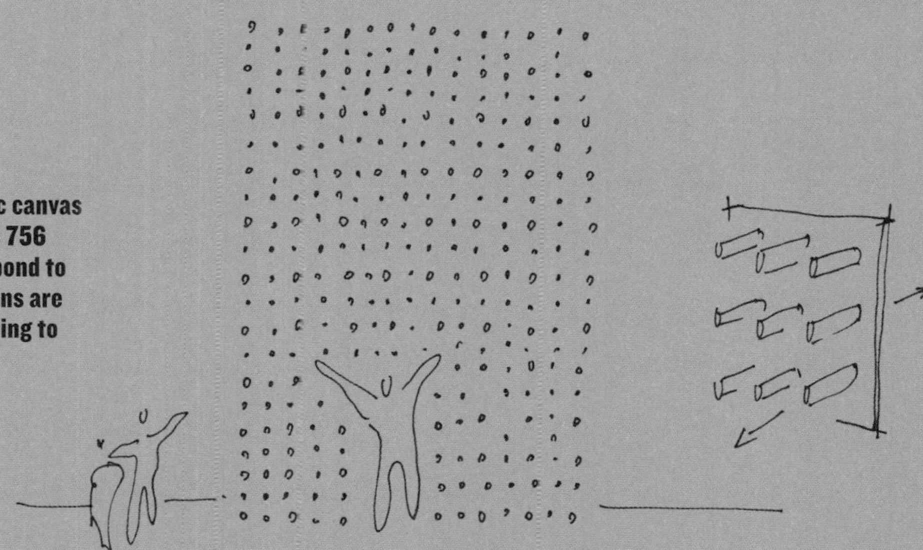

2018

CONSTELLATIONS

2018

Conceived for the celebration of Frankfurt's 'newly rebuilt' old town, the *Constellations* drone show is an urban, multimedia event which utilises drone assemblages to celebrate the history and culture of the city, shaping indistinct swarm-like masses into outlines of known objects – crowns, birds, flowers that order lights into figures with precision. PAGE 129

das aktuelle
SPORTSTUDIO

das aktuelle
SPORTSTUDIO

The expressive possibilities of organised space and matter are wide-ranging: architecture communicates ideas through colours, materials, proportions, structures, openings and patterns. Multiple, intricate, lush – patterns have constantly participated in the creation of architectonic experiences. They can be defined through simple features, which most often include repetition, joints, order and scale. They bring to mind imageries of textiles and decorations; of ornaments and craft. They evoke rhythms, symmetries, fragmented dimensions.

A PATTERN CONSISTS OF THE UNSWERVING WAY IN WHICH SOMETHING IS DONE OR OCCURS: IT IS SOMETHING WHICH HAPPENS OR EXISTS IN A REGULAR AND REPEATED MANNER.

For designers and architects, a pattern is associated with visual pleasure – it is a potent artistic tool. In her seminal text *Grids* (1979), art theorist Rosalind E. Krauss reminds us of the power of patterns. Commenting on grid-like arrangements, she speaks of the ways they give observers the ability to think they are dealing with materialism (or science, or logic) while simultaneously providing them with a true release into belief (or illusion, or fiction). This is the beautiful dialectic of patterns in space. In their systematic organisation, they offer us the ordered world of science and logic. In their aesthetic expression, they resuscitate pictures and emotions which surpass their factual order, and plunge us into compelling, multidimensional fictions. The projects featured in the following chapter are characterised and evaluated through this double meaning of patterns: two simple interrogations arise. First, what is the particular organisation of matter at play in the project's concept? Second, what is the affect or illusion which it creates? It is only after answering these questions that one can attest to – and appreciate – each project's value. Atelier Markgraph's ventures into the universe of patterns exist as many concrete proofs of the office's ability to situate its designs at the rich encounter of science and illusion; at the rich encounter of logic and fiction.

002

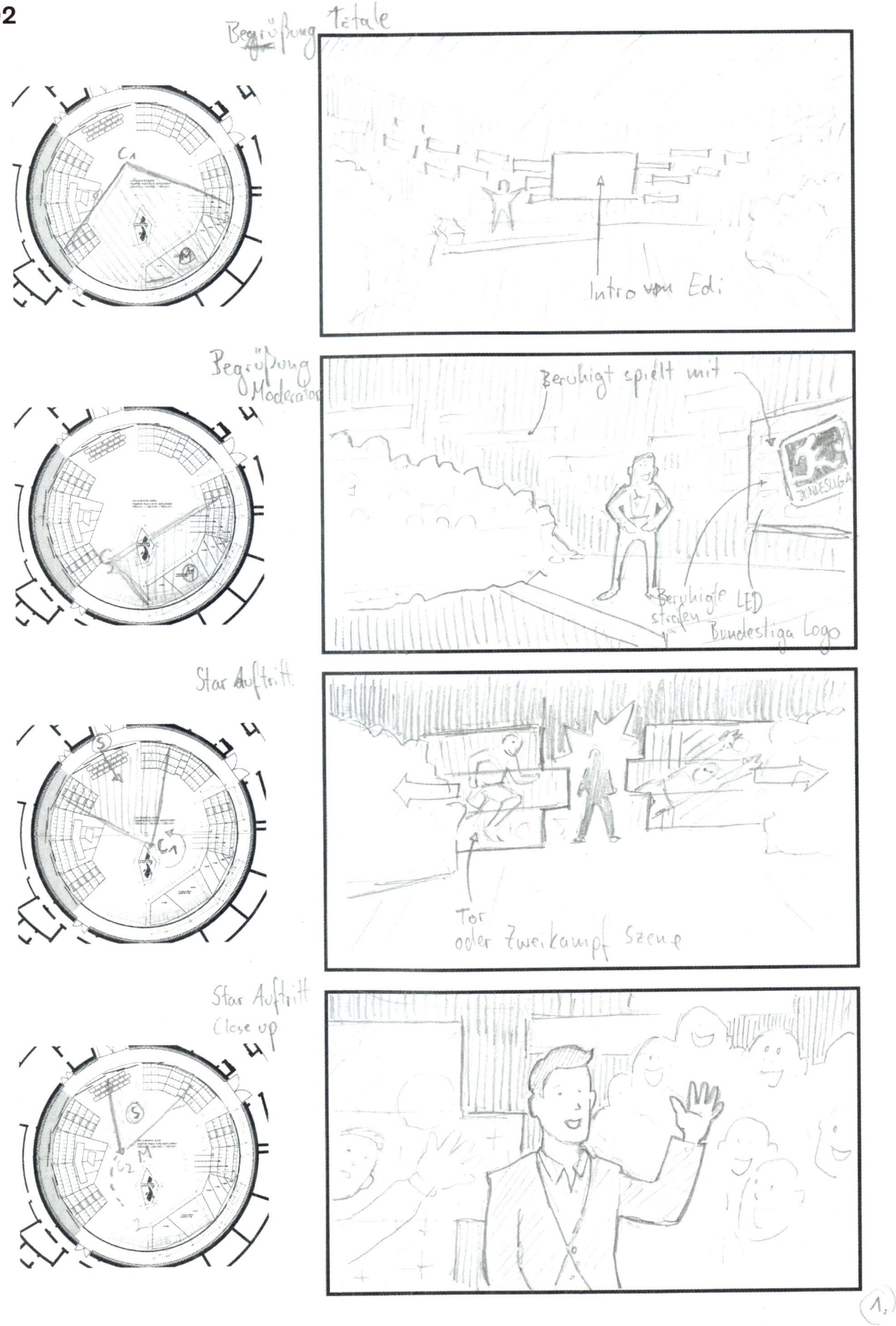
Begrüßung Totale
Intro von Edi
Begrüßung Moderator
Beruhigt spielt mit
Beruhigte LED Streifen
Bundesliga Logo
Star Auftritt
Tor
oder Zweikampf Szene
Star Auftritt
Close up

003

das aktuelle ZDF sportstudio
ZDF
tudio

004

005

001 Markgraph's conceptual 3D model shows the studio doubling as sport stadium: the sweeping curve, the open field and, up in the bleachers, the multitude of layered, stretched-out banners.
002 Markgraph's team of creatives often makes use of hand-drawn storyboards to convey key design features: here, sketches contrast the work's final aesthetic. They show patterns in context, with figures and textual cues.
003 ZDF Sport's studio makes for a simple, effective visual composition where crowd members are not quite anonymous; they rather express a social identity which links back to sportive experiences of celebration, excitement and solidarity.
004 Members of the project team stand with television host Sven Voss at the premiere of the new studio.
005 The modules are bent softly, thus adapting to the radius of the studio's stands. They are set with a slight variation in depth, which tricks viewers' eyes into a perspectival effect reminiscent of real-life crowds of fans.
006 A profuse collection of screens and panels saturates the studio space, an effect enhanced by the floor's reflective surface. Multiple and luminous, the 'scarfs' blend with nearby media objects, creating flashy patterns which catch the eye – space, hardware and software are well interrelated.

Pattern pioneers of the past took an interest in the figurative quality of their designs. Koloman Moser, William Morris and Maurits Cornelis Escher referenced both the animal and natural world in their works: shells, plants, bugs, birds, fish, flowers and human faces are arranged in symmetrical, grid-like repetitions that make for evocative artworks. Here, patterns are references, derived from real object sources – they are representational. They simplify and idealise this object source at the heart of their actuality, while retaining something of its essence. Their subject matter is both transformed and recognisable. Such a figurative approach to the creation of patterns guides the design of the ZDF television broadcast studio (2017). Markgraph's concept for the well-known media set is effective: new LED modules are multiplied and arranged in a dynamic motif that recalls the waving of scarves by football supporters. A visual phenomenon shifts from the stadium to the television set, with the repetition of numerous curvy, rectangular screens. In effect, the Atelier's ZDF set constitutes a true figurative exercise, arranging forms in a manner which reminds the viewer of important real-life objects: the colourful stripes of fabric that stretch proudly in the hands of fans are duplicated, rematerialised. Importantly, the power of the pattern directly links back to the nature of the portrayed phenomenon: the power of the scarf lies in its very accumulation. As it evokes the arena's community and embeddedness, camaraderie and synchronicity, it is the totality of scarves – the totality of units; a pattern – which impresses and affects. In one prompt image, discord ceases to exist. With its fitting circular arrangement (Atelier Markgraph refers to it as a 'fan curve'), the totality of bright screen modules creates an overall composition which similarly impresses and affects. The engulfing logic of the scarf swarm is refashioned in the broadcasting studio to harmonious ends.

Patterns present us with the art of repetition. An instance occurs; again and again, an object is ceaselessly duplicated. Repetitions are a form of training, where multiple iterations of the same element participate in its improved understanding. This, in part, explains the popularity of patterns for children and young teenagers. As a group in a constant state of learning, they are well suited to interact with patterned environments, where repeating and reproducing is the rule. Such is the case with Atelier Markgraph's design and realisation of the *MINISCHIRN* play course for

006
das aktuelle
SPORTSTUDIO
das aktuelle
SPORTSTUDIO
BERNAT

BORUSSIA
MÖNCHENGLADBACH
1900

007 Wide looking-glass, multisized spheres and circles, coloured openings: the patterned rooms of the *MINISCHIRN parcours* produce true eye-popping effects.

008 The world of the *MINISCHIRN* is composed of an enfilade of cosy rooms, each characterised by distinct formal arrangements and tonic colours. This makes for a markedly entertaining, child-friendly architectural experience – one which is partly inspired by Loris Malaguzzi's Reggio Emilia approach.

kids at Frankfurt's KUNSTHALLE SCHIRN (2014). Here, visual motifs are arranged sequentially, in a *parcours* which stimulates little bodies and minds. Green latticed triangles and yellow curvy lines form playful tridimensional mosaics; circles are carved and extruded out of furniture or walls, making for an eye-popping experience. Mirrors and toys, cranks and slides – all follow the logic of patchworks, grids and tessellations. To progress up and down the *MINISCHIRN* promenade is to be faced with systemised, kaleidoscopic universes where architecture proves to be an adventure. As patterns, shapes and colours become rich and intricate, allowing for an enhanced formation of knowledge and thus fostering basic aesthetic abilities and intuitions; namely, patterns achieve their pedagogical aims. Markgraph really does hit the nail on the head –

THERE EXISTS A STRONG AFFINITY BETWEEN THE ARRANGEMENTS OF PATTERNS AND THE IMAGINATION OF YOUNG ONES, AND THE ATELIER MAKES THE MOST OF IT.

By way of repetitive, haptic experiences, children encounter (and gain) new conceptions of matter, space and art. What's more, they have fun while doing so.

Fun and liveliness also lie at the core of Atelier Markgraph's vision for the Sparkasse-Gruppe (also referred to as their 'digital powerhouse') at the 2018 Finanz Informatik convention, though different means. The serious landscape of IT and economics is enlivened by a bold, spirited addition: floating above the cubicles and passages, hundreds of crimson squares and stripes form a fragmented swarm. The overall effect is intricate, attention-grabbing and remarkably dynamic. To be sure, pattern formations and the emergence of swarms constitute an impactful architectonic strategy – one which has been extensively explored in recent years, to varying degrees of success. In the case of Finanz Informatik, the strategy works. Modular behaviours of discrete elements make up for a playful totality; lumps and slivers are sublimated by their belonging to a cohesive group. The bright-red squares are described by

009 In the 'triangle universe,' green tetrahedrons can be reconfigured in new, endless ways, thus conferring the fun power of space transformation to its young users.

010 Given their size, observational capacities and varying motor skills, kids have a unique perspective of place and design; physical models show a change of architectural language which reflects this perspective. Markgraph's model works for the *MINISCHIRN* demonstrate the Atelier's ability to understand well (and enhance) this perspective.

011 Stark and bright objects or surfaces help children to make sense of their environments: the stimulating reds and yellows of the climbing nook modulate its space in playful ways, transforming it into a worthy destination.

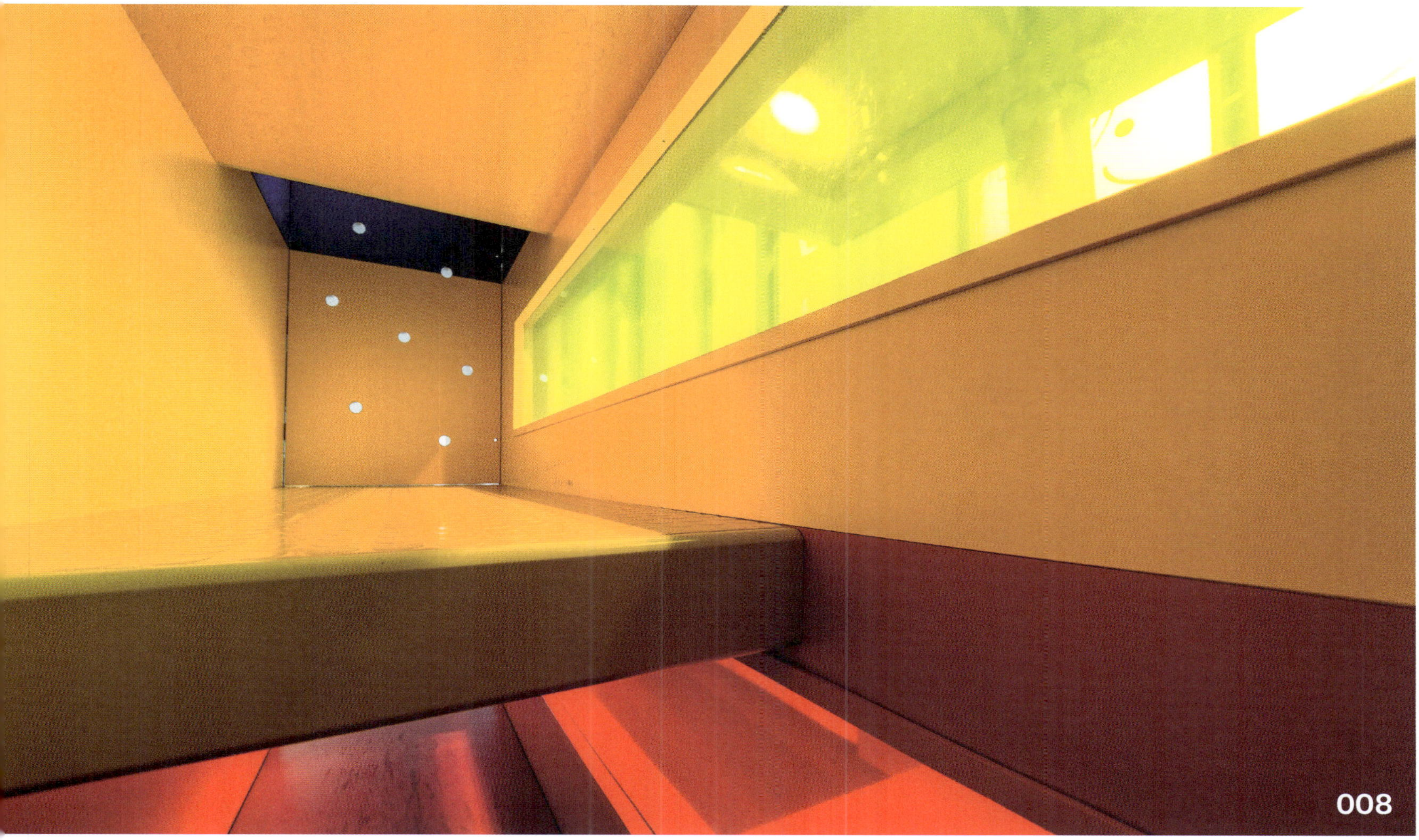

008

009

010

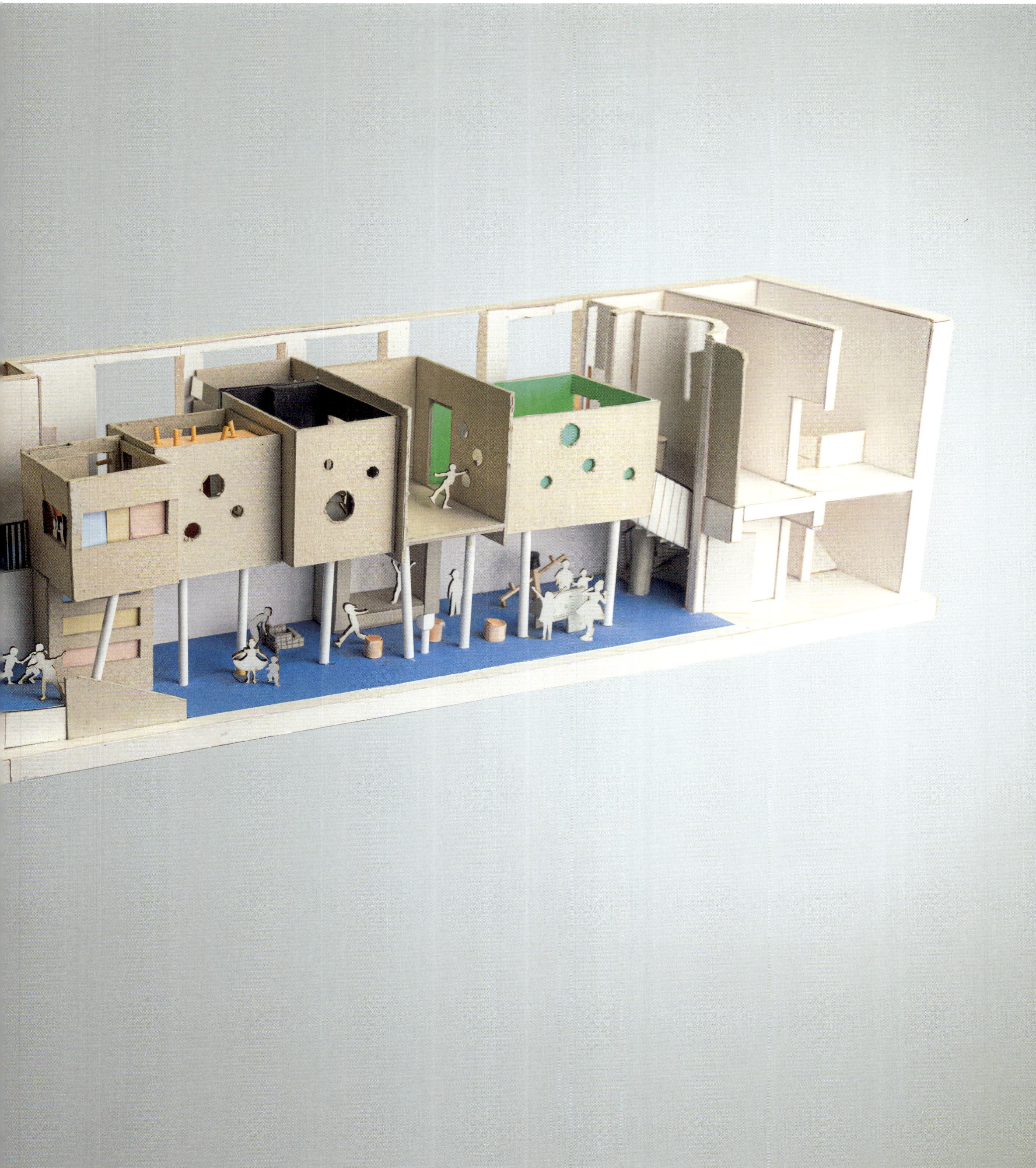

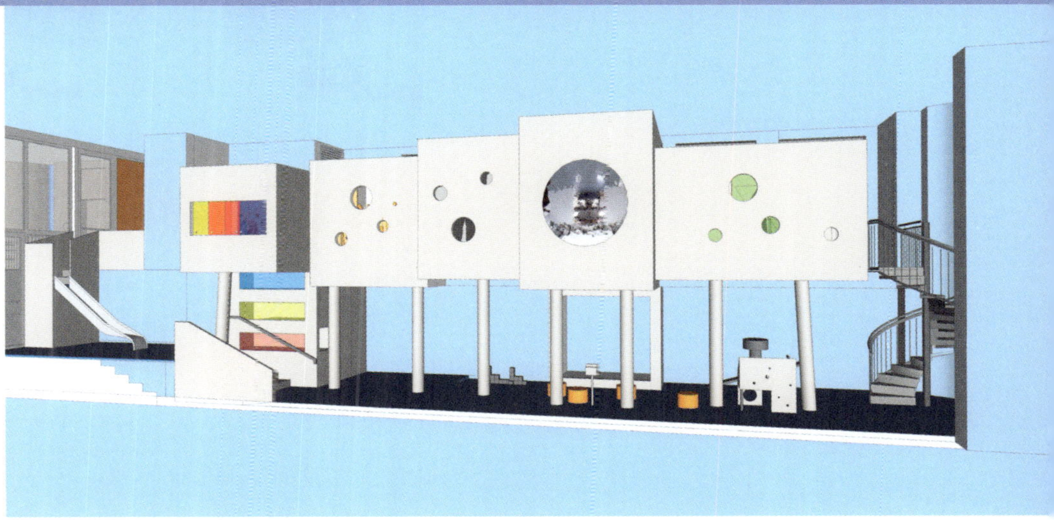

011

Das Internet ist wie eine Welle:
Entweder man lernt, auf ihr zu schwimmen,
oder man geht unter.
Bill Gates

Das Sammeln von Daten allein
reicht nicht – wichtig ist auch, zu wissen,
was man mit ihnen machen kann.
Michael Jiresch

013

014

012 At the end of the long, tunnel-like passage, the ceiling installation immediately grabs one's attention.
013 The sheer number of fragments that constitute Markgraph's sculptural intervention evokes an aesthetic of organicness, diversity and abundance.
014 Like an attractive and heavy snake, the red installation steadily threads its way into the open space of the fair. It is only through close proximity that visitors fully recognise its granular, pattern-like composition.
015 The pattern logic of the sculptural swarm is echoed in various ways throughout the FI promenade; soft projections are broken down into small, punctual pixels of light, which multiply one's vistas of swarms.
016 Hundreds of fine cable lines catch the red glow of the squares which connect them to the upper rails. The overall visual effect is complex, delicate and evocative.
017 Patterns occupy the ceiling space; they also leak along the walls, formed by clouds of small, see-through boxes. Red acts as a visual link between these different design moments.

Markgraph as 'festoons;' this is an appropriate qualification. Indeed, a festoon (from the Latin word 'festum,' or feast) refers to a tradition of decorative arts, where spaces and surfaces are adorned with hanging wreaths or garlands. Festoons are carved ornaments depicting specifics arrangements: small flowers, interlaced foliage or fruits are bound together and suspended, presenting viewers with one unified, organic pattern. Like their conceptual ancestors, the squares and swarms which form Atelier Markgraph's installation are bound together and suspended. In the horizontal field of the convention centre, the red swarm unfolds like a pulsating ribbon: it mobilises the gaze and, in its contrast with the slick, sombre world below, acts as an unmissable point of reference throughout one's exploration of the space. Inasmuch as it is necessary to the nature and quality of the architectural experience, the Finanz Informatik pattern bears a marked resemblance to the best decorative works – remove the swarm, and you are left with significantly less.

The type of encounters examined in this chapter are constituted through the viewer's discernment of a repeated module, the arrangement of which produces meaning. It relates to eloquent groupings and collections; to telling signs and swarms. Motifs can surpass their embellishment function, providing project users with an additional, informational layer. In effect, they form a composition that is more than the sum of its parts. This phenomenon is well exemplified in the impressive *Constellations* drone show, conceived by Markgraph for the celebration of Frankfurt's 'newly rebuilt' old town. An urban, multimedia event which was held in 2019, *Constellations* utilises drone assemblages to celebrate the history and culture of the city. In poetically surreal visions, points of lights hover and shift positions: from indistinct swarm-like masses, they then organise to create outlines of known objects – a crown, a two-armed scale, a bird, a pointy flower. Really, the scene amazes. There is a high degree of order and precision in the different placements of the drones; it is equaled by the degree of emotion and wonder experienced by viewers.

BEING PRESENTED WITH A PATTERN-LIKE FORMATION IMPLIES A TWOFOLD ENCOUNTER OF SPACE AND TIME.

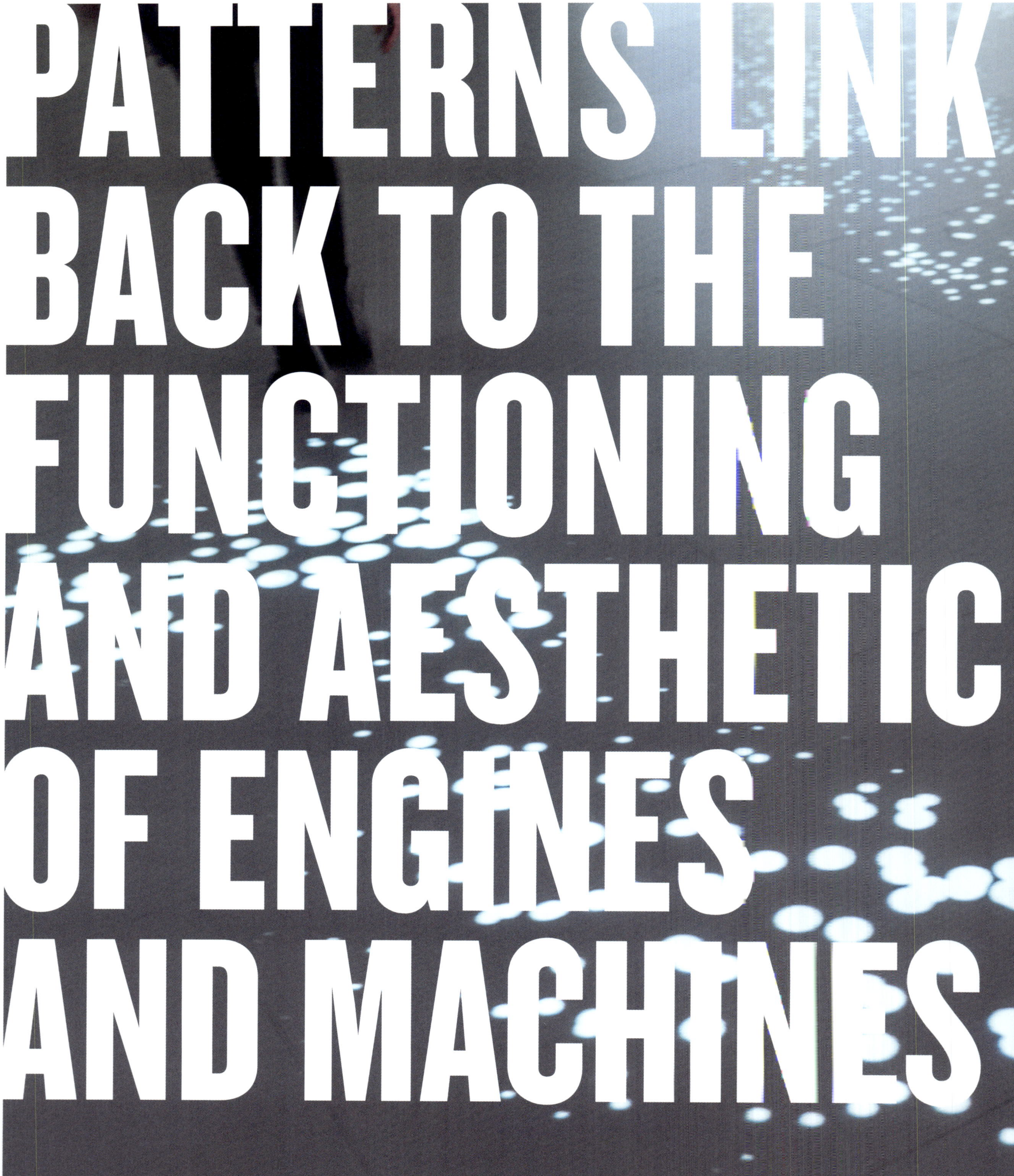

PATTERNS LINK BACK TO THE FUNCTIONING AND AESTHETIC OF ENGINES AND MACHINES

016

017

Atelier Markgraph's drone deployments demonstrate that ultramodern, technical feats can also double as poignant moments of storytelling. As such, *Constellations* is the undisputable heir of another large-scale night show: fireworks. Dozens of drones emerge as the 21st-century-outburst of shapes and colours and lights; a generous display that links to traditions of impartiality and inclusivity in cosmopolitan, artful celebrations. Everyone is welcomed, and the more the merrier. For what proves to be a striking moment of *vivre ensemble*, Frankfurt's residents and tourists are invited in masses to look up and enjoy the spectacle of luminous patterns in a dark sky.

The production processes of pattern-adorned objects – wallpapers, prints, woven textiles – generally consist of the motorised repetition of a unit which covers a small portion of the object's surface. In that sense, patterns link back to the functioning and aesthetic of engines and machines; of cogs and automatons. To reclaim German Jewish philosopher, cultural critic and essayist Walter Benjamin's famed term (1935), it can be said that pattern works capture something of the essence of art in the age of mechanical reproduction. This phenomenon was confirmed in the last decades, with computerisation and the general sophistication of digital technologies. The *EQ Teaser* installation (2018), a parametric canvas developed for Mercedes-Benz by Markgraph, features 756 individual LED pins which are programmed to respond to visitors' motions and impulses. In a manner reminiscent of *Constellations*, these pins are treated like pixels, advancing and receding with soft muffled noises to create depictions of silhouettes and gestures; mechanically transforming their pattern expression to form dynamic portraits. Complex rules of software, sensors and motion graphics inform the realisation and final appearance of the design, with its tubular lights, synthetic textures and dotted matrix.

A black wall becomes an interactive starry sky, with machine-driven constellations and movements. Colour gradients and waving RBG channels generate lively, candied vistas. These vistas' qualities are augmented by the fact that they mirror the human figure that stands in front of it. *EQ Teaser* is an imperfect mirror to be sure, but one that generously adapts and morphs to its audience's movements. Atelier Markgraph hints at desirable futures for the practice of pattern making – big, playful, rhythmic and, most importantly, user-friendly.

There exists a strong aesthetic enjoyment in viewers' recognition of patterns. A unit is repeated methodically; a thrill is felt. However, the power of organised, visual repetitions goes beyond mere beautification.

018 Different arrangements of luminous drones resuscitate simple symbols and figures, which all link back to Frankfurt am Main's past and future. Following the logic of patterns, it is the ordered placement of distinct elements which gives rise to meaning and recognition.

019 There exists a stark contrast between the lightness of drones and the heavy rootedness of the architecture of the city.

020 Drones await take-off on the old stones of the Main's banks, in a memorable time-collapsing tableau. 110 singular, automated flying devices were necessary to the creation of the many sky patterns of *Constellations*.

021 The waters of the Main reflect the presence of the drone assemblages, nicely doubling their visual impact.

022 Occupying the wide stage of the city's airspace: this is Markgraph's powerful strategy to multiply the amount of individuals who can take part in the celebration. The scale of *Constellations* ultimately matches the ambition of its conceptors; to Frankfurt residents and visitors, it offers an enthralling, ephemeral spectacle – an urban moment to share, cherish and remember.

110

021

022

ARCHITECTURAL PATTERNS ARE MORE THAN DECORATIVE; THEY INFORM AND SITUATE. ARCHITECTURAL PATTERNS ARE MORE THAN SKIN-DEEP; THEY EXTRUDE, RECONFIGURE AND REACH OUT.

Successful projects which abide by the logic of motifs, grids and orderly figures are joyful invitations into a world of recognition and knowledge; of narratives and reverie. *ZDF Sport*, *MINISCHIRN*, *Finanz Informatik*, *Constellations* and *EQ Teaser*: these five realisations by Atelier Markgraph exemplify intense, evocative, tridimensional encounters – and show us the variety and true power of the pattern.

023 A sophisticated motherboard softly deforms the Teaser wall to 'reflect' the bodies and objects which stand in front of it – this mirroring effect incites visitors to move in new ways.

024 Various software are used to capture and make sense of the installation's immediate environment. Bodies and movements swiftly transform into data.

025 The patterned nature of *EQ Teaser* appeals to audiences of varying ages. Through the use of software technology, sensors, processors and effectors playfully organise movements and pulses. This dynamic approach was already present in Markgraph's installation for Mercedes-Benz Museum *MYTHOS 6*.

026 With its illuminated ceiling of starry lights, *MYTHOS 6* epitomises pattern-informed designs. It illustrates Markgraph's years-long experience in creating installations which thread the line between physical and digital realms.

027 With its intermittent flashes and chasing lights, the LED pattern reminds of the design of marquees which crown the entrance of hotels, theatres or casinos – it links back to the aesthetic of signage, entertainment and glamour.

028 A bright, diffuse cloud is formed by the accumulation of the pinheads. From certain angles, basic grid structure of *EQ Teaser* blurs into a unified surface of light.

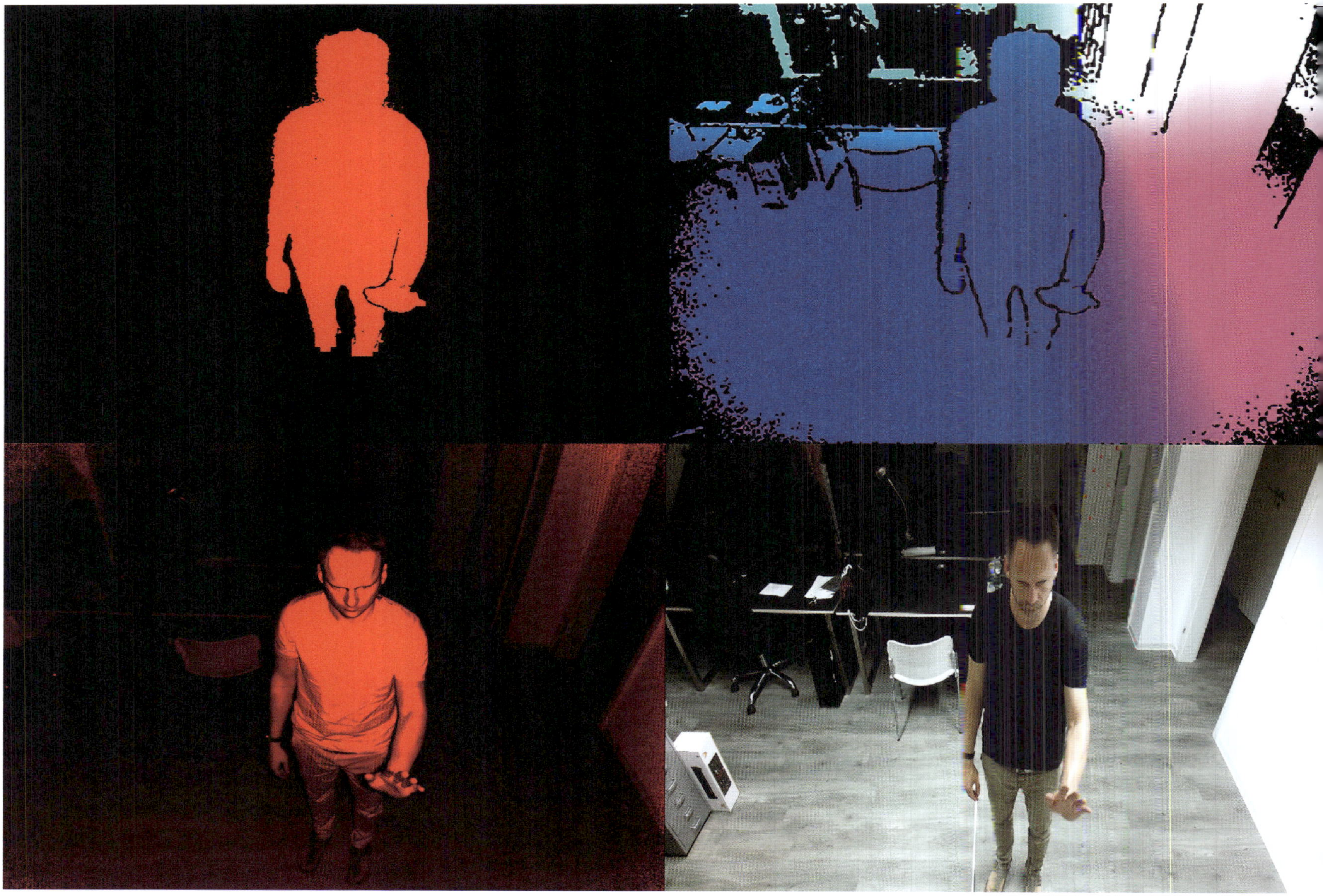

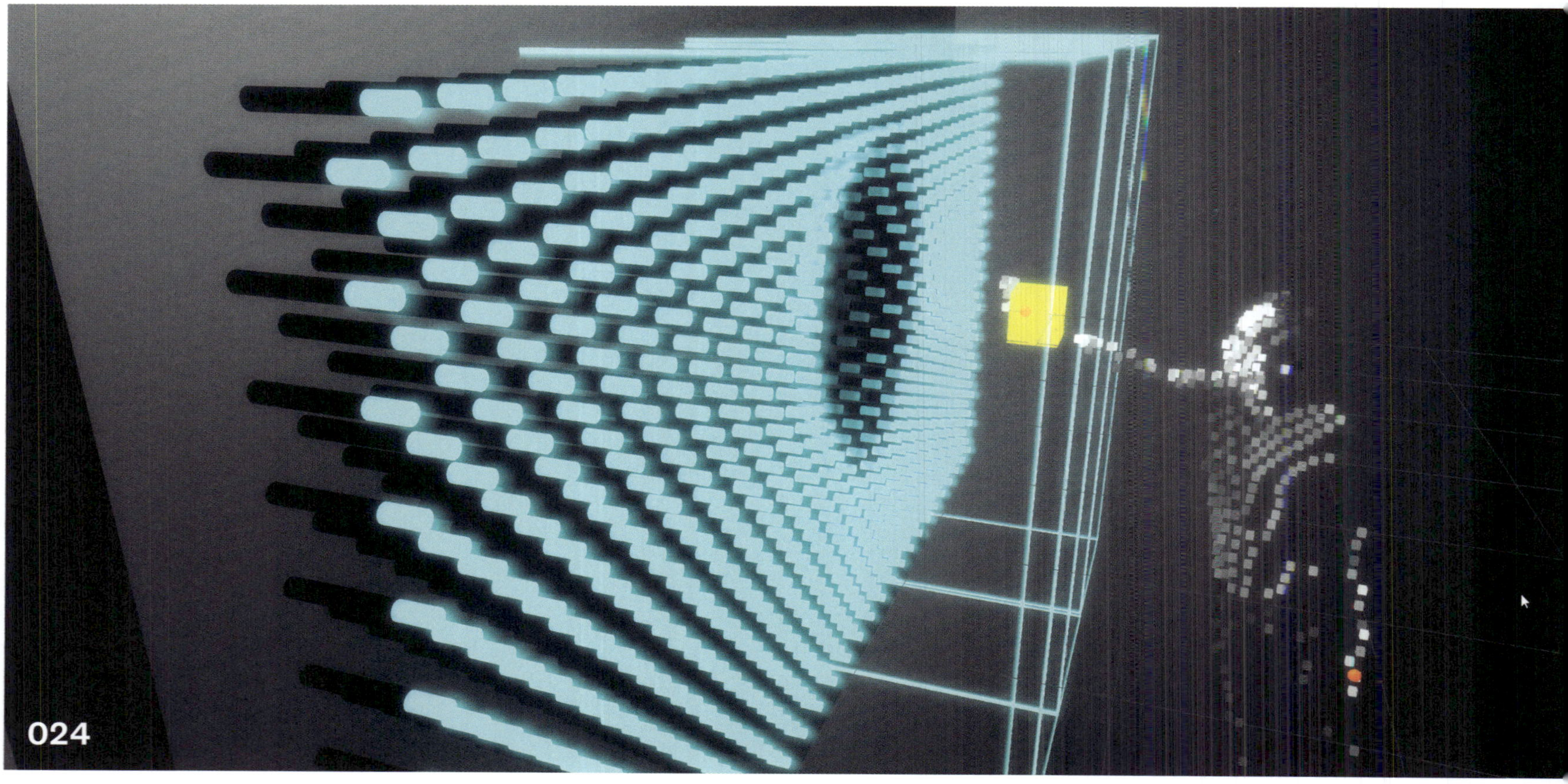

026

027

CONVIVIA

encou

ALITIES

friendly

nters

FRANKFURT KITCHEN

The Frankfurt-based restaurant Margarete pays tribute to Austrian architect and 'Frankfurter Küche' designer Margarete Schütte-Lihotzky 1897- 2000, her spirit permeating Markgraph's concept more than titularly: the space retains a sense of practicality, ergonomics and a welcoming nature, with wooden furnishings and warm-looking surface. PAGE 149

2012

2019

NETWORKING TOOLKIT

Created in dialogue with event-host Mercedes-Benz, the *EQ Networking Toolkit* gets visitors of various backgrounds and training to sport an interactive bracelet which allows them to casually connect and exchange information, creating a technology-facilitated experience of togetherness. PAGE 156

MARKGRAPH OFFICE

Situated in Frankfurt's busy Gallusviertel neighbourhood, Makgraph's Mainzer Landstrasse 193 office is a site of design praxis, where imaginative processes consist in space-bound, iterative combinations of activities and outputs. Generous windows, plywood surfaces, glass partitions and vividly painted walls give an overall impression of conviviality and creative energy. PAGE 160

2023

'SPIELFREUDE'

2023

The DFB-Campus is a place where young German football athletes can train and study. The design features sophisticated signage, typographical works, pattern designs, robotised wall drawings, immersive prints and contemporary references to the graphic identity of the Deutsche Fußball-Bund. The overall composition is an ostensible nod to the appreciable variety of individuals who are football players or fans. PAGE 172

ENCOUNTERS IN SPACE ARE AT TURNS UNEXPECTED, SWEET, MEANINGFUL, HOSTILE; THEY GENERATE NEGATIVE OR POSITIVE IMPRESSIONS FOR INDIVIDUALS WHO ARE SUBJECTED TO THEIR VARIOUS FEATURES.

The experience of discovering (and occupying) a well-built environment gives us a sense of happy satisfaction, of enjoyment – the pleasure is both physical and psychological, and participates in the preservation of human health. Pleasure, care, domesticity, conservation, comfort: these spatially sensitive notions have attracted renewed attention in our times of unkindly productivity, economic competition and ever-so-wearing performance of the self. Many contemporary architects, designers and theorists show interest in conceptualising spaces which also enable soft, affable dispositions. Interiors are to give off homely feelings; exteriors are to be 'warm' and truly hospitable. Yet, what does one mean, really, when she speaks of being in a welcoming place? How can conviviality translate into space? As is demonstrated in the following chapter, Atelier Markgraph's strategies for the making of convivial environments are multiple: they hint at creative attitudes or precepts which embrace the mundane, domestic and friendly side of architecture. By doing so, Markgraph takes part in a subtle enterprise of deconstruction, shifting value – hierarchical tendencies towards historically dismissed imaginaries. In effect, a search for spatial conviviality already hints at celebrations of femininity and intimacy; of camaraderie, gentleness and familiarity. This search therefore denotes a distinctly ethical position, and so, brings out a collection of human-centered endeavours.

A kitchen arguably constitutes the archetype space of conviviality: to many, it evokes feelings of familiarity and informality, of warmth and family life. Kitchens link back to the contentment of our most basic bodily needs; to

001
»All die guten Sachen zum Essen
und all die guten Sachen zum Trinken und
all die guten Sachen für die Gesundheit.«
Wer eine Kartoffel
so zu kochen versteht,
dass sie eine
lockende Nahrung
für sich darstellt,
beweist, dass er Sinn
für die Kochkunst hat
»Zuerst eine kleine Erfrischung
als Lohn für meine Mühe.«

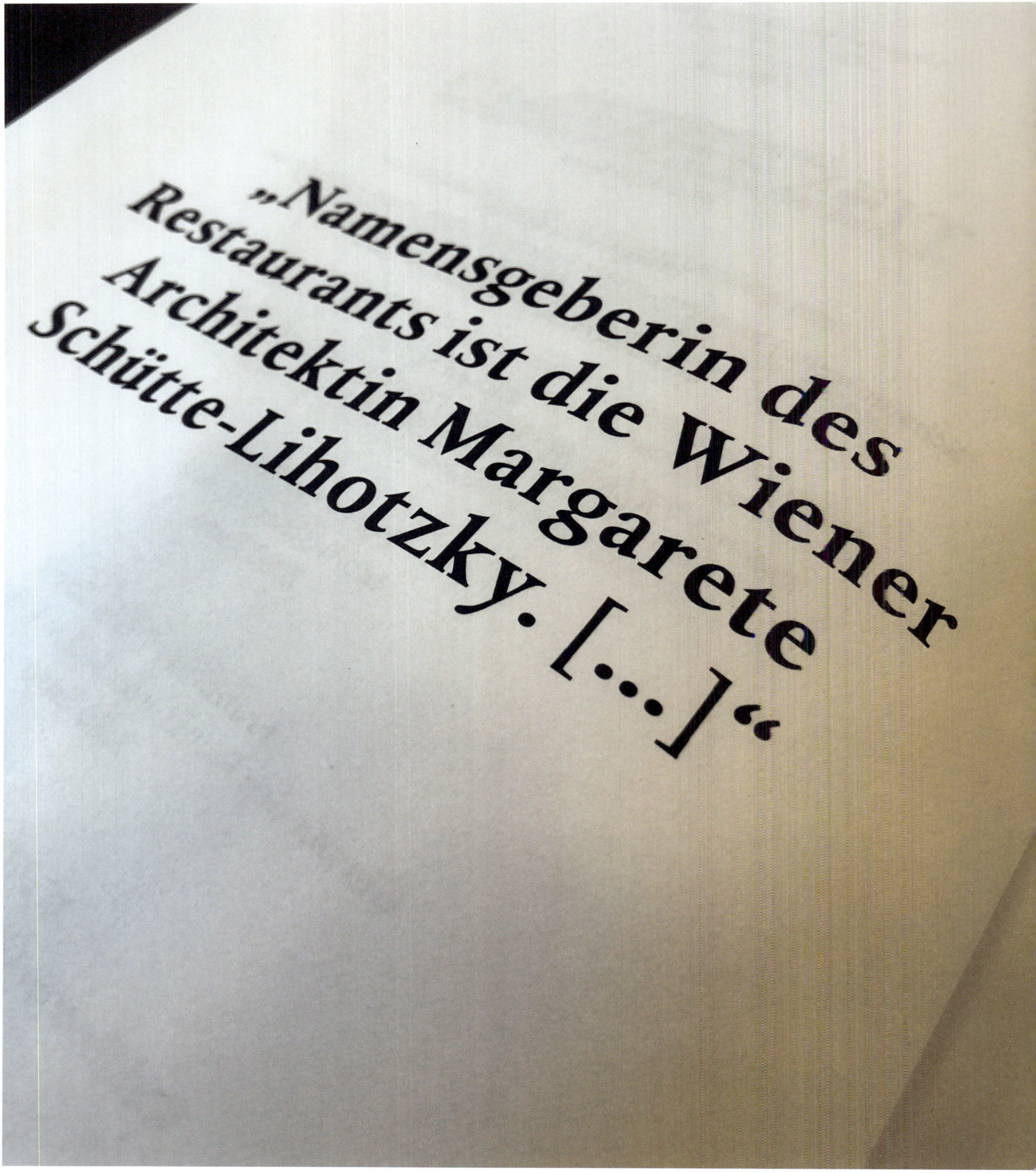
„Namensgeberin des
Restaurants ist die Wiener
Architektin Margarete
Schütte-Lihotzky. […]“

002

003

004

001 Architectural historians have noted that, in designing her kitchen, Margarete Schütte-Lihotzky drew inspiration from the kitchens of restaurant-cars in long-distance trains; with its tight, convivial rows of tables, the dining space of *Margarete* also reminds one of the restaurant-car spatial layout – and spirit.
002 Various wall openings and shelves allow guests to see the restaurant's insides or storage; lounging corners allow for different modes of spatial occupation.
003 A pioneer figure of human-focused architecture in 20th-century Europe, Margarete Schütte-Lihotzky is the inspiration behind features of Markgraph's spatial concept. Her famous 'laboratory of housework,' the Frankfurt kitchen, builds on design ideals of rationality, intelligence, social orientedness and elegance.
004 Simple, sturdy wooden chairs strengthen the impression of ergonomy and practicality, linking back to the architect Schütte-Lihotzky's Frankfurter Küche. Markgraph's selection of coarse, primary-coloured fabrics similarly suggests that functionality and use are prioritised as design principles.
005 The restaurant's principal room consists of one large, unbroken space. Its volume and table placement evoke collective dining experiences and typologies; by contrast, the shelving gives off an impression of homeliness and privy domesticity.

preservation, sustenance and care. As home environments, they are meant to be functional and orderly, comfortable and casual. These basic tenets of kitchen architectures are celebrated in Atelier Markgraph's concept for the Frankfurt-based restaurant *Margarete*, a project completed in 2012. The name of the establishment is a direct homage to Austrian architect Margarete Schütte-Lihotzky 1897–2000, a visionary woman who remains most known for her Frankfurter Küche – perhaps the world's first fitted kitchen, which was to facilitate the cooking and cleaning activities of working class dwellers. In truth, the spirit of Schütte-Lihotzky permeates Markgraph's design more than titularly: the restaurant retains a sense of its practical, welcoming nature. Gastronomy meets the crafty features of the contemporary Frankfurter Küche – circulation is facilitated through the ergonomic placement of furniture which orders the open dining spaces; custom built-in shelves provide for ample, visible storage. Wood elements confer a certain cosiness to the interior, while ample fenestrations ensure the good lighting of the space during daytime; details in copper and linen evoke local artisanal traditions, with an attention to the city's old book-making productions. Visual connections between guests (as well as with staff members) are encouraged by the large interior, which is left undivided. Lamp fixtures are positioned so that no strong shadow falls upon the tables, a subtle recall to Margarete Schütte-Lihotzky's light strategy for the Frankfurt kitchen. Finally, a small showroom (dubbed 'Fenster zur Stadt,' or window to the city) acts as programmatic connector, opening the space of *Margarete* up to urban wanderers, who are 'invited in.' This assortment of features demonstrates the convivial nature of Markgraph's restaurant design, in a clever homage to one of the oldest forms of encounters: making and sharing a meal.

Much has been written on the topic of developing digital technologies and their impacts on our capability for meeting meaningfully: one line of thought warns against cases of social isolation and dispassion through the use of new 'online' medias, which are taken to impoverish key moments of dialogues and other significant human exchanges. This form of argument often runs into reductive ends, but the point remains of interest – we ought to pay attention to the convivial qualities of digitally mediated encounters, and seek to strengthen these qualities when it is possible to do so. Atelier Markgraph conceived their *EQ Networking Toolkit* as such an exercise. Created in dialogue with event host Mercedes-Benz, the concept is

005

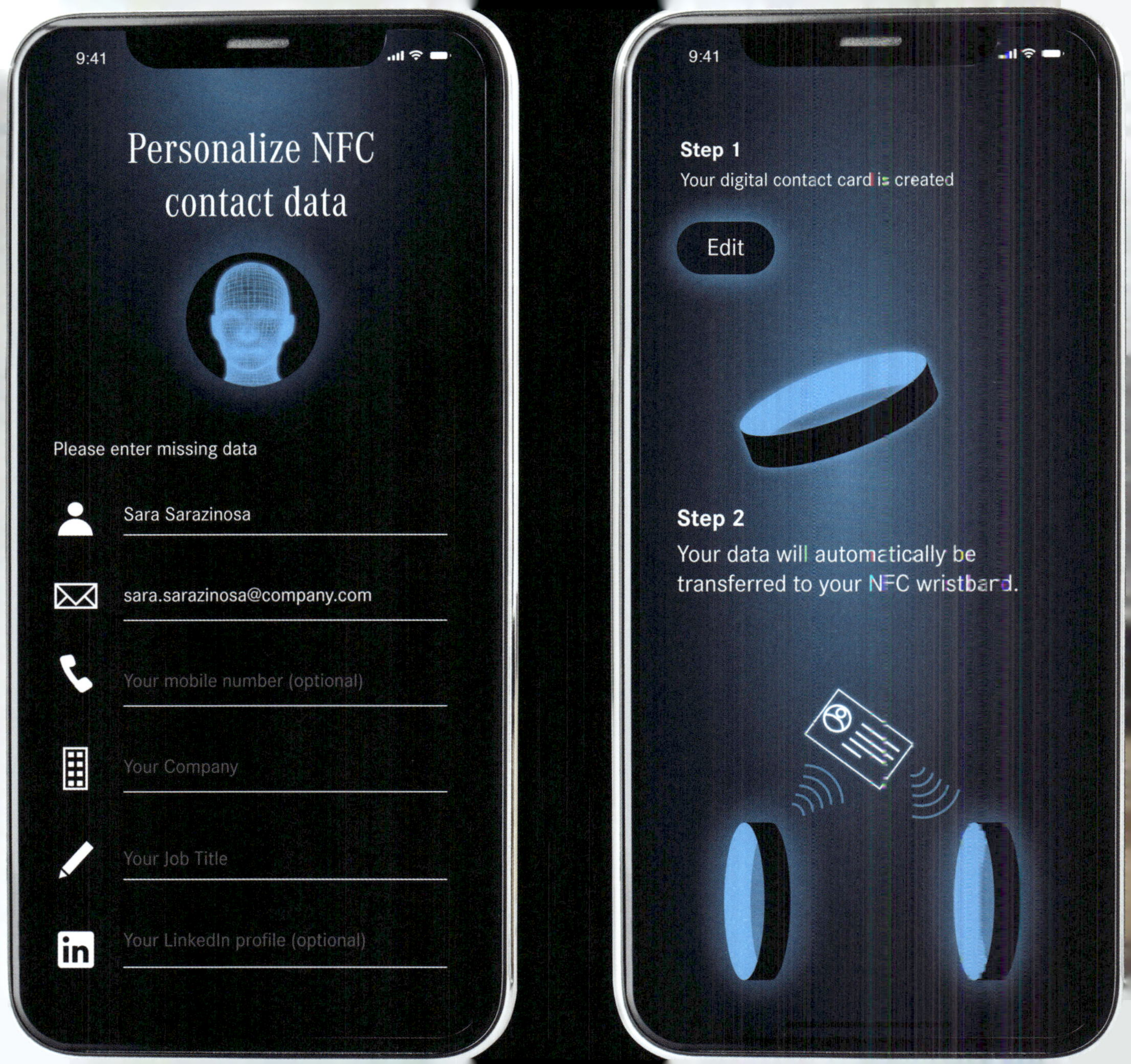
9:41
Personalize NFC contact data
Please enter missing data
Sara Sarazinosa
sara.sarazinosa@company.com
Your mobile number (optional)
Your Company
Your Job Title
Your LinkedIn profile (optional)
9:41
Step 1
Your digital contact card is created
Edit
Step 2
Your data will automatically be transferred to your NFC wristband.

Connect
First user, place your armband.

SHAPING THE FUTU

Guest list

Identified

Send your selected items to your mail
Take it home!

008

Connected

006 The recent integration of technologies into everyday life leads to a change in awareness and perception: Markgraph's *EQ Networking Toolkit* can be understood as commentary on and reminder of the complexities (and invisibilities) which arise from data-tracking and other datafication processes. All in all, it establishes the client's brand as both 'technologically advanced' and 'human centered.'

007 Participants' encounters are translated in fun, haptic ways. The users of *EQ Networking Toolkit* are in good, assisting hands; through their use of digital objects, they can keep the night going a little longer.

008 The concept mobilises various digital interfaces (phones, tablets, smart watches) in support of site-rooted, social encounters; the Atelier's creatives propose a vision of technological helpfulness which, in the image of their client's product, oscillates between the tools' accessibility and their sophisticated performance.

convivial indeed: through the sporting of an interactive bracelet (a smart watch of sorts), guests can casually connect and exchange information, in ways which hope to help in the breaking down of certain social barriers and conventions. For the duration of one evening, in the fun space of the Amsterdam Vervako Shipyard warehouse, individuals of various backgrounds and training can experience a form of togetherness which is facilitated by – and not prevented by – their usage of digital technologies. The objective is simple: algorithms are deployed in the service of cosiness and informality; data and online messaging are automatised in order to lessen the conventionalism of common business exchanges. Recognising (and hoping to overcome) individuals' possible digital illiteracy, the user-friendliness of the software designed by Markgraph's collaborators, 3spin, smooths the experience for all participants. Here *EQ Networking Toolkit* signals a willingness to challenge the atomisation and individualism that can follow for interactions with some digital tools and interfaces, when these tools lead to a withdrawal from the physical 'here and now.'

INSTEAD OF BUSYING THEMSELVES WITH ADDRESSES, NUMBERS AND WEBSITES, PARTICIPANTS ARE FREE TO CONVERSE, PLAY, DEBATE: THEY ARE ENABLED TO MEET IN DIFFERENT – AND ARGUABLY MORE MEANINGFUL – WAYS.

'Practice what you preach' is a commonsensical adage which speaks of one's expectation that individuals (or groups) ought to act according to the way they tell other people to act – in the context of our examination of Markgraph's production, the adage could be reworked as follows: as a group of creatives, we expect the Atelier to organise its own workspace according to the way it shapes spaces for others. So, a closer examination of Atelier Markgraph's

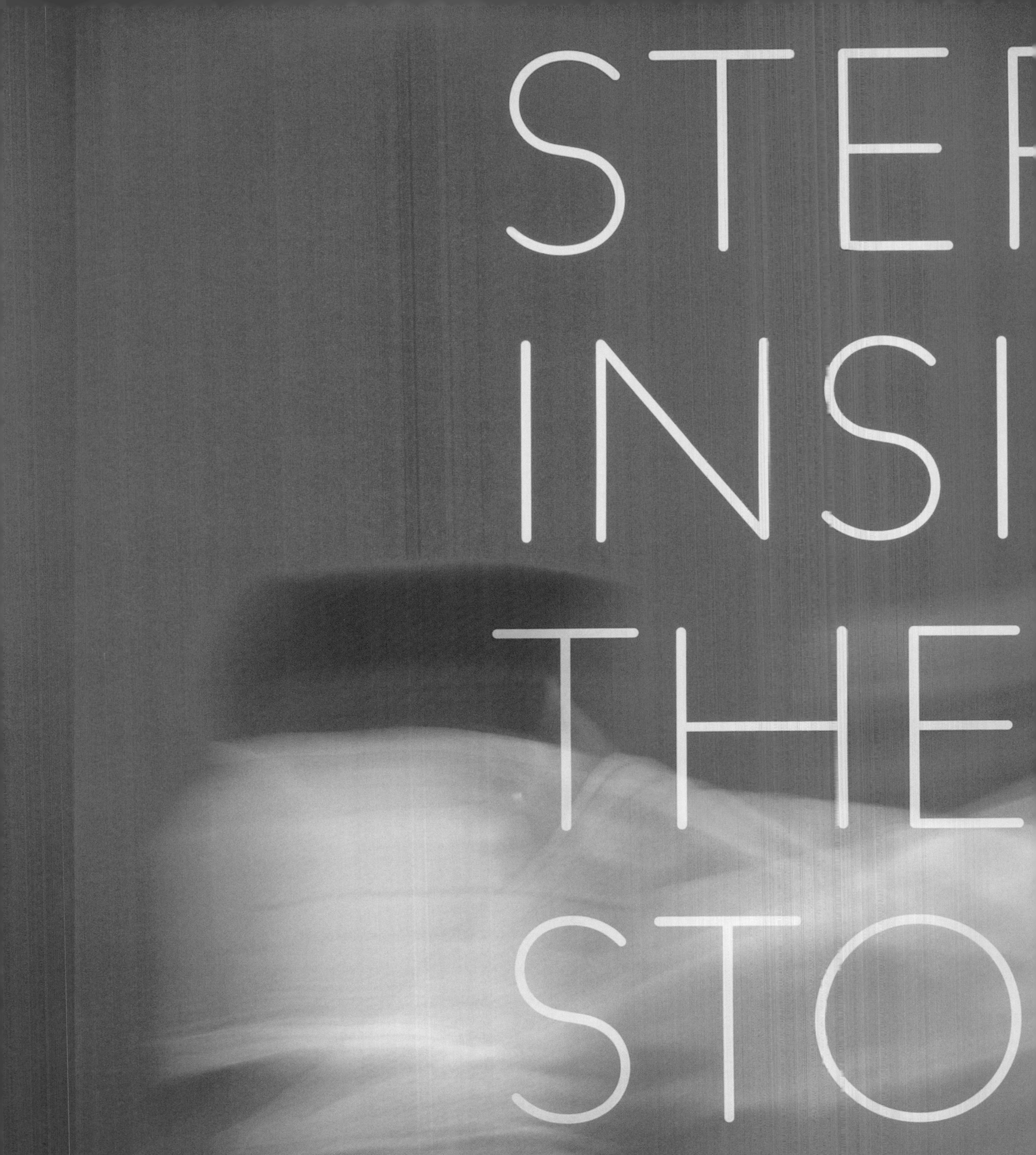
STE
INSI
THE
STO

009
DE
PATIAL
XPERIENCES
NCE
986
RY

009 A vivid red and other bold colours punctuate the spaces of Atelier Markgraph's office, making for a cosy and vitaminised experience for visitors and employees alike.
010 Glassy walls work to dematerialise the barriers between staff occupying different positions at Markgraph: open-plan rooms and smaller offices alternate in plan, but all connect visually.
011 Architectural interiors (styles, displays) and their various items represent something of a person's set of beliefs and values. Little toys, books, cups, posters: they also are a tangible extension of the individual who cumulates and displays them.
012 A fitting reflection of the Atelier's mixed-media production, digital and analogue tools are found in equal numbers in the Mainzer Landstrasse workspace.
013 Everyday sceneries at the Markgraph office prompt reflections on the post-pandemic version of the atelier; a shift to a 'non-territorial' office layout is gradually being implemented, with ramifying, freeing consequences for employees' occupation of their work space. Desks and equipment are constantly being reorganised, an organic answer to project demands and remote labour. What's more, employees are given the space to exhibit their personal objects, so as to share a bit of themselves with others.
014 An axonometric view of Markgraph's workspaces shows its longitudinal orientation, with ateliers *en enfilade* and many multi-sized room pockets.

most recent office, located in Frankfurt's busy Gallusviertel neighbourhood, is bound to speak volumes about core spatial principles, situations and attitudes which shape Markgraph's general production. In effect, the office – which occupies the third level at Mainzer Landstrasse 193 – is thought of as a site of true design praxis, where imaginative processes consist in space-bound, iterative combinations of activities and outputs. Importantly, such activities and outputs are highly collaborative. The challenge for the planners of the Mainzer Landstrasse's office consists of shaping spaces that can accommodate and encourage this spirit of iteration and collaboration. A visitor entering Markgraph's workstead first comes across a collection of varied features: generous windows, plywood surfaces, many framed posters, glass partitions, a vivid red wall. On the right side, a study room of sorts, its walls heavy with fully furnished bookshelves; on the left side, a large, see-through meeting room which doubles as a workshop and projection room. Glass partitions guide employees and guests further into the Atelier's world, toward the open desk areas, kitchens, technical rooms, archives and studios of varying scales. The overall impression is one of conviviality and creative disorder: everyday objects (project posters, machinery, catalogues, material samples and models, storybooks, utensils, music records, cables and papers, figurines) lay around, present at hand, easy of reach. Objects, furnishings, people: they are not artfully curated, but simply stumbled onto, in process. Numerous tables and seats signal a primacy of human encounters and dialogues; informal nooks and corners invite users to chitchat or daydream. Architectural interiors unfold in service of individuals' ability to interact creatively and autonomously with and in the company of others. In balance, Markgraph set up a work environment that appears both friendly and productive, thus living up to its very name: with its plethora of design items, tools and alcoves, this office does, indeed, function like an artist's atelier.

A variety of spaces can be associated with experiences of hospitality, care and sociability – we have seen that kitchens, warehouses or workspaces can, when successfully designed, foster warm sentiments of camaraderie and friendliness. To this collection of typologies, let us add the football pitch, which, as a space, perhaps best epitomises such convivial experiences and sentiments. In Germany and beyond, the symbolic importance of 'football architectures' no longer needs explanation: these are sites where people meet and connect in deeply spirited, solidary and meaningful manners.

011

bauhaus
Das Bauhaus
FUTURE SYSTEMS
10 x 10
archive
it's all
about
communi

TO BE SURE, THE VALUE IN PRIOR COMMUNALITY, HOSPITALITY W IN CREATIVE AC

RE IS TRUE
TISING
CARE AND
EN ENGAGING
S

NACKTE
Genius Challenge @ IAA 2019

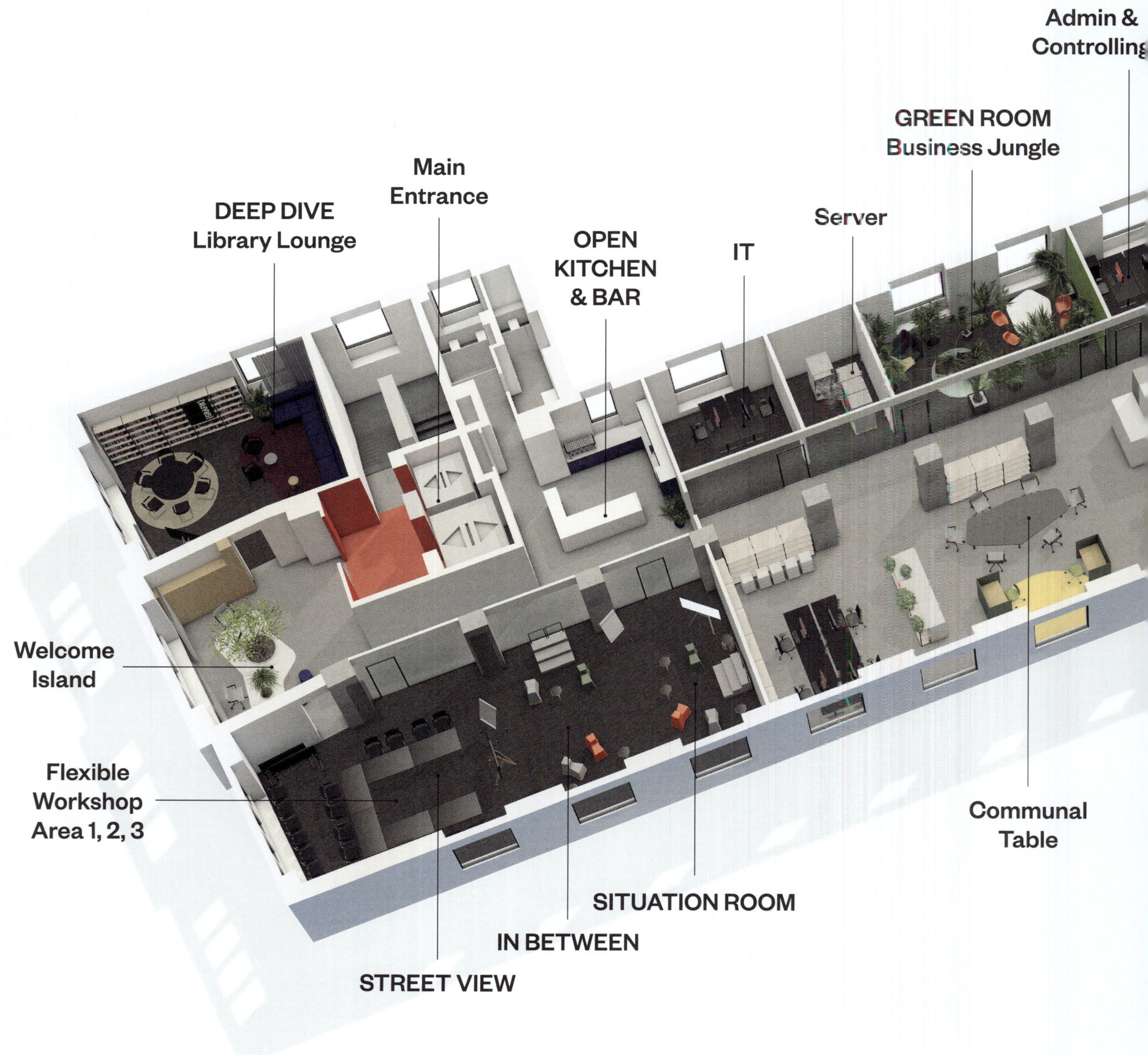
Admin &
Controlling
GREEN ROOM
Business Jungle
Server
IT
OPEN
KITCHEN
& BAR
Main
Entrance
DEEP DIVE
Library Lounge
Welcome
Island
Flexible
Workshop
Area 1, 2, 3
STREET VIEW
IN BETWEEN
SITUATION ROOM
Communal
Table

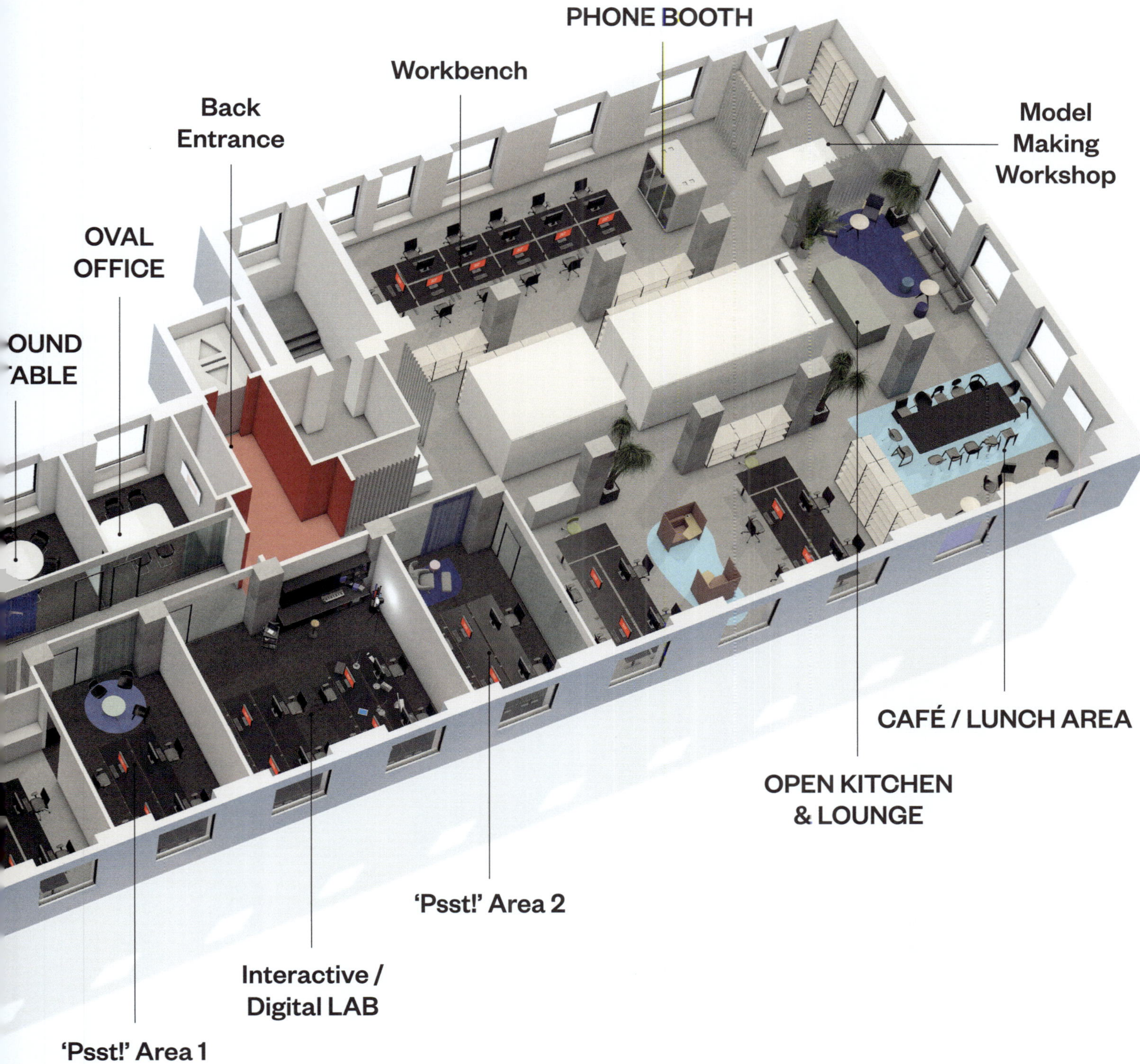
PHONE BOOTH
Workbench
Back Entrance
Model Making Workshop
OVAL OFFICE
OUND
'ABLE
CAFÉ / LUNCH AREA
OPEN KITCHEN & LOUNGE
'Psst!' Area 2
Interactive / Digital LAB
'Psst!' Area 1

FITNESS »
015

FAIR-PLAY AND TEAMWORK, BROTHERHOOD AND SISTERHOOD AND JOVIALITY – THEY ARE THE RULES OF THE FIELD, THE COMMANDMENTS OF THE BIG, STUNNING WORLD OF FOOTBALL.

Atelier Markgraph's concept for the Deutsche Fußball-Bund Football Academy, the *DFB-Campus* (2023), builds on such insights. An academy is a place of study or training in a special field. In the present project, it is a place of training for talented, young German football athletes; a boarding school of sorts. Based in a peripheral area of Frankfurt, the Football Academy also hosts the institutional headquarters of the Deutsche Fußball-Bund (which translates to German Football Association), with its public and private programs. The ambitious building complex by kadawittfeldarchitektur totals 50,000 m^2, and features a half-dozen football fields. Markgraph's team insisted that the spatial expression of the newly upgraded Football Academy be rooted in key notions of friendly performance, diversity, joyfulness and responsibility. Through a series of human-centred interventions, the Atelier transformed the Academy's generic existing interiors into places of excitement and identity. Sophisticated signage and typographical works, pattern designs and robotised wall drawings, immersive prints and contemporary references to the graphic identity of the Deutsche Fußball-Bund: these interventions signal a desire for users' inclusivity. Smooth surfaces of concrete create a fun contrast with mundanely green patches of astroturf; large atriums assemble and unite bodies, allowing for a visual reciprocity which recalls that of football stadiums. Press studios, conference rooms and exhibition areas tell a visual story of athletic heroism, history and sportsmanship. Here Atelier Markgraph does not hesitate to deploy heterogeneous tools, an ostensible nod to the appreciable variety of individuals who are football players or fans. The overall composition is a welcoming invitation to celebrate and appreciate the beauties and pleasures of the sport.

015 Conviviality consists of the quality of being friendly and making people feel good and welcomed; it captures the human dimension of encounters. Large wall projections (and many other visual representations found throughout the project) show individuals united, and happy to be so.

016 Detailed, colourful objects give off a feeling of familiarity, dynamism and movement. In that sense, Markgraph's design inspirations echo the sport featured and honoured: in the built environment of the Deutsche Fußball-Bund Academy, football is ever present.

017 Large signage and prints adorn the walls of the *DFB-Campus*, creating immersive and adorned atmospheres. Their visual variety echoes something of the variety of actors who participate in the life of the Academy; athletes, researchers, trainers, administrators, medical experts, coaches and referees make for a truly diverse group.

018 The Atelier's approach to creating the different spaces of the *DFB-Campus* evokes at times maximalism, with its many filigree illustrations, layered patterning, bold colours, geometric accessories and geometric furniture.

019 The building's conceptual imagery nicely links to the lively experience of playing or watching football together, which Markgraph's Deutsche Fußball-Bund design celebrates.

020 Staff and visitors' overall impression of the Football Academy's many spaces is one of energy, fun and abundance.

GALERIE

REGE
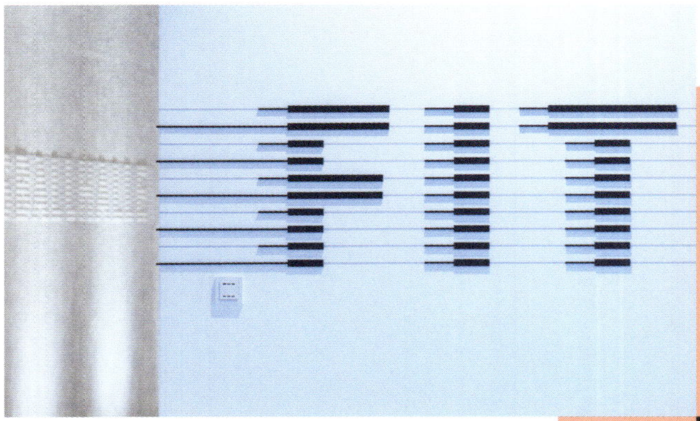
FIT

ARCHIV
B.U01-16.1-14

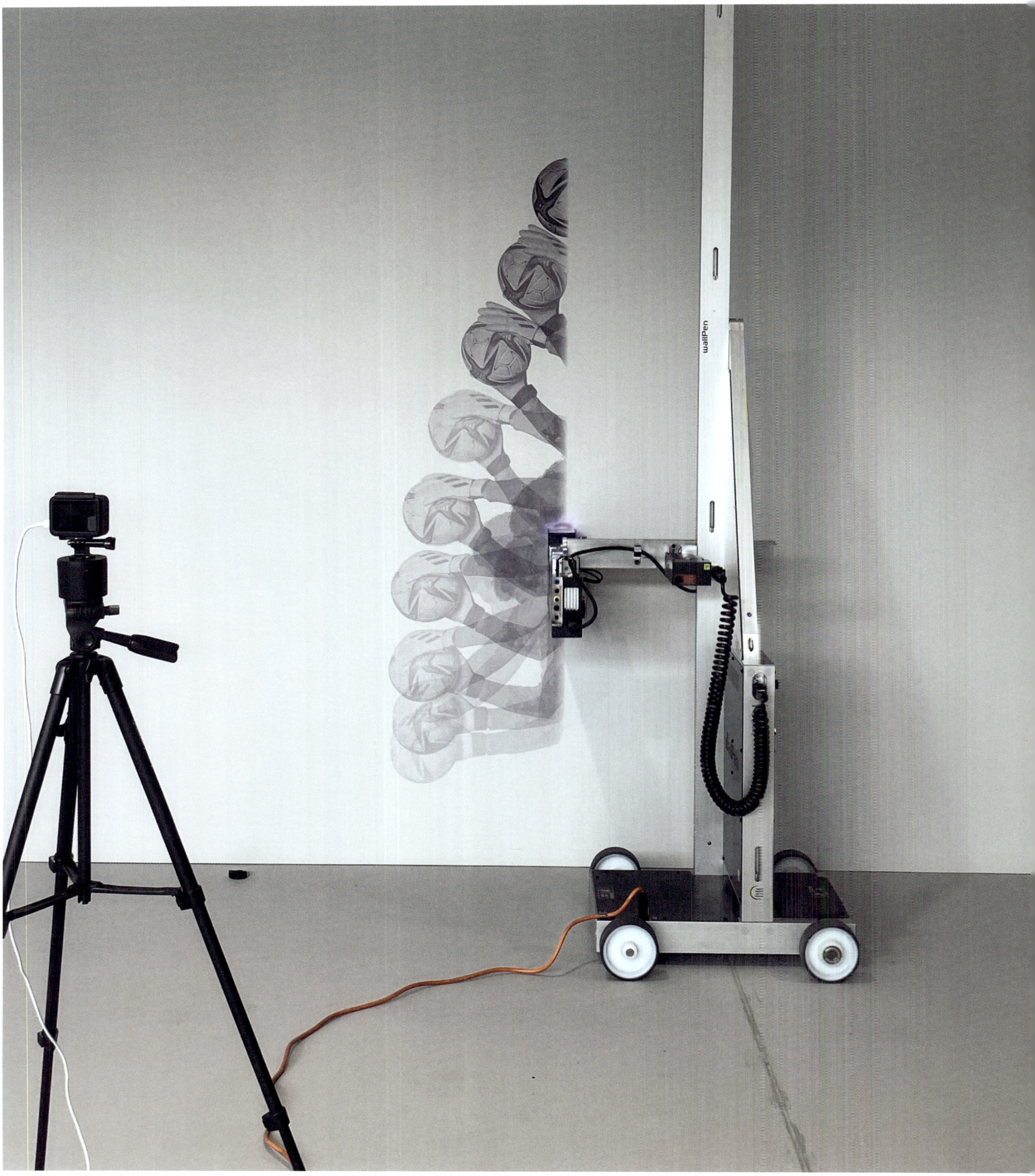
wallPen

The cultural imagination of conviviality often situates individuals in small-scaled, domestic environments – yet, as shown in this chapter, Markgraph makes the appealing case for an understanding of architectural conviviality which surpasses typological definition. Designers (and their collaborators and clients) who candidly seek the creation of people-centric spaces, events or encounters can begin by focusing on the basic, convivial principles identified through our examination of *Margarete*, *EQ Networking Toolkit*, the Atelier's office on Mainzer Landstrasse and the *DFB-Campus*. While they deploy different aesthetics and scales, these four projects deal with their users with respect and a distinctly marked affection. In that sense, they echo recent theorising on playful, comfortable 'third spaces,' which are thought to fortify human exchange and civil engagement. To be sure, there is true value in prioritising communality, care and hospitality when engaging in creative acts.

THE LATIN WORD 'CONVIVIUM' MEANS 'TO LIVE TOGETHER:' MARKGRAPH'S DESIGNS FOR INTERIORS, BRANDS OR EXPERIENCES DEMONSTRATE THE RICH, VARIOUS MANNERS IN WHICH SPACE INFORMS KEY FEELINGS – AND THE ENJOYMENT – OF TOGETHERNESS.

Queer Football

UN
BERECHENBAR
PERFEKT

V I E L F A L T

2 0
12.10.2003
WM-FINALE FRAUEN
DEUTSCHLAND VS. SCHWEDE
HOME DEPOT CENTER CARSON
USA

MIGRATI

encounte

ONS

mobile

rs

2016

TRIUMPH OF IMAGERY

***Athens. The Triumph of Imagery*, an art show presented in 2019 at Frankfurt's Liebieghaus Skulpturensammlung, utilises clever exhibition design to invite visitors on a time-collapsing journey to Ancient Greece's capital city; twelve adorned rooms feature an array of colours, lights, drawings, diagrams and media items mobilised to celebrate the strong, sculptural 'pictoriality' of the classical period.** **PAGE 196**

UNDERSTANDING VALUE

The Financial Investment travelling exhibition captures the fluctuations and activities which typify financial investments and trade, translating them into a simplified informative sequence. Pedagogical content and adaptable furniture ensure its grand-public informative aspect and transportability. **PAGE 219**

2018

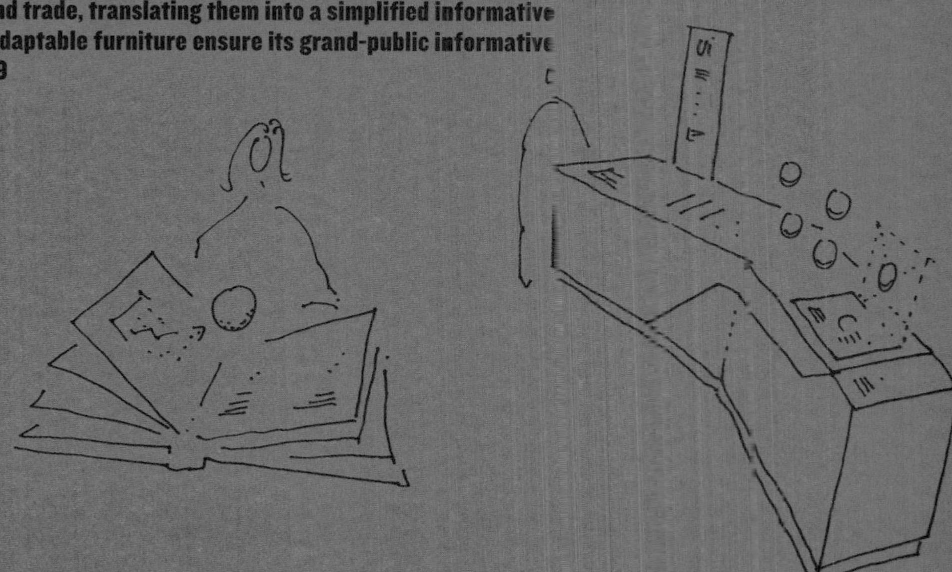

REACTIVE IDENTITY

Atelier Markgraph's corporate redesign, led and realised by independent Frankfurt-based studio Schultzschultz, simultaneously celebrates individuality and interdisciplinary cooperation with stretching, swirling, fluctuating graphics. **PAGE 188**

2017

ROADSHOW IN FESTIVAL FORMAT

CONTINUOUS

One of Atelier Markgraph's many container projects, aspires to formalise future experiences of mobility by arranging recycled intermodal boxes along vertical and horizontal axes, with their sides opening and swivelling according to programmatic demands. 'Plug and play' is the pavilion's axiom: new combinations and layouts are set up on open-air sites in various cities. PAGE 209

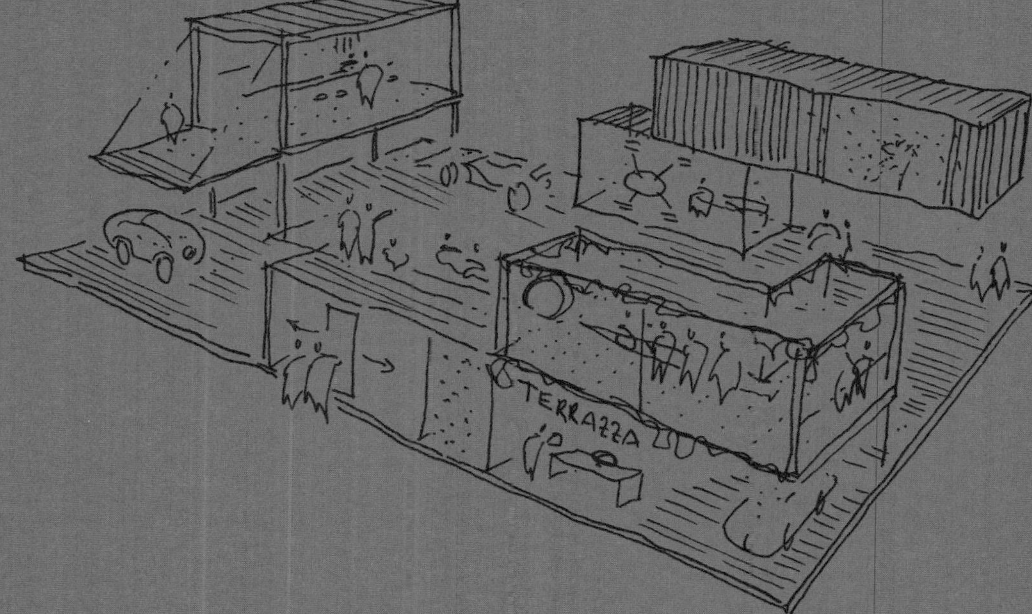

THREE-POINTED STAR

The strategic and spatial conceptualisation (and evolution) of brands' image and presence in the world follow the logic of dynamism and mobility – thus tasking the team of Markgraph creatives with conceptual guidelines and reappraisals. PAGE 226

CONTINUOUS

‘Afoot and light-hearted I take to the open road; healthy, free, the world before me; the long brown path before me leading wherever I choose.’ With the first words of his beautiful Song of the Open Road (1856), the poet Walt Whitman evokes the joy of journeys; the lively, hopeful feeling of being on the move. To be mobile, untethered; to multiply one’s possible trajectories – Whitman reminds his readers of the stirring freedom associated with voyage and movement.

THE WALKER OF THE OPEN ROAD REJECTS PERMANENCE AND ROOTEDNESS IN FAVOUR OF DYNAMISM AND MIGRATION, ASSERTING THE FLEXIBILITY (AND LIBERTY OF CHOICE) WHICH FOLLOWS FROM BEING IN TRANSIT.

We can begin to imagine the breadth of forthcoming encounters which await this walker along the way. Mobility links to open-ended situations; nomadic agents and beings multiply opportunities for meeting. The story of the present chapter is a story of journeys, trajectories, movements – of dynamic features and nomadism: projects by Atelier Markgraph are singled-out and examined in light of their distinctive mobility. What are the advantages and drawbacks of mobile architectures? How does motion inform Markgraph’s selected designs? ‘Wherever I choose,’ writes Walt Whitman – can projects, in effect, migrate seamlessly from one site to another, wherever one decides on? How do seasonal travels, circulation or movability translate formally? The five following works by Atelier Markgraph make for different evocatory responses to many mobility-oriented questionings.

Contemporary identities are fragmented, multiform, elastic. Persons, brands and institutions engage in their continual renewal, as we increasingly encourage dispositions of flexibility and adaptability, of swiftness and readiness. In a similar manner, architectures and styles adjust to an appreciable

LOGO UNTIL 2018

MARKGRAPH

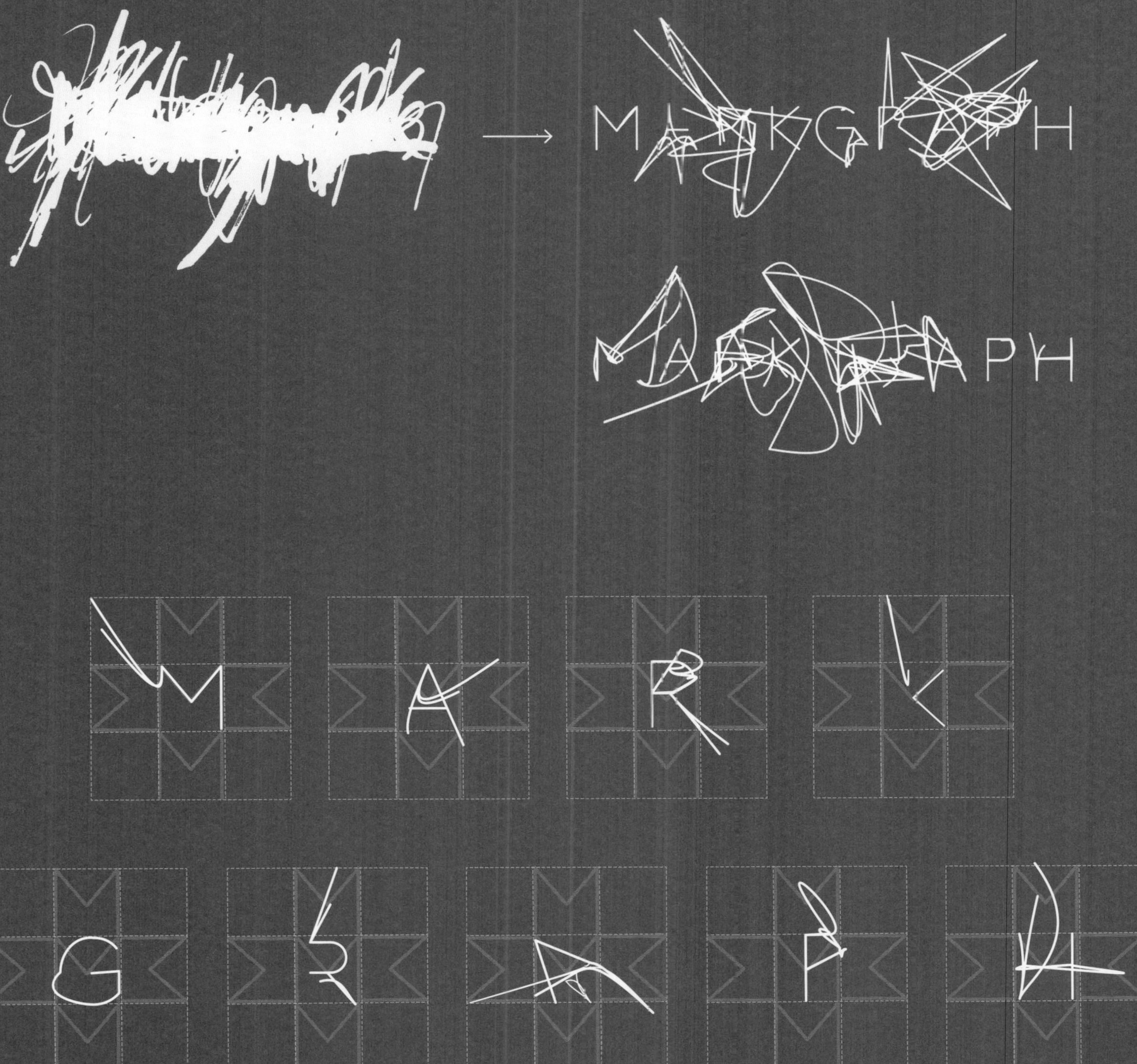

002

003

CUSTOM TYPEFACE MARKGRAPH

CHARACTER SET
LIGHT

Capital letters

AÀÁÂÃÄÅĀĂĄÆǼBCÇĆĈĊČDĐEÈÉÊËĒĔĖĘĚFGĜĞĠĢH
ĤĦIÌÍÎÏĨĪĬJĴKĶLĹĻĽĿŁMNŃŅŇŊÑOÒÓÔÕÖŌŎŐØǾŒPÞ
QRŔŖŘSŚŜŞŠẞTŢŤŦUÙÚÛÜŨŪŬŮŰŲVWŴXYŶŸZŹŻŽ

Lower case

aàáâãäåāăąæǽɑɑ̀ɑ́ɑ̂ɑ̃ɑ̈ɑ̊bcçćĉċčdðeèéêëēĕėęěfffffiflftg
ĝğġģhĥħiìíîïĩīĭjĵkķlĺļľŀłmnńņňŋñoòóôõöōŏőøǿœpþqrŕŗ
řsśŝşšßtţťŧuùúûüũūŭůűųvwŵxyŷÿzźżž

Proportional numerals	Tabular numerals	Subscript	Superscript	Fractions
0123456789	0123456789	1 2 3 4	1 2 3 4	¼ ½ ¾

Symbols and mathematic characters

& % ‰ § @ € $ ¢ £ ¥ ¤ © ® + - ± × ÷ ∂ ∏ ∑ √ ∞ ∫ ≈ = ≠ ≤ ≥ Ω µ π ∆ ◊

Punctuation and others

. : , ; · ¡ ! ¿ ? … ‐ – — _ ' " ‚ ' „ " " ‹ › « » ( ) [ ] { } * ° / \ • | ¦ † ‡ ¶ ™ ← ↑ → ↓ ↔ ↕ ↖ ↗ ↘ ↙

CHARACTER SET
BOLD

Capital letters

AÀÁÂÃÄÅĀĂĄÆǼBCÇĆĈĊČDĐEÈÉÊËĒĔĖĘĚFGĜĞĠĢH
ĤĦIÌÍÎÏĨĪĬJĴKĶLĹĻĽĿŁMNŃŅŇŊÑOÒÓÔÕÖŌŎŐØǾŒPÞ
QRŔŖŘSŚŜŞŠẞTŢŤŦUÙÚÛÜŨŪŬŮŰŲVWŴXYŶŸZŹŻŽ

Lower case

aàáâãäåāăąæǽɑɑ̀ɑ́ɑ̂ɑ̃ɑ̈ɑ̊bcçćĉċčdðeèéêëēĕėęěfffffiflftg
ĝğġģhĥħiìíîïĩīĭjĵkķlĺļľŀłmnńņňŋñoòóôõöōŏőøǿœpþqrŕŗ
řsśŝşšßtţťŧuùúûüũūŭůűųvwŵxyŷÿzźżž

Proportional numerals	Tabular numerals	Subscript	Superscript	Fractions
0123456789	**0123456789**	**1 2 3 4**	**1 2 3 4**	**¼ ½ ¾**

Symbols and mathematic characters

 # & % ‰ § @ € $ ¢ £ ¥ ¤ © ® + - ± × ÷ ∂ ∏ ∑ √ ∞ ∫ ≈ = ≠ ≤ ≥ Ω µ π ∆ ◊

Punctuation and others

. : , ; · ¡ ! ¿ ? … ‐ – — _ ' " ‚ ' „ " " ‹ › « » ( ) [ ] { } * ° / \ • | ¦ † ‡ ¶ ™ ← ↑ → ↓ ↔ ↕ ↖ ↗ ↘ ↙

MARKGRAPH

EMPFANG
Das G wurde von Uta Brinksmeier gesprochen.
KONFERENZ 1–3

ELLWERKSTA
TERIALBIBLIO
rde von Stefan Pach gesprochen

001 A collection of the small business cards printed with Markgraph's changing logo shows the fun and subtle variations (or iterations) between each visual signature.

002 Visualisations of Schultzschultz's creative process show the multifold transformation of the old Markgraph logo into the current one.

range of users and needs, always reinvented, accelerated, created anew. For good or ill, there exists a sense of movement and indeterminacy which characterises many a celebrated action or work – and this sense is reinforced through our daily passages between physical and digital environments. These timely features are referred to in Atelier Markgraph's 2017 corporate redesign, led and realised by independent Frankfurt-based studio Schultzschultz. The design's centrepiece is the new Markgraph logo, which consists of an imbrication of shapeshifting letters spelling out the company's name; the eye meets 'glyphs on the move,' stretching, swirling, fluctuating in a series of playful open-type deformations.

LIKE A SOUND WAVEFORM, THE LOGO REACTS TO DIFFERENT VOLUME LEVELS AND FREQUENCY RANGES, WITH THE LETTERS' INDIVIDUAL BARS BOUNCING IN ALL POSSIBLE DIRECTIONS.

Individuality and interdisciplinary cooperation are celebrated simultaneously, in a dynamic visual translation of the word 'Markgraph' spoken by the Atelier's employees. It is the unique pattern of each voice which animates the logo's form and content in live time. The quality and character of a particular individual which distinguishes them from others are overlaid; they accumulate in a half-digital, half-analogue representation which becomes more than the sum of its distinctive parts. The effect is one of energy and fruitful exchange. Schultzschultz's logo cleverly captures the dual spirit of Atelier Markgraph. It is both precise and indeterminate, constant and in flux – it moves between individualism and teamwork, between fiction and reality; between technological and cultural universes. With its 'monolinear' and geometric construction, the custom typeface developed for the redesign also joins tradition and

003 As a specifically designed typeface, the 'Markgraph' not only embodies a modern objectivity, but also enables the interplay of different (logo) states. It exists in 9 fonts (6 pt to 72 pt) at two styles each (light and bold). The typeface is based on a 'monolinear' and geometric construction. It thus stands in the tradition of popular fonts such as Futura, Gill Sans and Avenir.

004 Matt blacks or shiny reds make a fine background to Atelier's new font shape and style.

005 Eye-catching, fun features of the graphic relaunch of Atelier Markgraph include the insertion of 'dynamic letters' into the sober body of a written word. The effect is surprising and hints at a creative disorder of sorts.

Telesterion
Auswahl

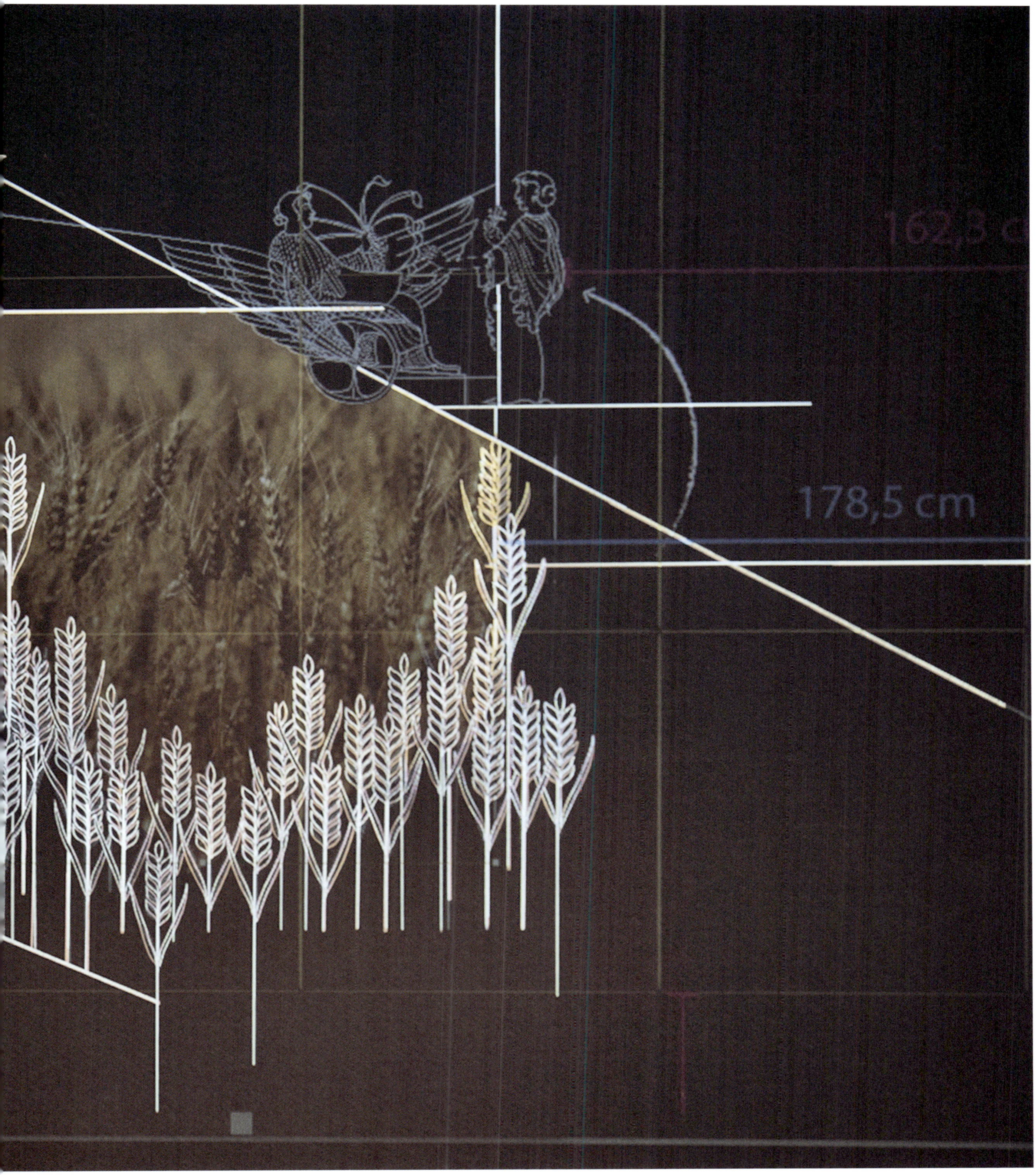
162,3 c
178,5 cm

SKENOGRAPHIA

„ATELIER DES PHIDIAS“
DER GROSSE PLAN
Athena
Atropos

006 A nice mix of digital and analogue representation technologies are used to create the wall graphics.
007 The placement of objects, texts, scales, sketches and photographies is often unconventionally asymmetrical, irregular, expansive: this gives a work-in-progress, informal quality to visitors' encounters with the featured content.
008 In various rooms, Atelier Markgraph's team opted for dark, blueish surfaces; the colour contrasts nicely with the whiteness of antique frescoes and statues, as well as with the white lines of the wall words and illustrations.

modernity; details such as rounded corners, height-adjusted middle strokes in capital letters and overall optical sizing confer rhythm and an impression of fluidity to the graphic project. This, truly, represents a corporate identity in motion – open-minded and hopeful, rapid and ready; shapeshifting, and generously so.

Mobile encounters also occur when objects and agents move and meet across geographies and spaces; they take place when objects and agents move and meet across time.

DIFFERENT ERAS ARE BROUGHT TOGETHER THROUGH NEW PROXIMITIES; CONTEMPORARY MINDS TRAVEL BACK IN TIME AND START TO CONVERSE WITH PAST INDIVIDUALS OR HISTORIES – THIS IS ALSO AN ACCOUNT OF DYNAMISM AND MIGRATION.

009 Some media projections bring an additional layer of colour and information to the walls of the exhibition.
010 As science fiction works have hypothesised journeys into the past or the future, Atelier Markgraph's design makes for a certain time-travel experience into ancient Athens.
011 The schematic logic of diagrams – a simplified drawing showing the appearance, structure or workings of something – is one of the project's principal representation strategies.

Atelier Markgraph's spatial design for *Athens. The Triumph of Imagery*, an exhibition presented in 2019 at Frankfurt's Liebieghaus Skulpturensammlung, builds from the intuition that individuals have the strong capability to 'move back' and 'travel' to different epochs and cultures. In the case at hand, Liebieghaus visitors are invited on a time-collapsing journey to Ancient Greece's capital city; they are to make their way through twelve adorned rooms, which correspond to the twelve months of the Attic (or Athenian) calendar. In collaboration with scholar Vinzenz Brinkmann, who acted as curator of the project, the Markgraph team here creates a vivid visual and spatial experience. An array of colours, lights, drawings, diagrams and media items are mobilised to celebrate the strong, sculptural 'pictoriality' of classical Athens, along with its processions,

Kopfgeburt
Poseidon
Athena
Salzquelle

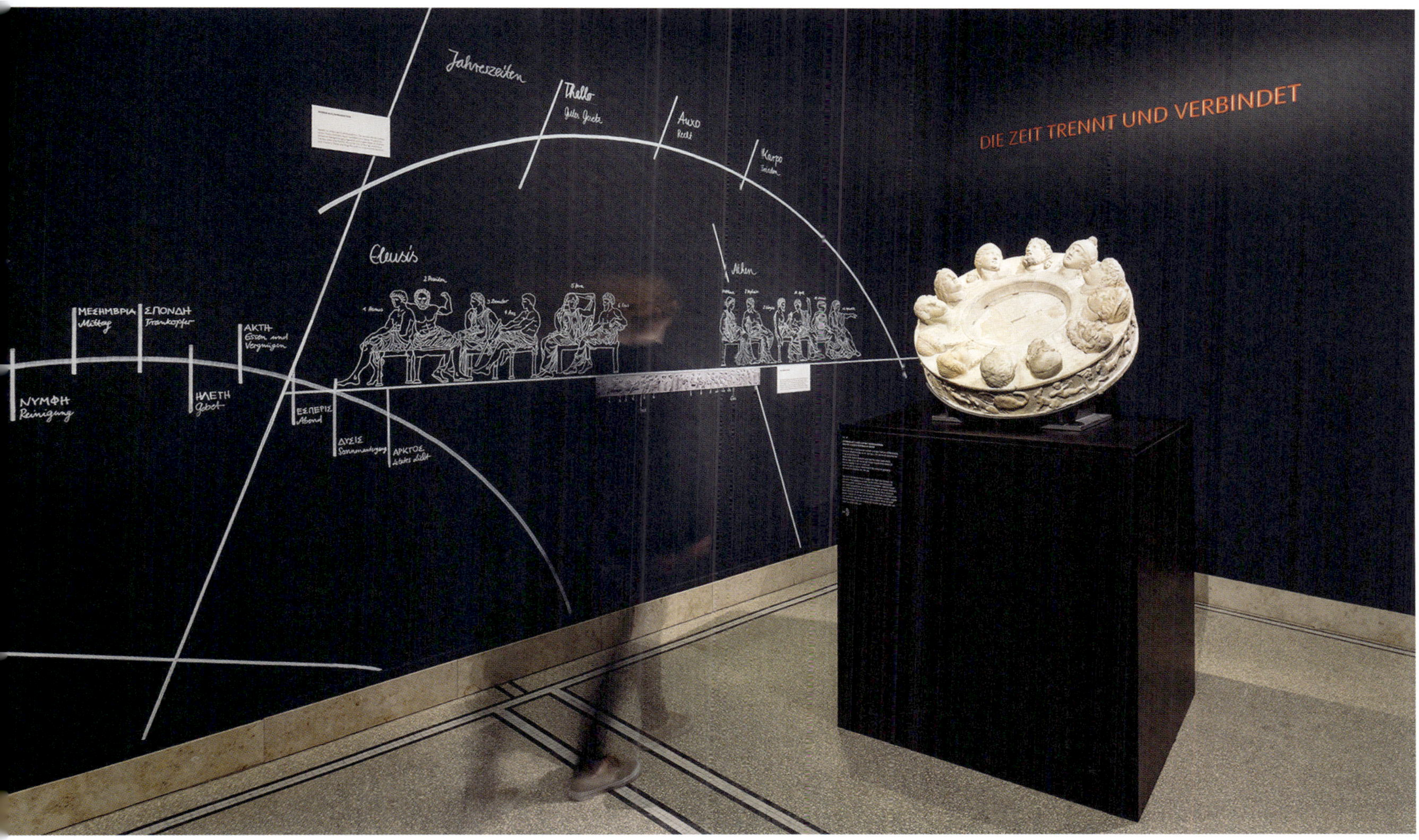
DIE ZEIT TRENNT UND VERBINDET
Jahreszeiten
Thallo
Auxo
Karpo
Eleusis
Athen
ΜΕΣΗΜΒΡΙΑ
Mittag
ΣΠΟΝΔΗ
Trankopfer
ΑΚΤΗ
ΝΥΜΦΗ
Reinigung
ΗΛΕΤΗ
Gebet
ΕΣΠΕΡΙΣ
Abend
ΔΥΣΙΣ
ΑΡΚΤΟΣ

SKIROPHORION
ΣΚΙΡΟΦΟΡΙΩΝ
Juni/Juli
12
EROS MIT DEM SONNENSCHIRM
DER LETZTE DIENST DER ARRHEPHOREN

009
Kap
Sunion

ATHEN
ZEUS
ERECHTHEUS
EUMOLPOS
ATHENA
POSEIDON
ASIEN

BEFREIUNG VON SCHULD

010

Olymp
Berggipfel

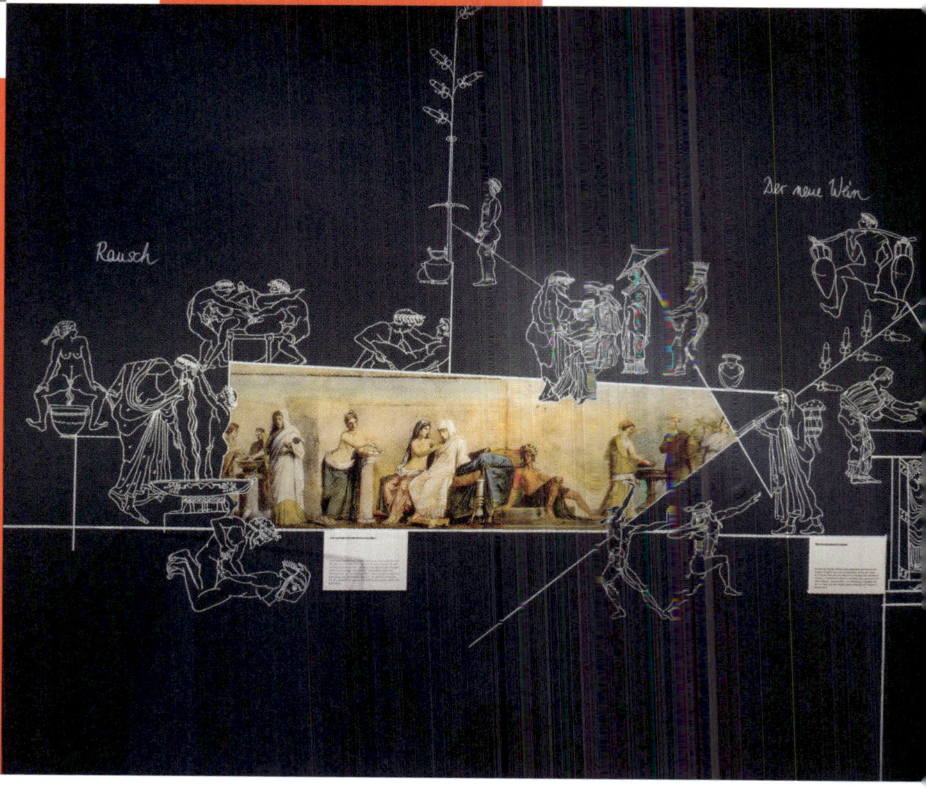
Rausch
Der neue Wein

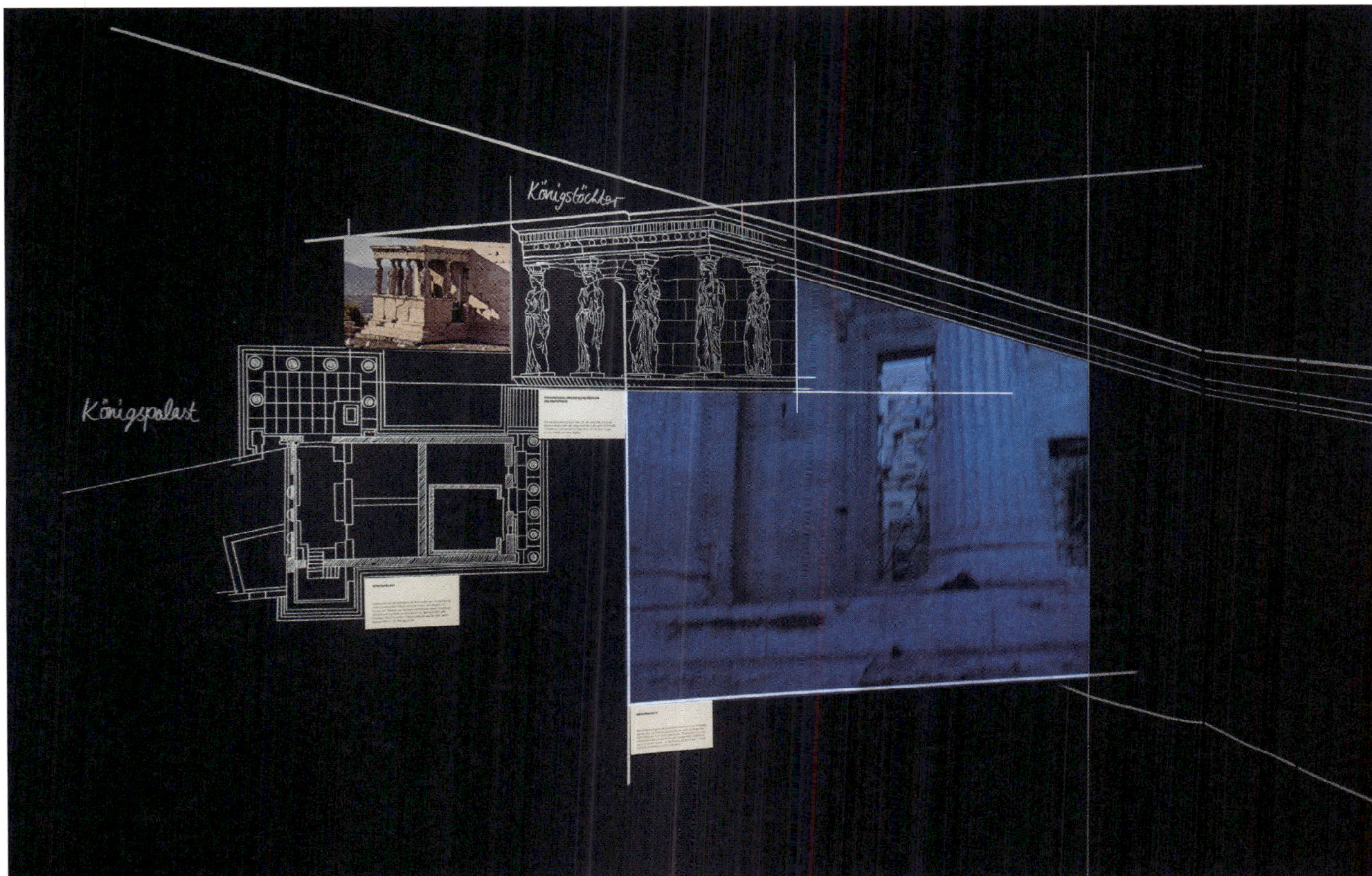
Königstöchter
Königspalast

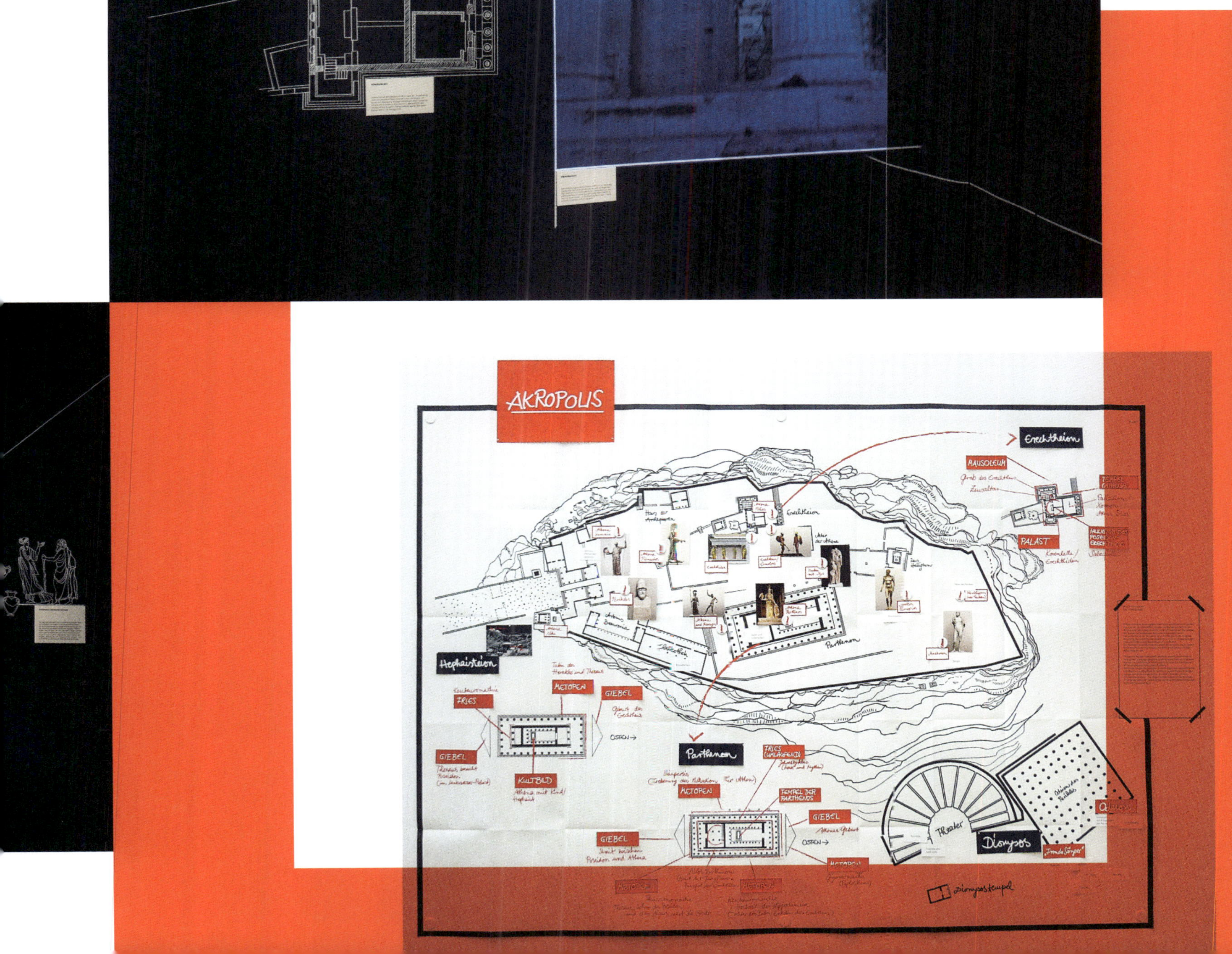
AKROPOLIS
Erechtheion
MAUSOLEUM
PALAST
Hephaisteion
FRIES
METOPEN
GIEBEL
KULTBILD
OSTEN→
Parthenon
Theater
Dionysos

MOBILITY LINKS
ENDED SITUATIO
AGENTS AND BE
OPPORTUNITIES

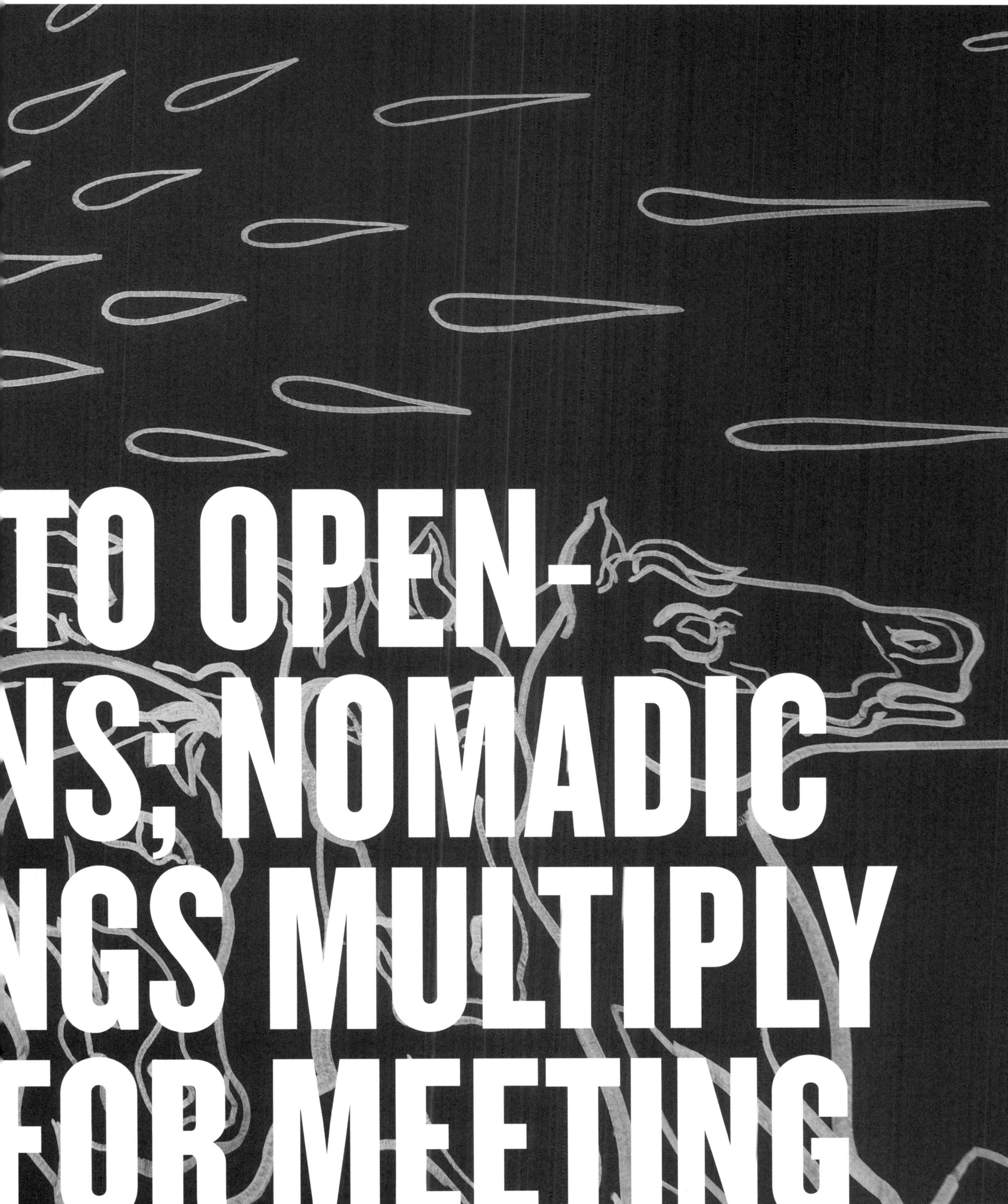

TO OPEN-
NS; NOMADIC
NGS MULTIPLY
FOR MEETING

sacrifices and festivals. In effect, this scenographic staging offers a new look on – and so retells – the fascinating myth of the metropolis' origin. Wall illustrations are especially energetic, making use of strong, crisp lines which recall architects' perspectival studies. Artefacts transform into dynamic subjects, their placement and contextualisation enhanced through fun graphics and fresh hues. The encounter is fruitful: one's experience of the exhibition benefits from Atelier Markgraph's fluid situation of its subject through alternate, widely dispersed geographies and temporalities. *Athens. The Triumph of Imagery* makes the persuasive case for time migrations through acts of design.

Now, freight containers have come to represent the mobile architectural object *par excellence*. Containers' size, modularity and industrial components greatly facilitate their installation and dismantlement. By nature, they are meant to be moveable, lightweight; lifted, towed or floated away. The industrial, standardised shipping container has fascinated architects and makers of space for decades: countless projects (housing, museums, shops, schools) feature stacks of corrugated boxes, conjuring value-laden imaginaries of trade, globalism, efficiency and reuse –

CONTAINER ARCHITECTURE HAS CERTAINLY BECOME A STAND-ALONE STYLE, AN AESTHETIC CATEGORY WHICH CAPTURES WELL THE SPEED AND SPIRIT OF OUR FAST-CHANGING TIMES.

Atelier Markgraph's own history of design with shipping crates unfolds over twenty years, through an iterative series of works which utilise these crates as building material and room definers: roadshow pavilions like *LAB.01* (2001), *Sound of Squares* (2007) or the Mercedes-Benz *Roadshow in Festival Format* (2019) demonstrate how Markgraph capitalises on the aforementioned characteristics of

ROOFTOP

Batteria
Capacità della batteria
>450 km

Soggiorno
Salon

TERRAZZA

Ufficio

012 Screens are mounted directly onto the containers' walls, animating lower and upper spaces with fluctuating light and content.
013 Markgraph's three-dimensional model shows different zones and levels, as well as possible activities for users; the project's aesthetic arguably hints at the easy assembly and dismantlement of the project.
014 A play of exterior and semi-covered areas enlivens one's progress through the pavilion.
015 Children, too, are guests of honour: shiny, circular slides and colourful, faceted climbing walls allow them to 'occupy' a nice number of surfaces and zones.
016 Energy considerations are parts and parcels of the Atelier's understanding of the project: sustainable exchanges and power saving measures represent essential and integral components of its in-flux vision of architecture.
017 Public activities are programmed throughout daytime and the evenings; they are supported by various mobile furnishings and good storage capacities.

temporariness, transportability and high spatial flexibility. The Atelier's most recent container project, *Roadshow in Festival Format*, created for Mercedes-Benz to accompany the year's Formula E race series, aspires to formalise future experiences of mobility. Recycled intermodal boxes are arranged along vertical and horizontal axes, their sides opening and swivelling according to programmatic demands. Visitors flow up and down a series of stairs, stages, climbing walls, bars and slides: these elements also suggest different speeds of use and movement, an aspect of the concept which naturally ties back to the surrounding car-racing events. 'Plug and play' is the pavilion's axiom: new combinations and layouts are set up on open-air sites in the cities of Rome, Paris, Berlin and Bern. As such, Mercedes-Benz *Roadshow in Festival Format* reprises the successful formal exercise of *LAB.01,* a striking, sprightly container building which was successively installed in Cologne, Hamburg, Warsaw, Berlin, Dresden, Barcelona and Hanover in the year 2001. Both Markgraph works take advantage of freight boxes' dynamic design properties; they both nicely evoke constructivist assemblages – as do the red, corrugated volumes of the 2007 *Sound of Squares* migrating pavilion. These three projects form a simple and coherent typological family, immersing users' bodies in a built environment of efficient engineering and circulation; of freedom of assembly and usage. They constitute, in literal and symbolic ways, an architecture of transit.

Journeys, trajectories, movements: as was stated before, mobile encounters come with their share of uncertainty and indefinition. Open-endedness and dynamism are attractive concepts in numerous settings, but they can also be associated with a disagreeable feeling of risk and unease – too much flow, too great a freedom, and individuals become weary. It is such specific, negative feelings toward uncertainty and indefinition which are tackled in the *Financial Investment* travelling exhibition. Realised by Atelier Markgraph with the support of MESO Digital Interiors, the project captures the fluctuations and activities which typify financial investments and trade, translating them into a simplified, informative sequence. To cite Markgraph's client, 'Union Investment Privatfonds,' most Germans lack the skills necessary to grow their own wealth – they might be great savers, but hesitate when it comes to investing and yielding return on money. With its four built stations, *Financial Investment* is designed as a pedagogical ensemble of 'portable objects,' one which can be deployed across the country

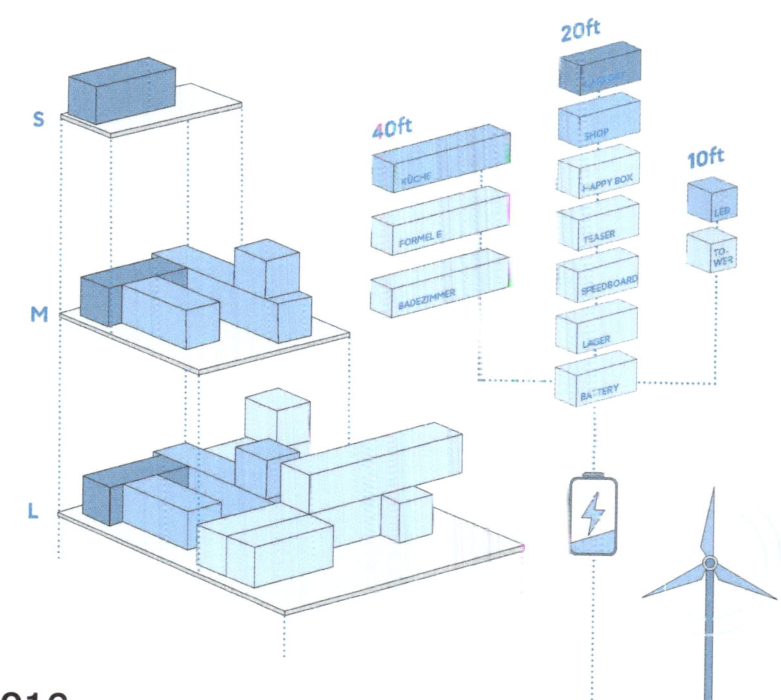
S
M
L
40ft
KÜCHE
FORMEL E
BADEZIMMER
20ft
SHOP
HAPPY BOX
TEASER
SPEEDBOARD
LAGER
BATTERY
10ft
LED
TO-
WER

017

and harvest visitors' personal experiences in the hope to undo these prevalent prejudices toward capital increase. The specific shape of the exhibition furniture ensures its adaptability in different spaces: the blocks can be nested, in a tight bracket configuration, or set side-by-side, in a long and linear circuit. Given its temporary deployment across 200 German bank branches, this flexibility of assemblage is key to the work's success. Fittingly, the apparent simplicity of the design hides sophisticated technical boards, which quantify and decipher the various haptic input generated by visitors. This content is declinated through additional mediums and formats: in addition to the large-scaled *Financial Investment* exhibition, lightweight 'explainer boxes' and pop-up books – as well as a user-friendly web platform – allow for further dissemination. Atelier Markgraph envisions various iterations of 'financial advice on tour,' ensuring its broad public informative aspect and portability are maintained. Factor time, value preservation, risk spreading, compound interest: these notions transform into intuitive spatial modules and items. The analogue nature of Markgraph's exercise is noteworthy:

FINANCIAL MARKETS' DYNAMISM IS OFTEN EXPLAINED THROUGH (OR EQUATED TO) DIGITAL TOOLS, BUT FINANCIAL INVESTMENT SHOWS THAT SUCH DYNAMISM IS SOMETIMES BEST CAPTURED WITH SOLID, PALPABLE – AND PORTABLE – OBJECTS.

Back to beginnings: the first project listed in this chapter, Markgraph's graphic redesign, told a story about the challenges of picturing a company's core identity; these challenges are commonplace at the Atelier, which is itself

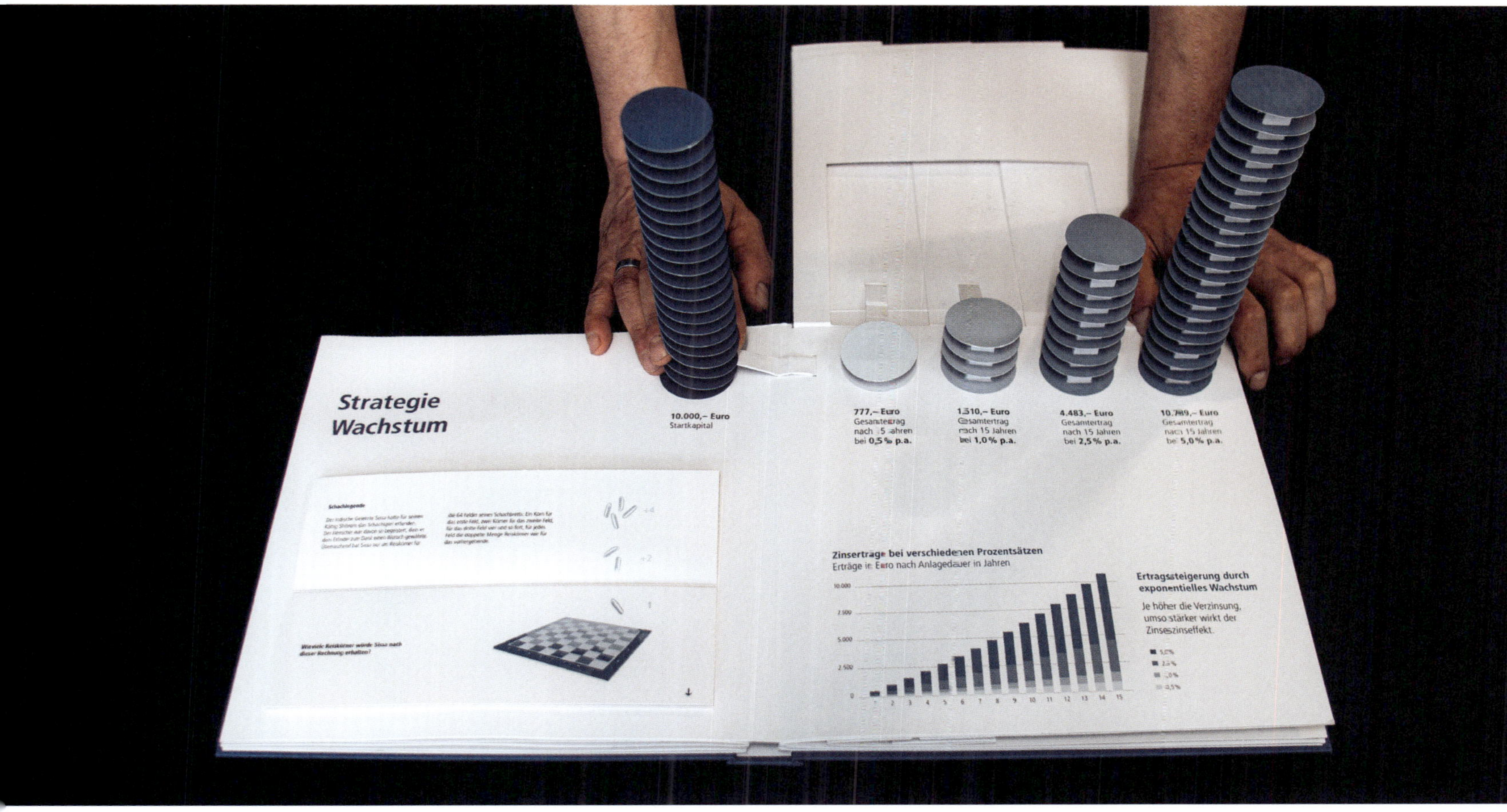
Strategie
Wachstum
10.000,– Euro
Startkapital
4.483,– Euro
Gesamtertrag
nach 15 Jahren
bei 2,5 % p.a.
Zinserträge bei verschiedenen Prozentsätzen
Ertragssteigerung durch
exponentielles Wachstum
Je höher die Verzinsung,
umso stärker wirkt der
Zinseszinseffekt.

018

Strategie
Wachstum

Struktur
Stabilität
Testen Sie Ihre Wertanlage.

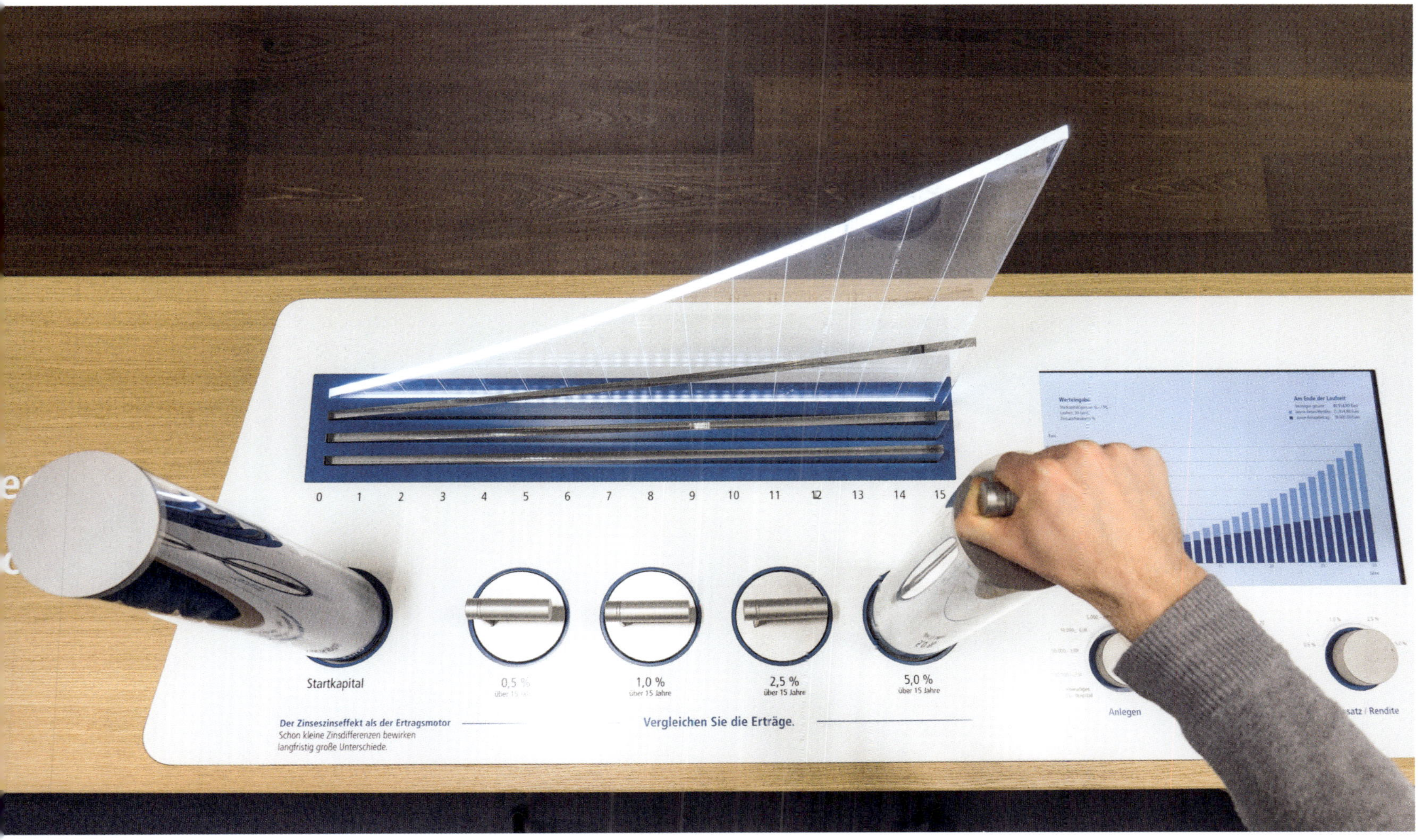
0 1 2 3 4 5 6 7 8 9 10 11 12 13 14 15
Startkapital
0,5 %
1,0 %
über 15 Jahre
2,5 %
über 15 Jahre
5,0 %
über 15 Jahre
Der Zinseszinseffekt als der Ertragsmotor
Schon kleine Zinsdifferenzen bewirken
langfristig große Unterschiede.
Vergleichen Sie die Erträge.
Anlegen

Risiko
Chance
Schwankungsbreite
Ausdauer
Erfolg
Geben Sie Ihrer Wertanlage Zeit
Der Aktienmarkt
← DAX
← S&P 500
Schon ganz schön gut …
Eine kürzere Haltedauer ist gewagt.
Das kann gutgehen – oder auch nicht.
9 8 7 6 5 4 3 2 1
Anlagedauer in Jahren ↓

018 Visitors are tasked with a variety of hands-on actions, which then translate into bits of practical knowledge. This is facilitated by proportionately accumulated objects; they allow for simplicity without simplicism.
019 Markgraph's spatial design include a sober colour palette, with blues, beiges or whites gicing off an impression of calm, resolution and knowledge.
020 The project's team of creatives multiplied sizes, textures and formats to ensure a good communication of data and other numerical figures.
021 The 'underside' of the tabletop reveals the mechanical intricacy required in the design of effective interactive exhibits.
022 A pop-up book was designed by Atelier Markgraph to accompany the exhibition: three-dimensional structures rise up when a page is opened, in the hands-on spirit of the overall concept.

often tasked with the development of corporate identities. Prominent business clients, such as Mercedes-Benz have called upon Atelier Markgraph for the conceptualisation and evolution of their enterprise's image and presence in the world. This type of strategic and spatial work follows the logic of dynamism and mobility – while corporate trust builds upon experience and service quality, the relevance of companies directly depends on their respective capacity to (quickly) adjust to immediate and global milieus. In such a context, the team of Markgraph creatives are tasked with constant and critical feedback; with conceptual migrations and reappraisals. They provide adaptive guidelines; rules, principles and pieces of advice which are to determine key logos, signage, public behaviours and other forms of communication. These rules are to determine, too, the new shape and feel of commercial spaces, physical and digital. In essence, the work is conceptual, architectural and atmospheric.

ATELIER MARKGRAPH'S LONG-TERM COLLABORATIONS WITH BRANDS ALLOW FOR A COMPREHENSIVE UNDERSTANDING OF THEIR PAST, PRESENT AND FORTHCOMING POSITION; OF THEIR DESIRABLE PLACE, SITUATION AND CHANGING STANDING IN THE MARKET.

This sort of work mostly unfolds over many levels of involvement and iterations – in the case of Mercedes-Benz, corporate identity pilots include the various works of

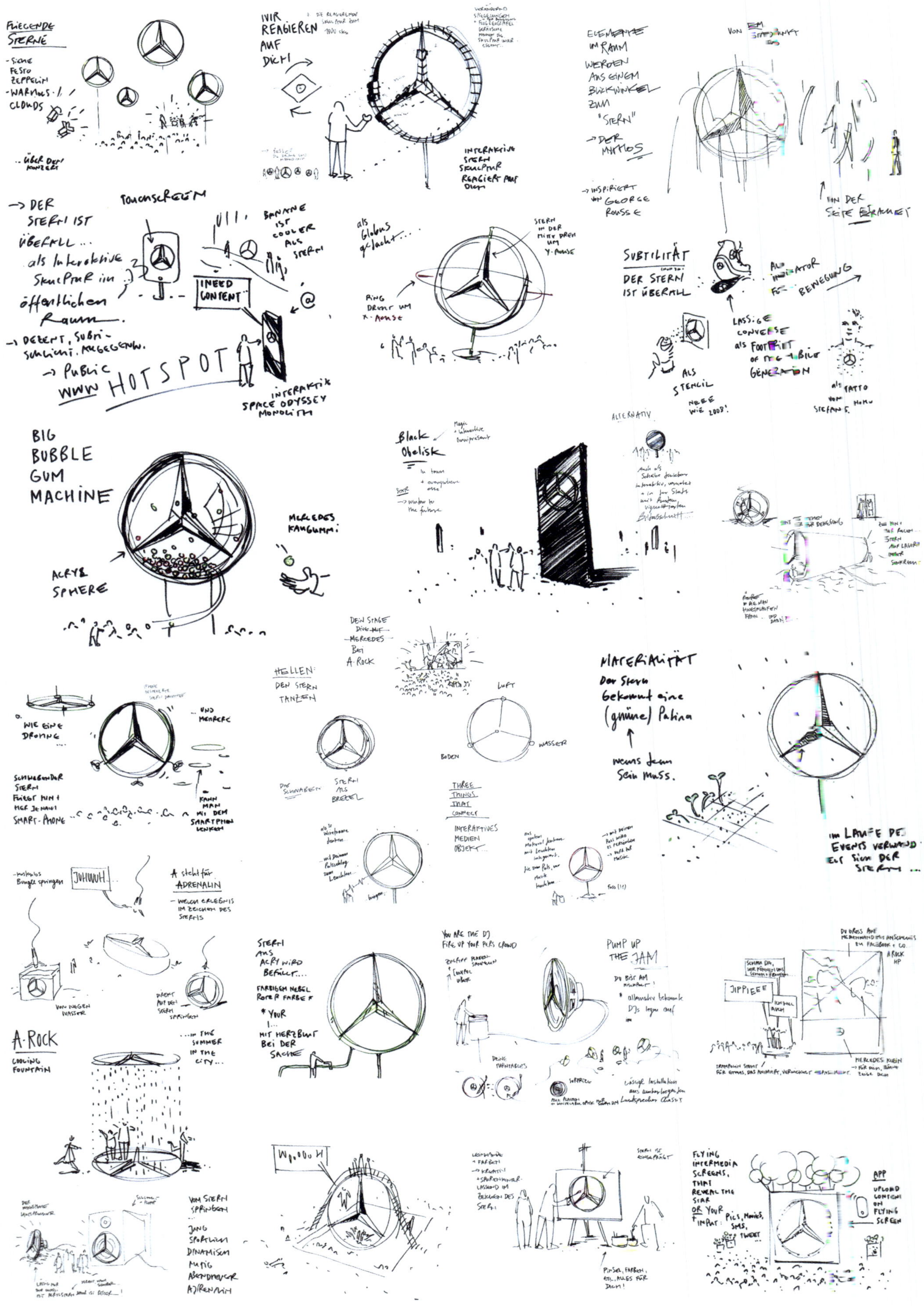
FLIEGENDE STERNE
WIR REAGIEREN AUF DICH!
INTERAKTIVE STERN SKULPTUR REAGIERT AUF DICH
ELEMENTE IM RAUM WERDEN AUS EINEM BLICKWINKEL ZUM "STERN"
-> DER MYTHOS
INSPIRIERT VON GEORGE ROUSSE
-> DER STERN IST ÜBERALL... als Interaktive Skulptur im öffentlichen Raum.
TOUCHSCREEN
BANANE IST COOLER ALS STERN
I NEED CONTENT
-> Public
www HOTSPOT
INTERAKTIV SPACE ODYSSEY MONOLITH
als Globus gedacht...
SUBTILITÄT
DER STERN IST ÜBERALL
LÄSSIGE CONVERSE als FOOTPRINT
ALS STENCIL
BIG BUBBLE GUM MACHINE
ACRYL SPHERE
MERCEDES KAUGUMMI
Black Obelisk
ALTERNATIV
MATERIALITÄT
Der Stern bekommt eine (grüne) Patina
wenns denn sein muss.
IM LAUFE DES EVENTS VERWANDELT SICH DER STERN...
HELLEN DEN STERN TANZEN
LUFT
WASSER
BODEN
THREE THINGS THAT CONNECT
INTERAKTIVES MEDIEN OBJEKT
WIE EINE DROHNE
JUHUUUH!
A steht für ADRENALIN
A-ROCK COOLING FOUNTAIN
... IN THE SUMMER IN THE CITY...
STERN ALS ACRYL WIRD BEFÜLLT...
PUMP UP THE JAM
JIPPIEEE
VOM STERN SPRINGEN
FLYING INTERMEDIA SCREENS, THAT REVEAL THE STAR OR YOUR IMPACT: PICS, MOVIES, SMS, TWEET
APP UPLOAD CONTENT ON FLYING SCREEN

023 Hand sketches and annotations reflect the team's various tests to re-imagine the three-pointed star.
024 A true exercise of visual rupture-and-continuity, the taped star shows its many colours; line patterns add to the overall effect of dynamism.
025 Atelier Markgraph's studies in light, texture and scale reveal the mood-changing potential that follows from the insertion of a signifier (here, the brand's logo) into a given space.
026 Guideline principles are identified and established with the intention of ensuring conceptual clarity: while branding strategies might make use of different formats, the overall understanding of meaning and message must remain constant.
027 Works by the Atelier's creative team consist in a reinterpretation of a simple geometric logic, which recalls Swiss architect and artist Max Bill's piece in the Stuttgart Mercedes-Benz Museum.
028 An old archival conceptual model (2013) tests out system flows.

Mercedes-Benz's sub-brands AMG, EQ and Maybach; an exercise in migrating a core concept into different relevant, site-informed formats. Alternatively, we can say that this exercise consists of creating dynamic encounters between the brand and its audience, between the brand and its environments – between the brand and itself. All projects examined here demonstrate a desire to pursue such dynamism, with results that are swift and lively; nicely reactive. They constitute design in motion: moving toward an increased public relevance and betterment.

025

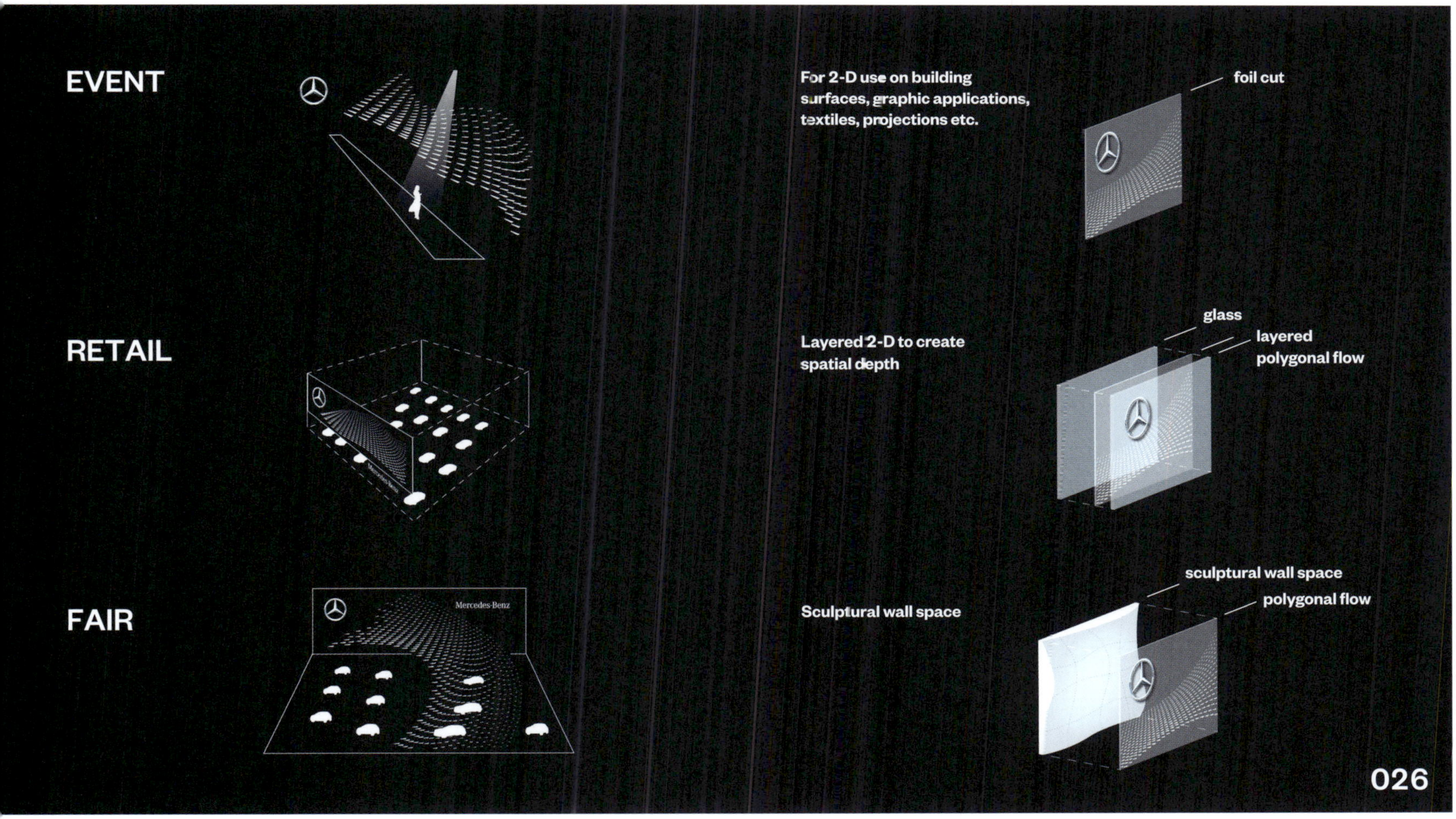
EVENT
RETAIL
FAIR
Mercedes-Benz
For 2-D use on building surfaces, graphic applications, textiles, projections etc.
foil cut
Layered 2-D to create spatial depth
glass
layered polygonal flow
Sculptural wall space
sculptural wall space
polygonal flow
026

027

028

PLASTIC

encoun

TIES

tectonic

ers

2013

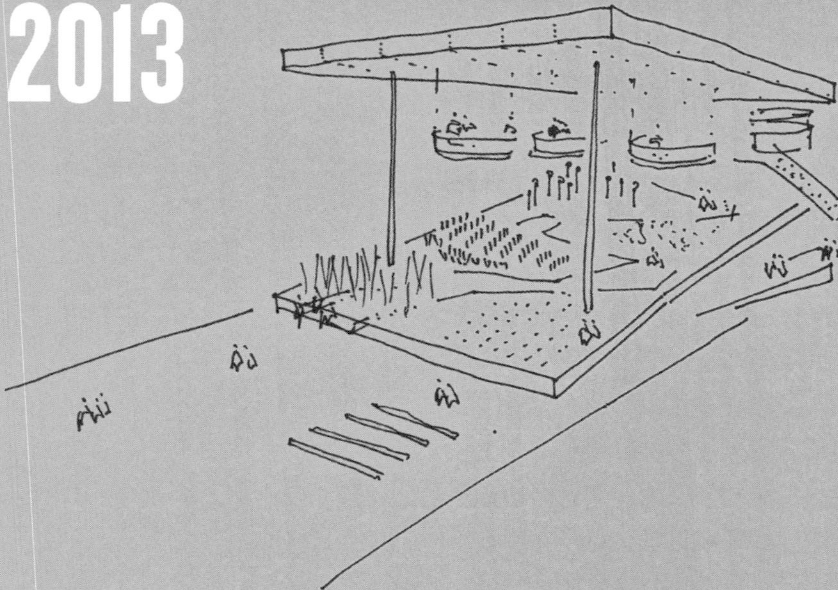

CULTURAL LANDSCAPES

The central themes of the 'Feeding the Planet, Energy for Life' World Expo in Milan shape the design proposal for the German pavilion. This pavilion is an assembled structure composed of slanted and sloped surfaces where visitors can explore and gain knowledge about sustainability and agriculture-related issues. Straddling the line between a building and a landscape, the project offers a playful assortment of exhibition and circulation spaces. This spatial diversity aptly mirrors the multidisciplinary nature of the pavilion's design team. PAGE 250

RETHINKING COOKING

The small-scale, multilevelled showroom for the 'Württembergische Metallwarenfabrik' group deploys tectonics at the scale of large objects, with its four floating, glacier-like blocks hovering over the counter spaces of the Frankfurt international consumer goods trade fair. Each polygonal 'glacier' acts as a screen-filled hood, marking key moments in the activity of making and enjoying food, and therefore symbolises meal-related pleasures. PAGE 256

2015

2017

BUILDING EXCELLENCE

Atelier Markgraph's Investa *Expo Real Munich* pavilion presents a classical 'plastic' vision of built space, with its gentle assembly of concrete-glazed plateaus, tone-in-tone logo insets and slick shadows: the small-scale, multilevelled showroom combines wood, glass and concrete surfaces to create an architecture of sobriety and simplicity – of sculptural solids and voids. PAGE 245

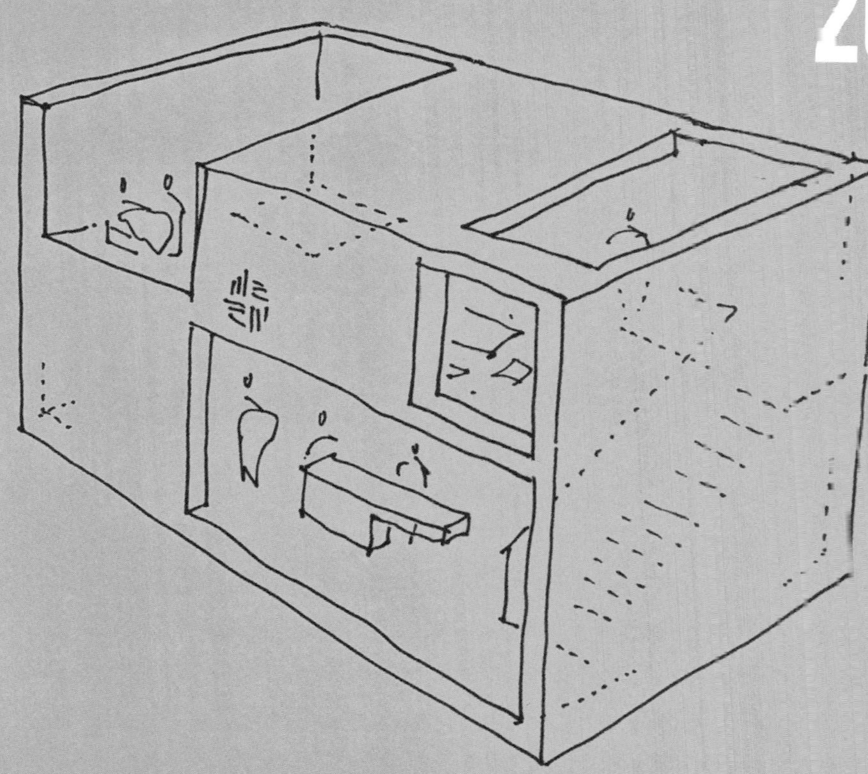

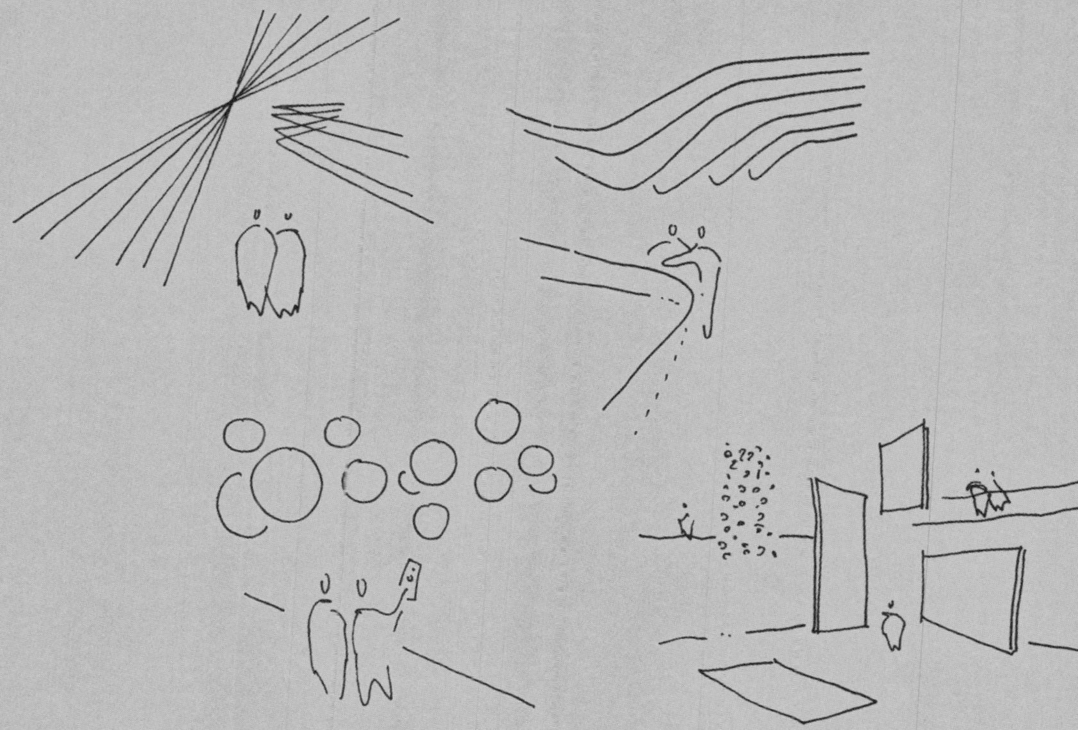

BEYOND THE CAR

2019

At the Internationale Automobil Austellung, *Mercedes-Benz Experience* presents a series of adaptive, monothematic environments where thick, extruded lines indicate connectivity and soft waves indicate wellbeing; where bouncing mirror balls indicate amusement and sharp squares indicate technology. Hues, lights and textures operate an alchemy of sorts, elevating visitors' experience of interior space. PAGE 262

2019

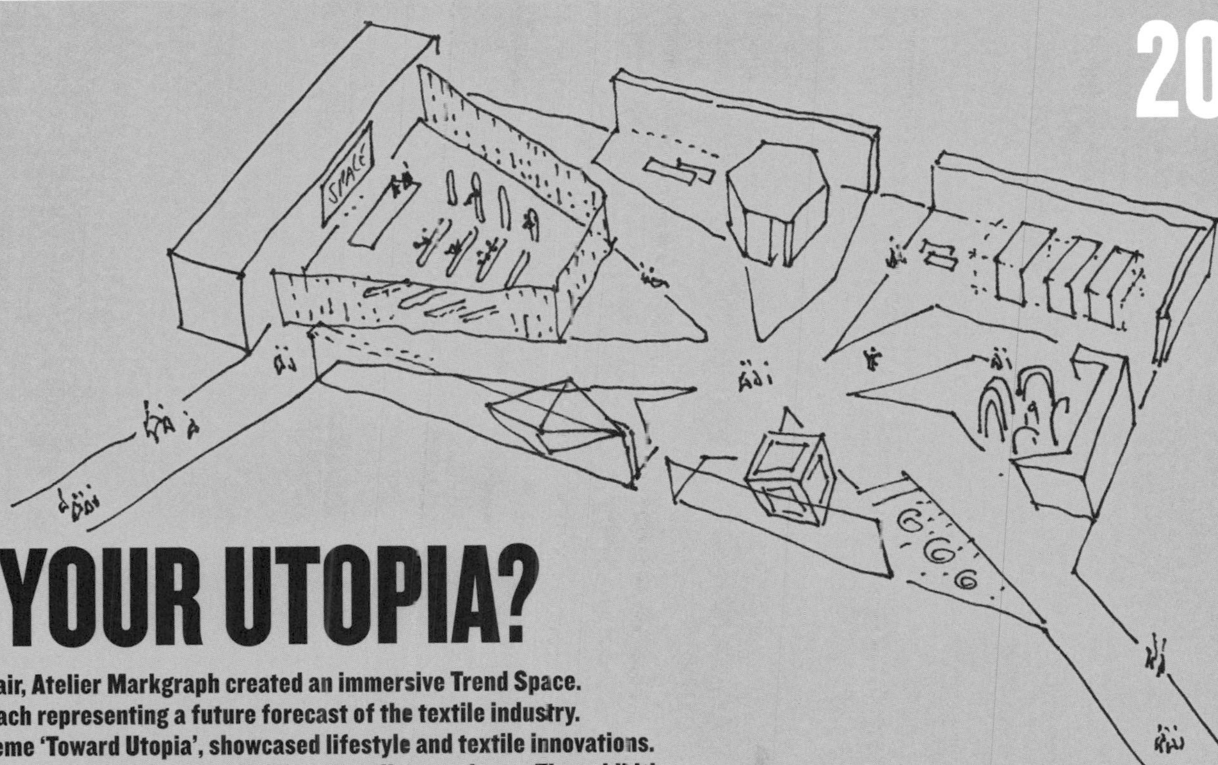

WHAT'S YOUR UTOPIA?

At the Heimtextil 2019 trade fair, Atelier Markgraph created an immersive Trend Space. It featured five microcosms, each representing a future forecast of the textile industry. The microcosms, under the theme 'Toward Utopia', showcased lifestyle and textile innovations. Each trend stage was marked by a unique landmark, providing a tactile experience. The exhibition also included interactive elements like selfie areas and an audiovisual installation. PAGE 236

001

Façades, interiors or volumes: time and again, architects refer to their works as 'sculptural' and 'sensuous,' their tectonic articulation set forth and praised.

TO ENCOUNTER A SCULPTURAL OBJECT, A SENSUOUS SPACE – THE MATERIAL EXPERIENCE AT PLAY OFTEN RELATES TO THE RICH QUALITY OF PLASTICITY.

This quality relates to the general property of being easily shaped or moulded; it is a token of softness and pliability. 'Plastic' items and environments are designed in ways that remind viewers (and users) of substance in formation, of various castings and mouldings, of supple fabrics and stretchy fibres. They exist in universes of reliefs and curves, of imprints and puffy fragments. Assuredly, three-dimensionality is crucial to people's appreciation of tectonic encounters: the famous words of Le Corbusier, who spoke of architecture as the soft, spatial play of light and shadow, ring true to this day. Several projects conceived by Atelier Markgraph make good use of the Swiss architect's intuition; these projects feature sensual, plastic expressions of matter, ones where built bodies are carved and bloated, stretched and contrasted. What are the implications and impacts of architectural plasticity? How does it manifest, physically and phenomenologically, in Markgraph's production? Do 'plastic' designs constitute the new creative norm? A closer inquiry into Heimtextil, Investa, WMF Ambiente and the Explore gallery of the Mercedes-Benz 2019 Internationale Automobil Ausstellung hall shows the range of possible, tectonic ways to build and meet.

Initiated by Messe Frankfurt as a supporting exhibition to the Heimtextil B2B event, Atelier Markgraph's *What's Your Utopia?* (2019) consists of a succession of five formalist vignettes. Each vignette forms an immersive territory, where a distinctive – and idealised – fashion trend is displayed and critically examined. In their own words, the Atelier's creatives here attempt at 'materialising' a spatial utopia of sorts; with spongy, foldable, elastic or form-fitting installations, they construct a 3,000m^2 vision of the future en vogue. Velour, nylon and thick yarn become sculpted landscapes.

001 Layers of folded, translucent surfaces add up to create an overwhelming interior; sense of scale and depth lessens to give way to a softer, organic experience of space.

002 Colours and shapes function to signal different thematic clusters across the large landscape of *What's Your Utopia?*

003 Lots of actual cloth pieces are directly hung from the gallery's walls; while they represent the main exhibited 'material,' they also modify the acoustic qualities of the space.

004 Architectural historian Gottfried Semper argued that enclosures (walls) were said to have their origins in weaving; the most basic form of a spatial divider still seen in use in parts of the world today is the fabric screen, as in the scene here depicted.

Ultimate playdate
Luxurious and indulgent

002
Pursue
Play

ENJOY YOURSELF
IN THE FLOW
OF NTASY.

Go
Off-Grid
People are rewilding their lifestyles, turning off-grid to re-establish a connection with nature. Trying to find out connections with humanity's primal roots, they are committed to being resourceful, active and fit, and seeking transformative experiences in remote places. Designs are drawing references from the practical aspects of outdoor textiles and workwear, their tech look suggests longevity and endurance.
Colour & Material

#thatsmyutopia
Perfect Imperfectionist
Ultimate Playdate
Back to nature

005 Thin, bent frames and a minimalist railing contrast the plastic relief of concrete-glazed MDF panels. The green-blue wall also works as a contrasting element, a strong backdrop for the pale greys.
006 There is something resolutely modernist about the project's push-and-pull articulation of concrete volumes, slabs and surfaces.
007 Atelier Markgraph decided to place punctual warm wooden elements as complements to the concrete, metal and cold green which dominate the space.
008 Imprinted concrete is textured, embossed or patterned to various aesthetic or discursive ends: in the case of Investa, the company's name and logo were casted as subtle, corporate imprints.

Draperies wrap in and around objects and rooms; the textiles of tomorrow are turned into haptic experiences. In the wide Messe hall, high visibility is ensured by a custom ceiling piece, where plump air cushions seemingly float above visitors' heads, like outlandish cotton effigies, or cloud-like pendants (shapeshifters, lightshifters). The overall impression is one of style and suppleness; the grammar of Trend Space builds on the vocabulary of soft petticoats and ribbons, evoking the silky imaginaries of Christo and Jeanne-Claude, or the visual intensity of high-end fashion runways. Cosy, synthetic, queer, kitsch, green: the microcosms crafted by Atelier Markgraph build upon an aesthetic of tension and stretch – staged elements look as though they have considerable amounts of force or pressure under which they hang and deform elastically, thus making for an active viewing experience. In effect, clothes and other scenographic items are animated, chiselled by these physical forces. Such performance combines well with Heimtextil's thematic explorations; future-oriented design must accommodate change, and an environment of formal expansion and contraction demonstrates a true potential for malleability.

CONCRETE, CEMENT, RESIN, CLAY, PLASTER, MORTAR: GIVEN THEIR LIQUID-TO-SOLID CHARACTERISTIC, THESE 'SOFT' ARCHITECTURAL MATERIALS HAVE COME TO EPITOMISE THE CONCEPT OF PLASTICITY.

It should be stated that, as an industrial product, the former is not without its current challenges; most concrete infrastructures and objects are difficult to reuse and come up with environmental costs. Their construction should be limited, and strategically so. At any rate, the appeal of grey 'molten stone,' which impacted the architecture of modernism like no other, finds its roots in alluring tectonic qualities. With its gentle assembly of concrete plateaus and lines, its tone-in-tone

investa
REAL ESTATE
006

007

008

009

010

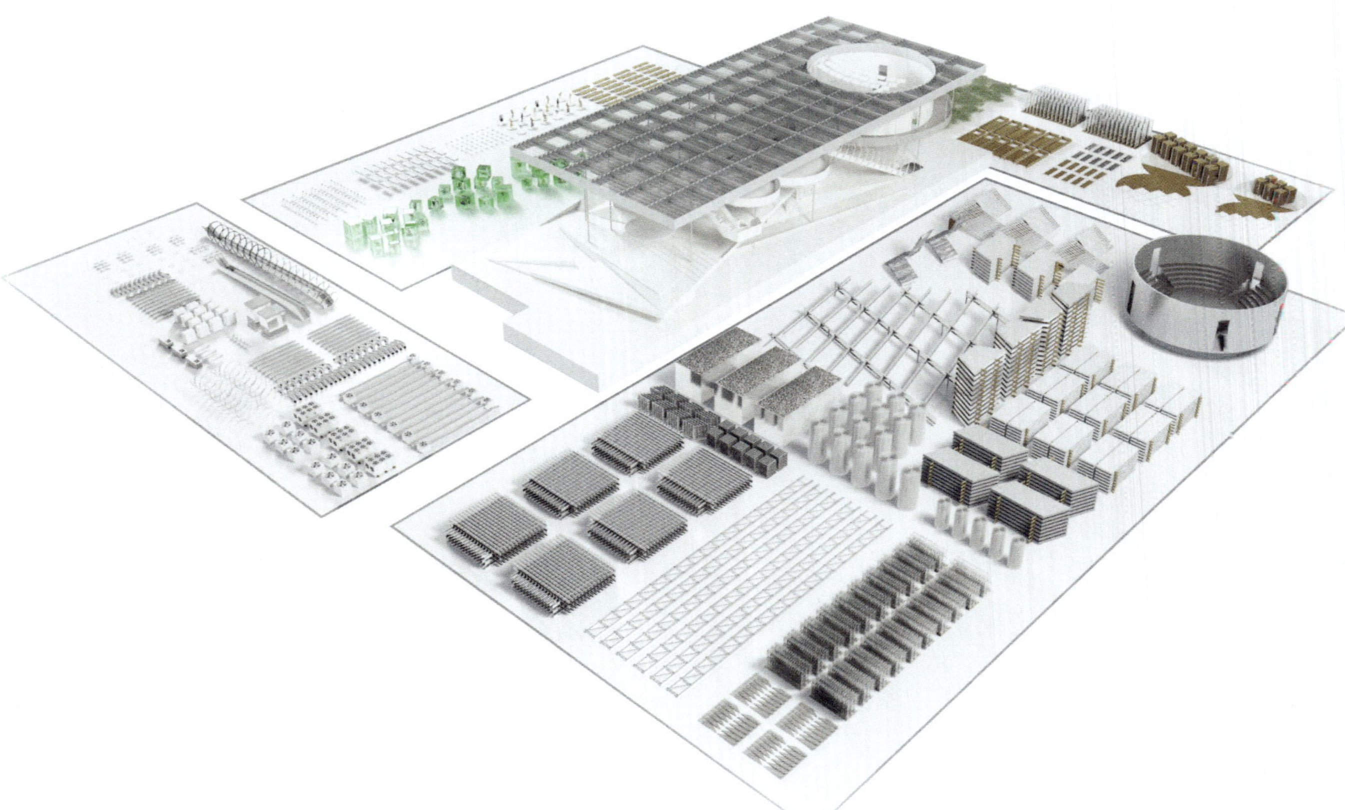

009 Visitors walking down the main axis of the World Expo's masterplan have a full view of the German pavilion, which appears to 'float' over a lush grassland.
010 All building components are modular: they were designed in ways which allow for easy assembling and dismounting, ensuring their post-Expo afterlife. This is part and parcel of an 'Energy for Life' vision for the built world.
011 A key component of the pavilion's spatial experience consists in seasonal changes in its lower landscape, which, over the duration of the World Expo event, shows new colours, heights, and densities. The diagram also documents the food that is planted on site, and harvested for the pavilion's restaurant.
012 Strong forms and contrasted materials are visible in the project's back elevation; the impression is one of productivity, heterogeneity, and grandeur.

logo insets and slick shadows, Atelier Markgraph's 2017 Investa Expo Real Munich pavilion makes for a classical 'plastic' vision of built space. The Atelier conceived a small-scale, multilevelled showroom which combines wood, glass and concrete surfaces. Orthogonal planes, colour blocks and square openings create an effect of sobriety and simplicity; minute design details – tectonic ornaments – are distributed evenly throughout visitor's *parcours*. In terms of finishing, the mixture of sand, cement and stone aggregates is at times polished, at times coarse: formwork planks' textured markings can be discerned on many poured walls of the Investa pavilion. These walls stand firmly, in a Euclidean interplay of solids and voids. Markgraph here illustrates how the plastic qualities of concrete need not be articulated in the contemporary language of curves and spheres; as was described, the tectonics of flat slabs and plates constitute an equally sensuous expression.

In 2012, Atelier Markgraph teamed up with architects haascookzemmrich STUDIO2050 and landscapers Bureau Baubotantik to conceive the competition design of the German pavilion for the upcoming 'Feeding the Planet, Energy for Life' World Expo in Milan. A state-of-the-art multilevelled vision, the submitted entry mainly consists of a series of slanted and sloped surfaces where visitors can roam and learn about various sustainability and agriculture-related themes.

HALF-BUILDING, HALF-LANDSCAPE, THE PROJECT'S FORMAL ARTICULATION ANCHORS ITSELF IN THE CONTEMPORARY LANGUAGE OF PLATFORMS AND PLAINS, WITH ITS LAYERED BODY TILTING, CURVING AND BENDING TO FORM DIVERSE POCKETS OF EXHIBITION SPACE.

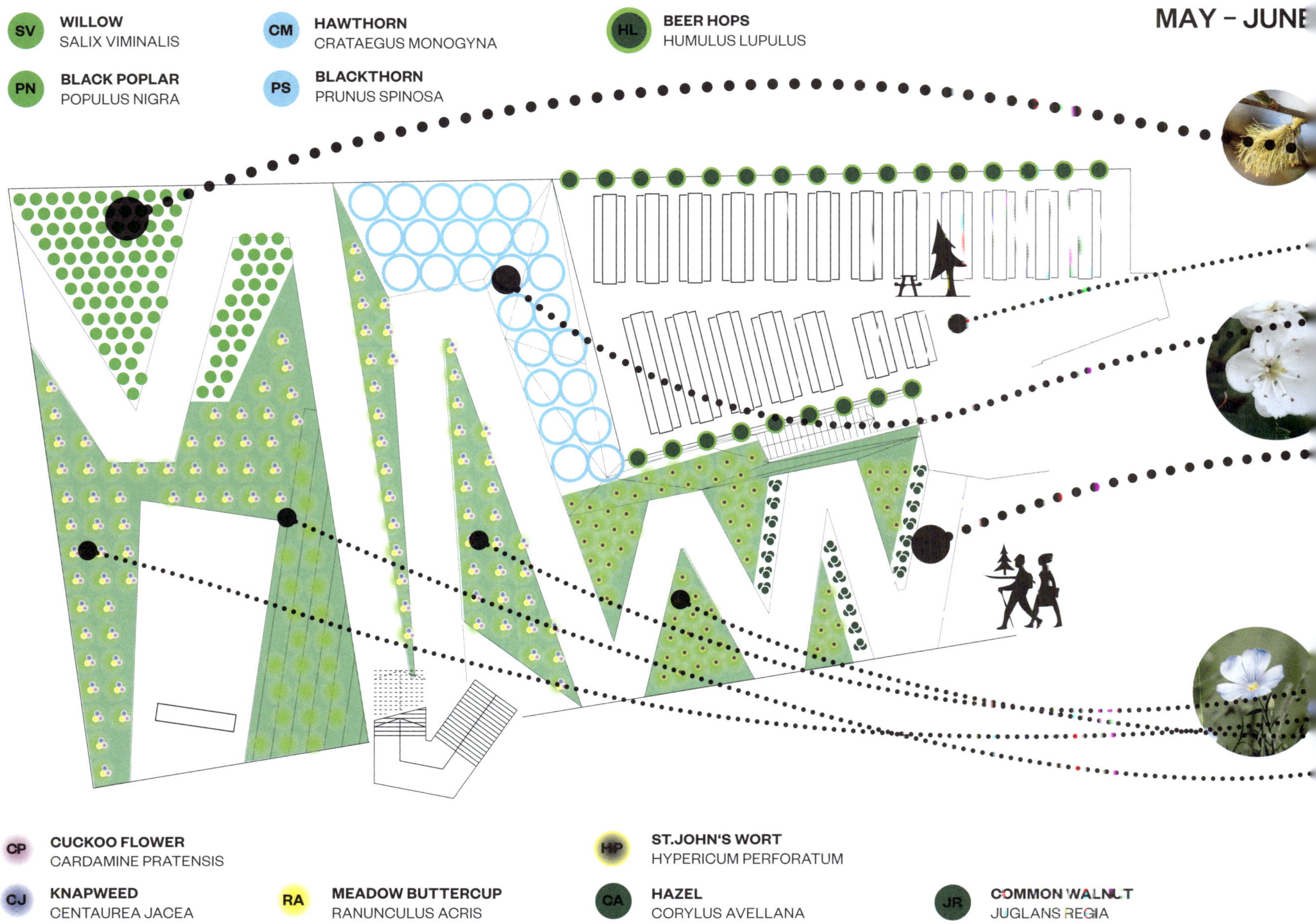
SV WILLOW
SALIX VIMINALIS
PN BLACK POPLAR
POPULUS NIGRA
CM HAWTHORN
CRATAEGUS MONOGYNA
PS BLACKTHORN
PRUNUS SPINOSA
HL BEER HOPS
HUMULUS LUPULUS
MAY – JUNE
CP CUCKOO FLOWER
CARDAMINE PRATENSIS
CJ KNAPWEED
CENTAUREA JACEA
RA MEADOW BUTTERCUP
RANUNCULUS ACRIS
HP ST.JOHN'S WORT
HYPERICUM PERFORATUM
CA HAZEL
CORYLUS AVELLANA
JR COMMON WALNUT
JUGLANS REGIA

011

JULY – AUGUST
SEPTEMBER – OCTOBER
WILLOW MEADOW
RESTAURANT
WILD BERRY HEDGE
EDGE OF THE FOREST
WILDFLOWER MEADOW
WILLOW SALIX VIMINALIS
BEER HOPS HUMULUS LUPULUS
BLACKTHORN PRUNUS SPINOSA
HAZEL CORYLUS AVELLANA
HORNBEAM CARPINUS BETULUS

GERMANY

WMF Group
WMF
Silit
cooking
Silit

013 The oversized bodies of the 'screen sculptures' float over a series of domestic setups, with fine-scaled cooking hardware and furnitures.
014 Four stations represent different steps in the act of making and enjoying food: preparing, cooking, dining and drinking. A glacier-like block hovers over each of these stations.
015 Architectural plasticity can refer to the capacity of spaces to adapt and accommodate various functions, activities or user needs: in a similar manner, a kitchen is not just a static, utilitarian space for food preparation, but a dynamic environment which evolves and adapts to the requirements and desires of individuals, thus catering to varied cooking styles, cultural practices and social interactions. WMF plastic qualities are both formal and programmatic.

Greeneries sprout from various plateaus, creating 'harvest fields' of a new, hybrid kind; circulation bridges are edged by see-through elements, which allow for open views toward the pavilion's grounds and larger Expo site. Rhythmic columns, soft bands of white steel and glass superimpose to create a sculptural (and highly functional) architecture, whose immersive qualities appeal to all senses; the range of space experiences reflects the multi-disciplinary profile of the competition team. Like a mass of robust, triangulated ribbons, the building's large roof trusses also enhance the sculptural feel of the architecture. The linear stacking of solid slabs and transparent railings creates something of the fun play of light and shadow which architects so often pursue and celebrate – it is visually dynamic, inherently three-dimensional and agreeably formalist. At night, the pavilion softly shines and glows, in a futuristic multimedia vista of the world of energy production and fertile lands. Overall, the design of the 'Milan 2015' German pavilion is rooted in a certain version of architectural plasticity – one where built shapes match and mix to layered, parallax-like effects.

The artistic rendering of three-dimensional form is occasionally spatial (architectural scale, rooms); it is frequently object-bound (sculptural scale, artefacts). Take the case of the Württembergische Metallwarenfabrik group – most commonly known as WMF – brand appearance, conceived in 2015 by Atelier Markgraph: here, tectonics deploy at the scale of large objects. Four floating, glacier-like blocks hover over the counter spaces of WMF at the Ambiente, a yearly international consumer goods trade fair based in Frankfurt am Main. Sturdily fastened to the ceiling, each polygonal 'glacier' acts as a hood of sorts, marking four key moments in the kitchen and dining room – namely, preparing, cooking, dining and drinking.

WITH THEIR EDGY, SENSUAL VOLUMES, THESE SCULPTURES ACT AS EYE-CATCHERS AND SYMBOLS OF VARIED FOOD-RELATED PLEASURES.

014
preparing
drinking
dining
drinking

dining

Storyboard (dining)

skills

products

applications

Moments of Delight

preparing

cooking

dining

drinking

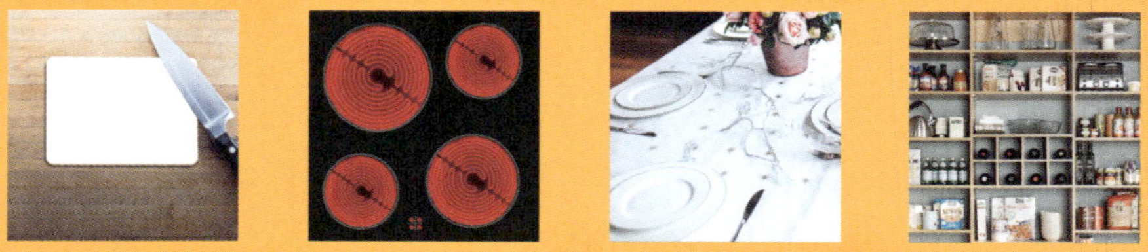

Spatial Design

WMF Group
WMF
Silit
ORIGINAL KAISER

drinking
dining

INSPIRING
EXPERIENCES
ex
cite

Rectangular screens are mounted on their underface; they animate the WMF tabletops, tasting stations and pedestals with the pleasant, pulsating light of media projections. Interestingly, the custom-looking shapes of the Ambiente 'glaciers' also function as a pictorial commentary on the age of mass production of food products, tableware and utensils; however, despite their sculptural, tailor-made appearance, the four blocks are actually conceived as a reusable, modular system. As such, formal plasticity does not equate to unicity. The Atelier's WMF project nicely reminds us of this key design lesson. Markgraph's approach to crafting scenographic environments for brand experiences often stems from a simple act of translation: that of a topic into form and space.

TECTONICS ARE ARTICULATED IN THE SERVICE OF AN IDEA; A STORY, A THEME OR A MESSAGE.

With their 2019 IAA (Internationale Automobil Austellung) Experience exhibition sequence for Mercedes-Benz – and their work on the Explore rooms in particular – Atelier Markgraph's team operationalised this translation skillfully, in a series of adaptive, monothematic environments. Thick, extruded lines indicate connectivity; soft waves indicate well-being. Bouncing mirror balls indicate entertainment; sharp squares indicate technology and urbanity. Throughout the IAA promenade conceived and planned in partnership with architects jangled nerves, hues, lights and textures operate an alchemy of sorts, elevating visitors' experience of interior space. In one gallery, an intricate layering of wavy wall panels plunges individuals in a uterine world, whose atmosphere changes with coloured projections – pinks, oranges, purples and blues animate the Explore ribs, to very plastic ends. The surfaces' modulations also confer special acoustic qualities to the rooms; this attribute benefits one's occupation of the architecture, reducing the noise from the high influx of passersby. After a walk throughout a long, grotto-like tunnel, visitors arrive at a mezzanine level which overlooks display areas. The Mercedes-Benz products, while present, do not dominate the space; priority is given to the various ornaments

016 Fun, chubby spheres hang from the ceiling of the 'Explore' gallery, reflecting the lights and bodies filling up the space below.

017 Making for a soft and layered veil of sorts, curvy ribs of pink or violet hues shape the multilevelled 'Energise' gallery: visitors move up and down; closer and away from the ribs. The space's changing colours adapt to nearby bodies, using and reflecting biodata (pulse, skin temperature).

018 As is commonly found in an Atelier Markgraph project, user-friendly stations offer a variety of participatory tasks and smooth hands-on tools, linking fleshy feels to the more abstract themes of the show. Using various biodata, interactive stations allow visitors to partially control the room's ambience.

019 Sculptural patterns of tessellation align with the structural logic and assembly of the gallery, enhancing its tectonic expression; beams of light too participate in dematerialising and rematerialising the space.

LET YOUR PULSE
SET THE TONE

en.er
gize

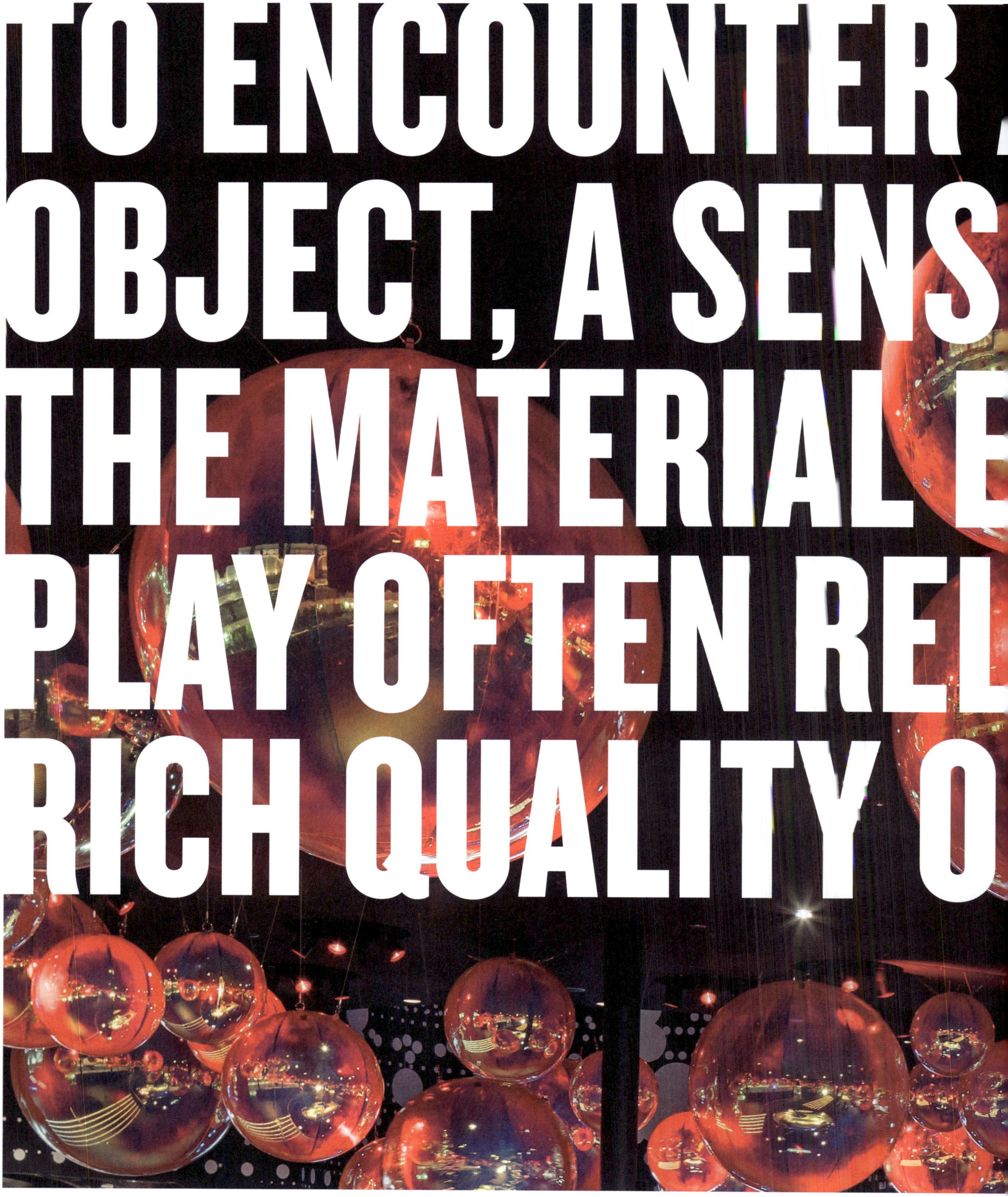

TO ENCOUNTER
OBJECT, A SENS
THE MATERIAL E
PLAY OFTEN REL
RICH QUALITY O

SCULPTURAL
OUS SPACE –
XPERIENCE AT
ATES TO THE
PLASTICITY

ener
LET YOUR PULSE

018

ENERGIZING COMFORT
BY MERCEDES-BENZ.

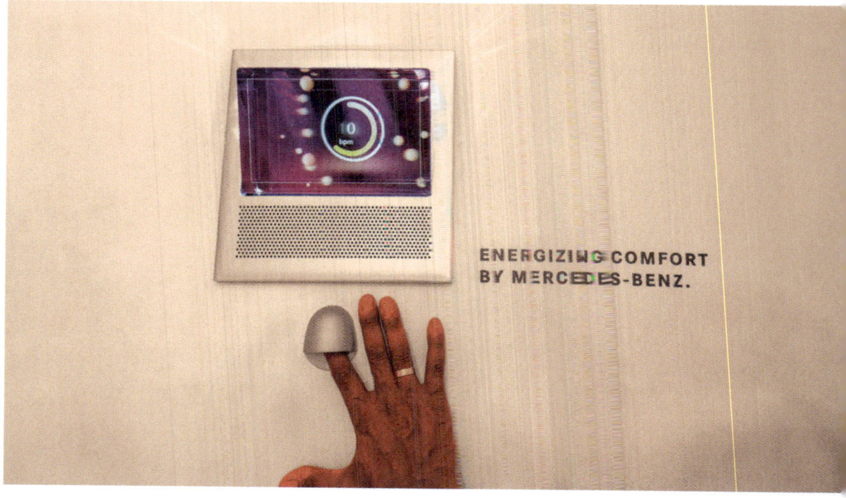
ENERGIZING COMFORT
BY MERCEDES-BENZ.

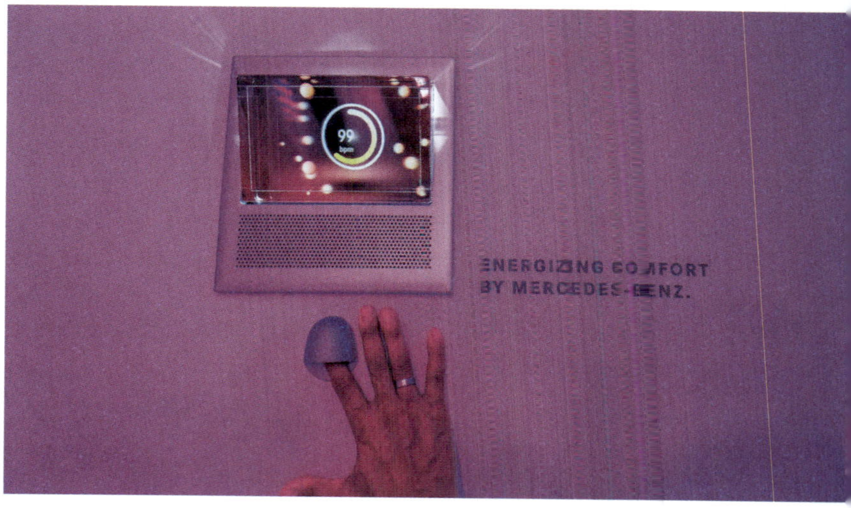
ENERGIZING COMFORT
BY MERCEDES-BENZ.

intui
tive
indiv
idual

PERSÖNLICH

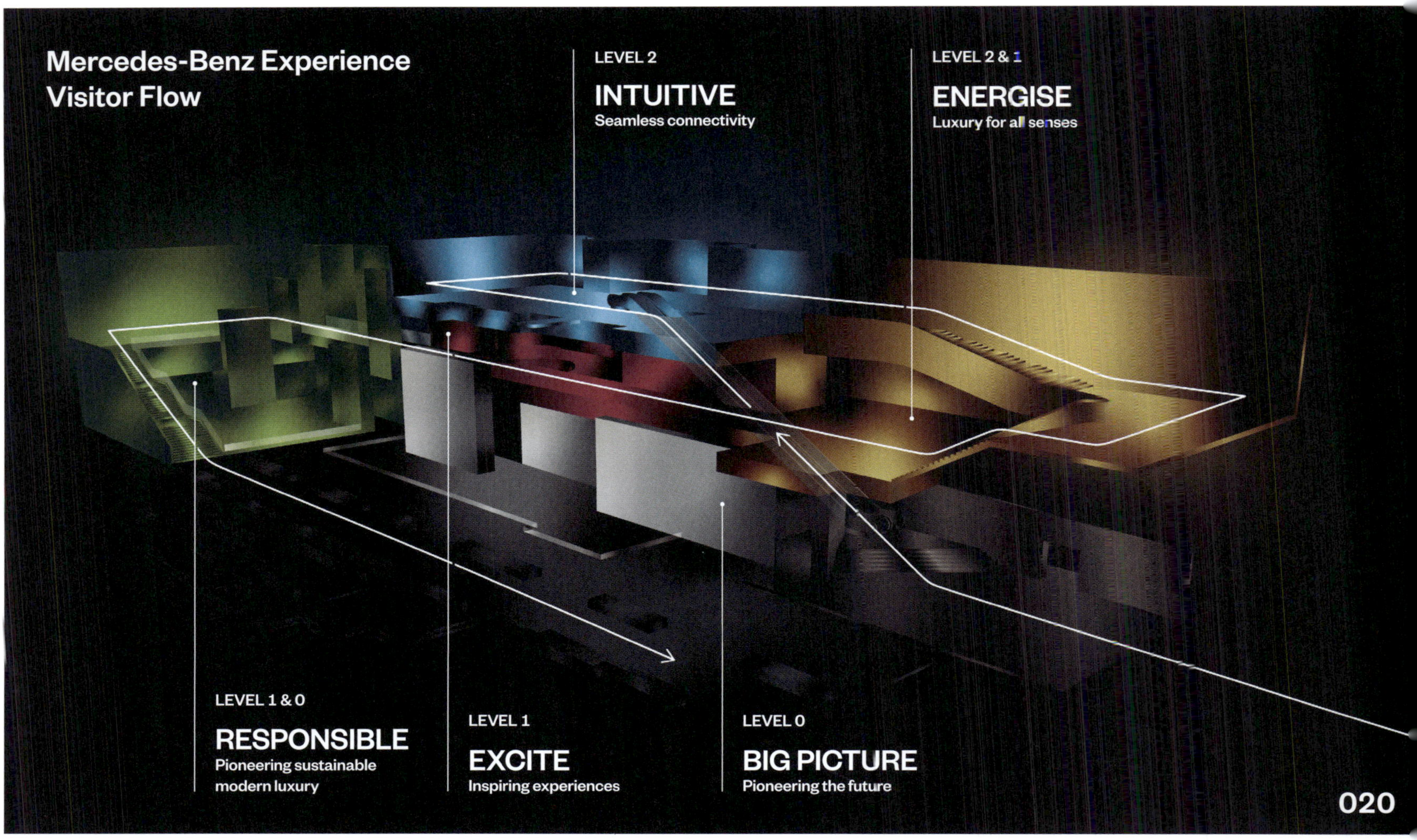
Mercedes-Benz Experience
Visitor Flow
LEVEL 2
INTUITIVE
Seamless connectivity
LEVEL 2 & 1
ENERGISE
Luxury for all senses
LEVEL 1 & 0
RESPONSIBLE
Pioneering sustainable
modern luxury
LEVEL 1
EXCITE
Inspiring experiences
LEVEL 0
BIG PICTURE
Pioneering the future
020

Kooperative und
sichere Mobilität
ESF 2019
021

and items, and to their sensory properties. As decorative elements, these ornaments and items entertain people's imagination in free play with ideas; they enable aesthetic judgements without a determinate end. Rooms like 'Explore' are staged as deeply immersive milieus, their sensuous and phenomenological features are felt as much as they are seen.

PLASTICITY CAN, INTER ALIA, BE UNDERSTOOD AS THE EXPRESSIVENESS OF THREE-DIMENSIONAL FORM IN BUILT DESIGNS.

The five works examined in this chapter exist as five distinctive manifestations of this property of architecture to modulate sculpturally and harmoniously according to different ambient conditions, effects or programmes; they exist as five distinctive tectonic encounters. The range of formalist strategies is appreciable and proves Atelier Markgraph's willingness to engage with diverse expressions of matter – through a contemporary array of styles, materials and colours, bodies and minds are aroused, invigorated; project users gain a new and valuable understanding of architectural space.

020 Axonometric studies show the movement flow through the space's different levels. As depicted in the diagram, the selected language pertains to seamlessness and sensual luxury, two concepts central to the creation of 'plastic architectures'.

021 The Mercedes-Benz *parcours* culminates in a large-sized showroom, where a highly glossy floor doubles objects, lights and bodies.

METABO

processe

e

.ISMS

s as

ncounters

A DIALOGUE PLATFORM

This Mercedes-Benz installation in Frankfurt features a multilevel, adaptable assembly of vertical and horizontal screens, which, overall, make for a large mobility-themed media spectacle. With its lifting and dropping surfaces, the design formalises important notions about the renewal of a physical environment, reminding visitors of theatre rigging and other mechanical behaviours. PAGE 309

2017

PIONEERING ORGANIC

The new Legau headquarters of Rapunzel Naturkost host a variety of public and commercial programs which make for an environment-friendly ensemble. In that context, Atelier Markgraph's design of the central visitor centre's permanent show features spaces where natural and agricultural processes are turned into a variety of sensory experiences, and where users encounter food matters in friendly industrial-looking setups. PAGE 277

2022

2021

GARDEN DELIGHT

Garden Delight **and the traveling modular exhibition** ***Environment, Climate & You*** **tackle issues of climate change, landscape resilience, housing shortage and 'green' metropoles through natural and playful aesthetics, engaging young visitors with the topic of urban landscaping. Markgraph's creatives show a marked focus on scale: flexible design elements break down the exhibition hall in smaller pockets of varied sizes, forms and colours. PAGE 284**

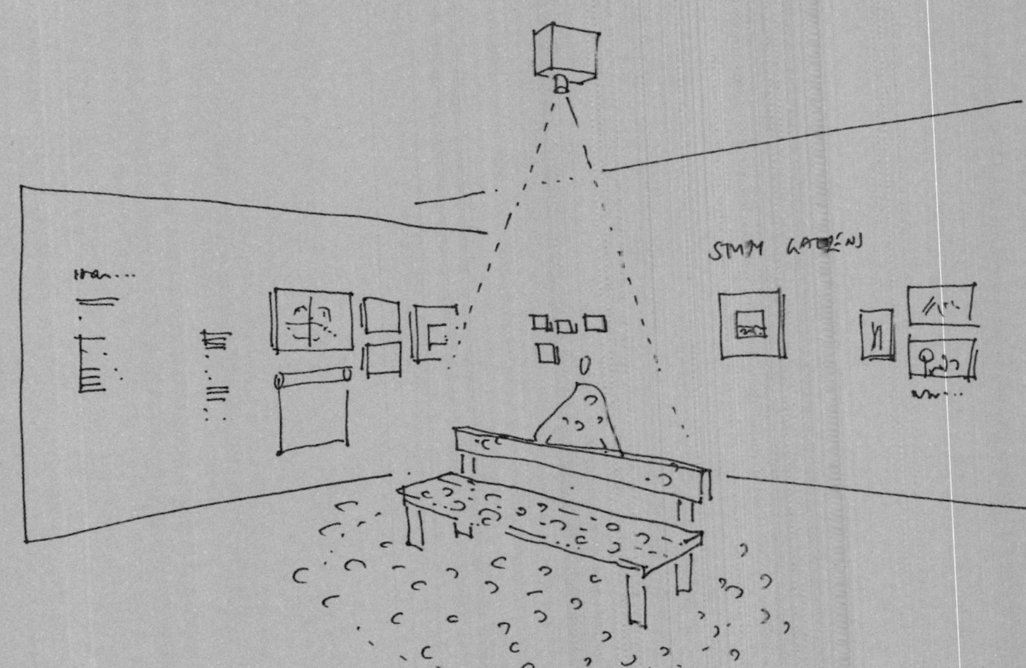

FUTURE FLOW

Atelier Markgraph's installations at the Viega Learning Centre convey impressions of fast connections and technological feats: through large-scale audio and sight pieces, a multisensory imagination of the future comes to life. This phenomenon is especially marked in the *Viega Sphere*, a panoramic moving image theatre which acts as a literal manifestation of immersive and circular design. PAGE 298

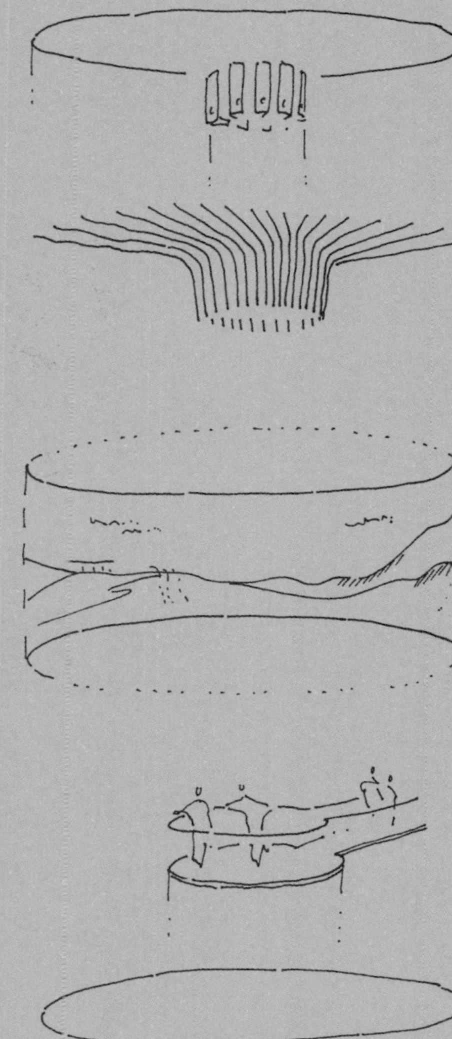

2023

CONTINUOUS

ENERGY TRANSITIONS

Through the use of hands-on artefacts, explanatory diagrams, and multimedia animations, a years-long collaboration between Atelier Markgraph and Viessmann works to reveal and explain complex energy exchanges and processes. A series of fair stands examines different human-machine symbioses, immersing visitors in physical environments which stimulate both thoughts and senses. PAGE 291

‘WE REGARD HUMAN SOCIETY AS A VITAL PROCESS – A CONTINUOUS DEVELOPMENT FROM ATOM TO NEBULA. THE REASON WHY WE USE SUCH A BIOLOGICAL WORD, THE METABOLISM, IS THAT WE BELIEVE DESIGN AND TECHNOLOGY SHOULD BE A DENOTATION OF HUMAN VITALITY.’

(Metabolism 1960: Proposals for a New Urbanism). These few sentences from Japanese architects, designers and theorists Kiyonori Kikutake, Fumihiko Maki, Kisho Kurokawa, Masato Otaka, Kiyoshi Awazu, Ekuan Kenji and Noboru Kawazoe capture well the appeal of ‘Metabolism’ as a concept for the development of spatial infrastructure. In their celebrated manifesto, these pioneers used biological metaphors to advocate for an architecture capable of regeneration. In current times of sustainability, environmentalism and general consumption awareness, the notion of buildings and spaces ‘capable of regeneration’ is attractive indeed; ecology, biology and the wide-ranging study of living organisms’ patterns of growth and renewal in their physical environment inform many contemporary designs. Continuous processes, reuse, circularity, vitality, evolution and degrowth – to organise and erect matter today often means doing so with eco-friendly, ‘Metabolist’ tenets in mind. Atelier Markgraph’s position on this topic is articulated and keen; its in-house Luminous Green approach tackles challenges of corporate and social responsibility in the face of a fast-changing material culture. Arguably, every recent Markgraph project shows a (degree of) commitment to sustainable principles; the following

001
Bio von Beginn an
Organics since the beginning

002

We legalized Müsli 1974

003

> VOM FELD IN DIE MÜSLISCHALE
> AUF MÜSLIREISE
> TRIFF UNSERE MÜSLI-BAUERN
VERTIEFUNG:
> DIE LÄNDER
> DIE PFLANZEN
> BIOKOOPERATIONS-PARTNER
RAPUNZEL
ORIGINAL
Müsli
DEU
POL
TSCH
SLOW
IT
TÜ
ÄGYPTEN
> HAFERFLOCKEN
> GERSTENFLOCKEN
> WEIZENFLOCKEN
> LEINSAAT
> SESAM
> BUCHWEIZEN
> SONNENBLUMENKERNE
> HASELNÜSSE
> SULTANINEN

001 The Legau-based Rapunzel Naturkost features a series of interior spaces focusing on sense stimuli. Spatial strategies include the visual accumulation of objects which evoke nature.
002 Natural qualities and themes are emphasised by the use of raw finishes, as well as a palette of bright, lively colours.
003 Members of the Markgraph team ensured an in-depth mapping of the Rapunzel networks at play, using various diagrams and pictograms.
004 A series of installations capture and re-translate the intricacies of agricultural and natural processes: fresh hues and user-friendly vignettes catch the public's eye and enable a spatial pedagogy of sorts.
005 Key moments of the Rapunzel experience denote Markgraph's general approach to exhibition design, where bodies and minds are both equally engaged.
006 Throughout the show, wall and floor textures, light fixtures and carefully selected furnitures come together in ways which recall food-oriented industry and production centres.
007 Children of all ages get to 'learn by doing and moving' in the exhibition areas, with cranks, levers and other fun-facts wheels.

selection is limited to five key projects, which best exemplify the 'Metabolist' mentality at play in their conception and realisation.

Opened in autumn 2022, the new headquarters of the organic manufacturer, Rapunzel Naturkost, in Legau host a variety of public and commercial programs: coffee roasteries, a cooking school, a bakery shop, exhibition areas, a roof terrace, offices, yoga studios, a café-restaurant, picnic fields, greenhouses and other extensive food growing facilities which make for an 'organic' and environment-friendly ensemble. Atelier Markgraph was tasked by Rapunzel to design and build the large, permanent show on display in the building's central visitor centre – in cooperation with Stuttgart-based architects haascookzemmrich STUDIO2050, Markgraph developed a space where natural and agricultural processes are translated into a sensory experience. In 'From the Plate Back to the Field,' visitors explore various stations equipped with product samples, tools and responsive, multimedia units; they encounter plant matters and waste in friendly industrial-looking setups. Effectively, the aesthetic language of the show more closely resembles that of food production spaces, rather than a traditional museum. Immaculate white walls and 'do not touch' signs are replaced by earthy props, recipe cartons and lively, transforming screens; audio recordings of soil organisms and dressed dining tables lead to novel learning opportunities. Through hands-on artefacts and telltale graphics, individuals of all ages get familiarised with holistic interpretations of agronomic heritage and sustainable cultivation, making good sense of the adage that it is the world which we absorb through food. With their spatial design for Rapunzel, the Atelier's creatives reveal the force of a fairer, greener vision of the human activity of agriculture, with all its potential impacts on biodiversity and health.

While most people associate planting, farming and harvesting with rural milieus, it is the case that cultivated nature has become an intrinsic part of cities' Metabolism. Urban greeneries and other ecological processes in densely built spaces are the focus of Atelier Markgraph's 2021 *Garden Delight* and *Environment*, *Climate & You*. Both exhibitions took place at the Historical Museum of Frankfurt, the latter within the children's branch, in the context of the yearlong initiative 'Die Stadt und das Grün' (or 'Vegetation and the City'). *Garden Delight* and the traveling modular exhibition *Environment, Climate & You* tackle the broad topics of climate change, landscape resilience, housing shortage

Auf die Nüsse, fertig, los!
Verfolge den Weg der
Haselnuss vom Strauch bis
ins Samba-Glas.

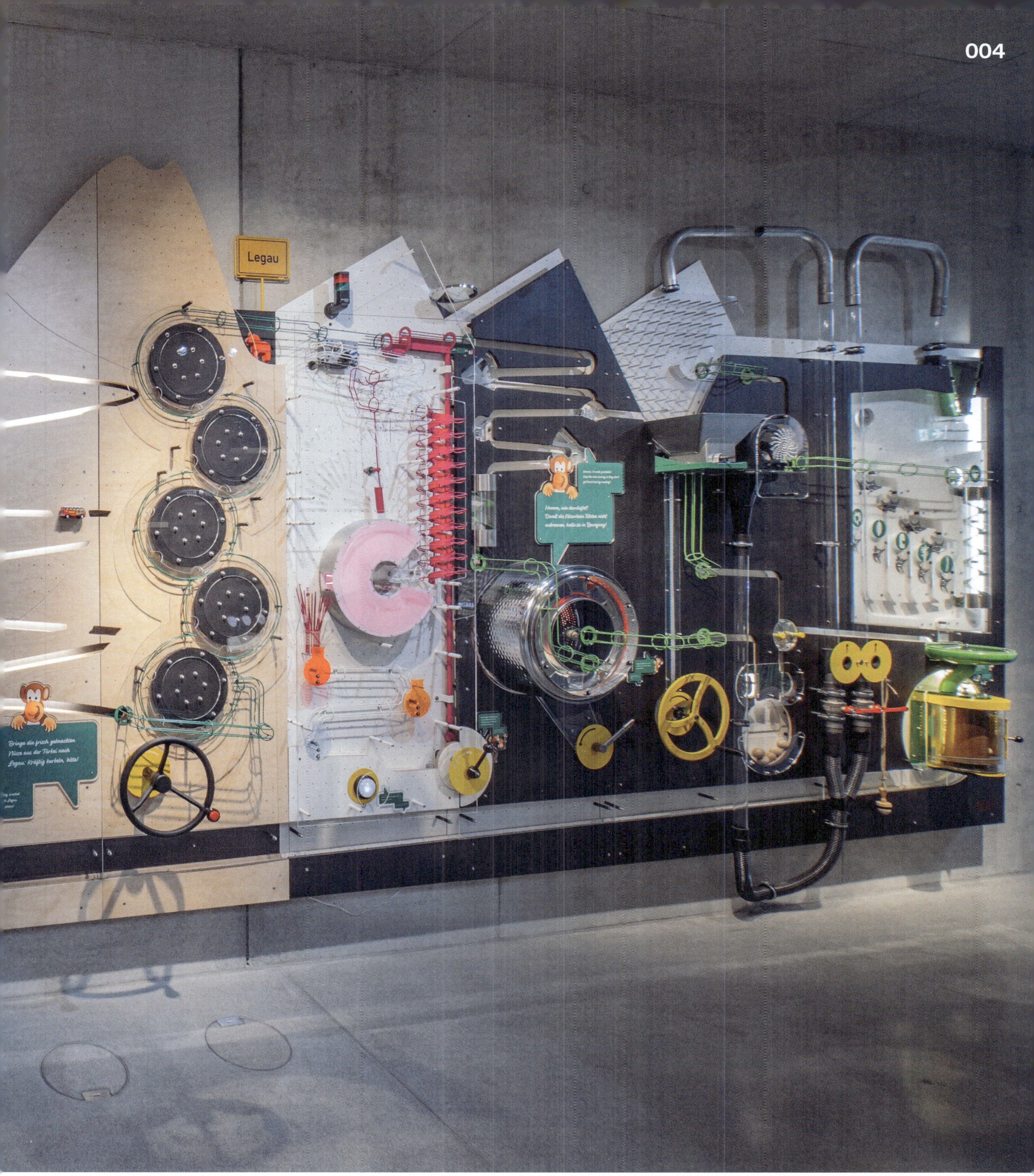
Legau
Bringe die frisch geknackten Nüsse aus der Türkei nach Legau: Kräftig kurbeln, bitte!

005

006

Bringe die frisch geknackten
üsse aus der Türkei nach
gau: Kräftig kurbeln, bitte!

Gesunde Böden — die Basis für eine nachhaltige Zukunft
Healthy soils – the basis for a sustainable future

007

GARTENKULTUR

008 Forest-themed wall prints, dark green hues and wooden elements come together to create an atmosphere which directly recalls nature.

009 A fun nod to 'outdoors aesthetics', a long park bench sits inside the *Garden Delight* galleries.

010 Graphic design decisions allows for the juxtaposition of romantic, traditional imageries of the natural world with more abstract and dynamic visual elements, like these bright blue outlines.

011 Tiny and colourful objects (Viessmann technologies and products) pop out in contrast with the dimmed, slick surfaces of walls or ceiling panels. Their function is to grab visitors' attention, as well as to symbolise green gardens, parks and squares.

012 Plywood is utilised throughout the exhibition rooms, in light of its natural and friendly-looking qualities: it conveys impressions of warmth and robustness to the users, who are therefore more likely to approach and touch it.

013 Creatives at the Atelier know that, for children, playing remains one of the most engaging ways to learn about an issue.

and 'environmentally conscious' metropoles; for the duration of an afternoon, visitors become researchers and activists who engage in different aspects of urban landscaping and greening – and so, of urban betterment. Markgraph envisioned the galleries as flexible, with dividers segmenting the exhibition hall into smaller pockets of varied sizes; a forum-like space provides groups with a cosy area for collective activities. Monitors and gaze curtains project and receive the light of pedagogical videos, with attention-grabbing effects. Case studies consider the past, present and future of public green squares and parks, examples of urban gardening in Frankfurt, or the applied ecological and socio-political dimensions of inner-city greening; social participation and its relation to civic spaces in the urban fabric is highlighted throughout the exhibition *parcours*. Additionally, in the rooms of *Environment, Climate & You*, large, colourful prints combine landscape planning visuals with biology textbook-like graphics; cartoons and anthropomorphised figures accompany children in their various thematic encounters. These two shows staged by the Atelier tell the story of a built world which we continuously nurture and negotiate – and they both manage to persuade viewers that this story can be a hopeful one.

AS THE SET OF LIFE-SUSTAINING TRANSFORMATIONS IN ORGANISMS AND SYSTEMS, METABOLISM IS CONCERNED WITH EXCHANGES OF ENERGY

– bodies convert food and drink into vital forces; material cells grow, reproduce and stay robust and healthy. To be sure, such exchanges demand high amounts of physical or chemical resources. To the everyman and woman, most Metabolist processes remain a little opaque, unclear; these processes are part of our daily lives, but they are also often hidden and misunderstood. Through a partnership which now spans over a decade, Atelier Markgraph and the German manufacturer of heating and refrigeration systems, Viessmann, have worked on revealing and explaining the many energy exchanges and processes which surround

BAUMPERSÖNLICHKEITEN
TREE PERSONALITIES

010

VERGNÜGUNGSORTE
PLACES OF LEISURE

011

ZIALE GRÜNFLÄCHEN
CIAL GREEN SPACES
GARTENBAU
AUBERGINE

GLOBALER WARENHANDEL
Waren reisen oft um die ganze Welt. Das liegt daran, dass der Handel und die Herstellung von Waren heute weltweit organisiert sind: Die Baumwolle für ein T-Shirt kommt aus den USA, genäht wird es in Bangladesch, verkauft wird es in Deutschland. Das ist für die Firmen wirtschaftlich sinnvoll, weil die Herstellung in einigen Ländern viel billiger ist. Viele kritisieren aber auch, dass die Arbeiter*innen oft schlecht bezahlt werden und unter schwierigen Bedingungen arbeiten.
Staaten. Im Internet ist die Welt miteinander verbunden. Es frisst aber auch viel Energie: Die Datenspeicherung auf großen Servern und die Netzstruktur machen 5% des weltweiten Stromverbrauchs aus. Das ist so viel wie Deutschland und Kanada zusammen verbrauchen.
Flugzeug
Mit dem Flugzeug werden empfindliche Waren transportiert: Medikamente, wichtige Post, aber auch Obst und Blumen. Das geht schnell, kostet aber viel Geld und stößt sehr viel CO_2 aus. Viele Waren fliegen mit einem normalen Passagierflugzeug mit: oben sitzen die Passagiere, unten lagern die Pakete. Am Frankfurter Flughafen starten und landen jeden Tag im Durchschnitt 1.400 Flugzeuge. Das Flugzeug bringt uns schnell an weit entfernte Ziele, ist aber auch das klimaschädlichste Transportmittel. Und das Problem: Erst mal ist auch keine umweltfreundlichere Lösung in Sicht. Da hilft nur, öfter auf's private Fliegen zu verzichten.

012

NACHHALTIGKEIT
NACHHALTIGKEIT
WIE HOCH IST DEIN CO_2-AUSSTOSS?
GLOBALISIERUNG

013

014 Curious and eye-pleasing objects are strategically placed in the bright gallery space; they stand out and slow visitors' path down, allowing them to better engage with informative content. As such, a spatial experience translates to a pedagogical one.

015 As they present a variety of colours, forms and materials, Atelier Markgraph's installations engage space users, bringing them to roam and explore the different booths and stands.

016 A rich collection of 'spatial typologies' inform the placement of Viessmann objects, wall partitions, sounds and texts: the fair stands' design can, at will, invoke the tango steps of a dancer, the urban grid of a North-American city, or the crevasse-like geology of a canyon.

017 At times, the large spaces of the exhibition hall call for the creation of similarly large visual markers; a balance of scales is achieved with smaller, user-friendly infills.

018 The bright hue of red, which is used by the Viessman group for their general visual identity, is recuperated by the Atelier and distributed calculatedly throughout the fair's open rooms.

us. A series of fair stands – 2007-2023, at the International Trade Fair for Sanitation, Heating and Air (ISH) in Frankfurt – jointly designed by Markgraph creatives and Viessmann experts examine the different human-machine symbioses which characterise contemporary life; these stands make good use of diagrams, action-oriented artefacts and multimedia animations to capture visitors' attention and interest. Playful ornaments, thumbnail illustrations and eye-levelled plinths function as facilitators for the passing of technical and industrial knowledge; projection mappings and VR simulations meet the universe of constructed pipes and machineries. Three-dimensional temperature maps and robotic cameras permit a new, concrete understanding of the aforementioned notions of reuse, circularity, vitality and degrowth. In effect, Atelier Markgraph has designed a wide array of scenographic objects to capture Viessmann's energy-related craft – its *Energy Shelf* (ISH 2007), *Hanging Cities* (ISH 2009), *Medial Dioramas* (ISH 2011), *Lanes of Innovation* (ISH 2013), *Technology Towers* (ISH 2015), *Central Forum* (ISH 2017) and *Partnership Lane* (ISH 2019) are diverse formal strategies which clarify and celebrate state-of-the art technological progress.

EXPERIENCES OF SPACE ALTERATIONS CAN BE FUNDAMENTALLY VISUAL – THE USER WITNESSES A RAPID SHIFT IN HUE, IN LIGHT; THE EYE FOLLOWS LINES WHICH DRAW THE GAZE UP OR DOWN.

019 Key transformational processes are featured and synthesised in the graphic and spatial concepts developed for the German brand.

020 Digital projections allow for a dynamic display of content, and complement the show's more 'static' title cards, prints and object labels.

They can also signify transformational processes and exchanges through the use of music, tones and other sounds. Key rooms at the Viega Learning Centre (2023), also known as Viega World, convey impressions of fast connections and technological feats through audio and sight pieces: like amalgams of visitors' perceptual qualities, installations

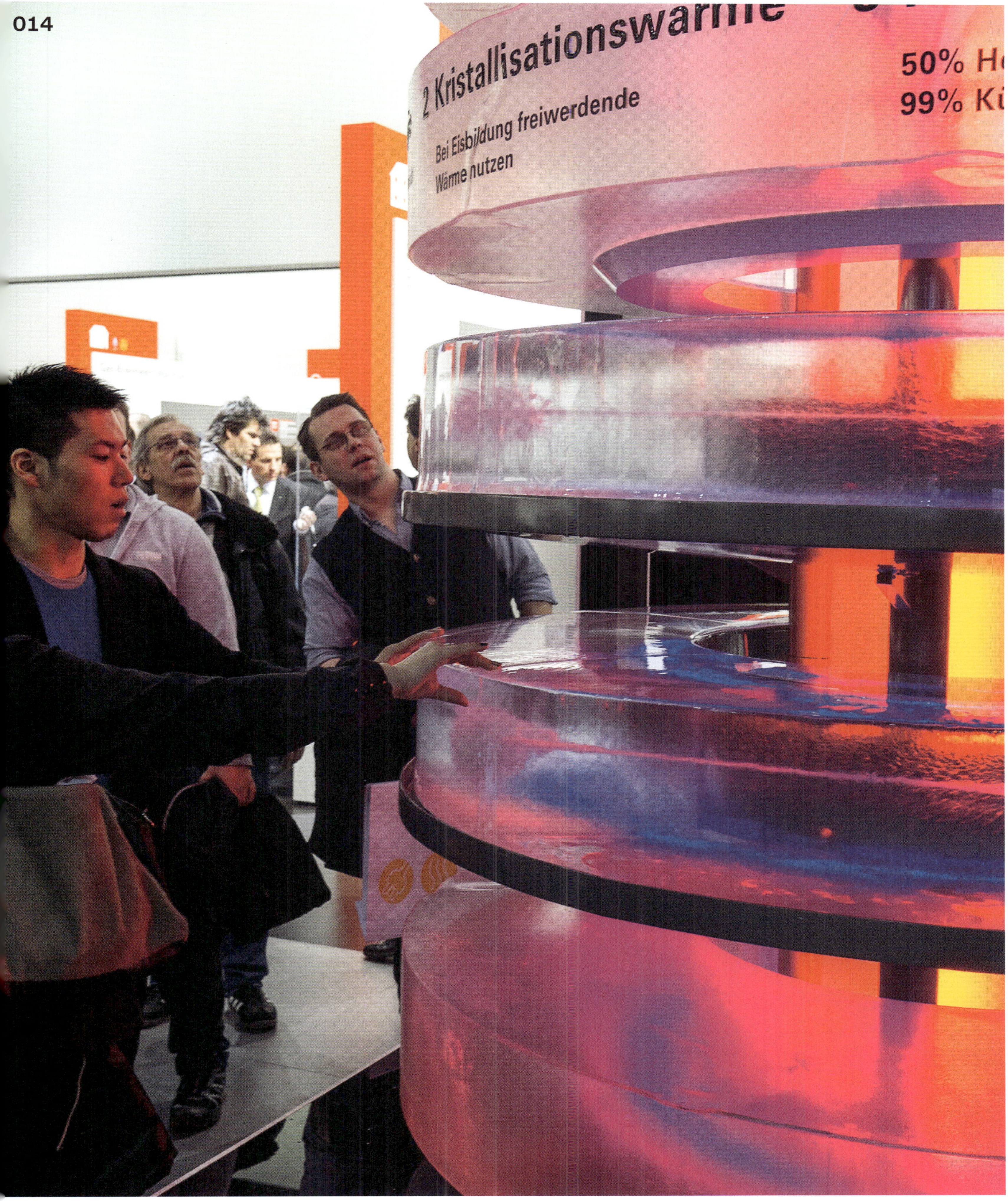
2 Kristallisationswärme
Bei Eisbildung freiwerdende
Wärme nutzen
50% H
99% K

FUEL CELLS
LLEN
BRENNSTOFFZELLEN
Modernisieren mit
der Brennstoffzelle
Modernising with
a fuel cell
RADSON
Anmelden Sign up

COMMERCIAL
GEWERBE / KOMMUNEN
MODERNISATION
MODERNISIERUNG
VIESSMANN
VIESSMANN

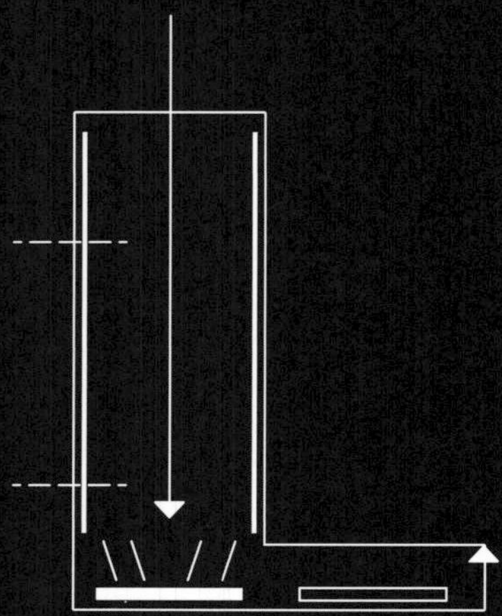

Frontal Approach

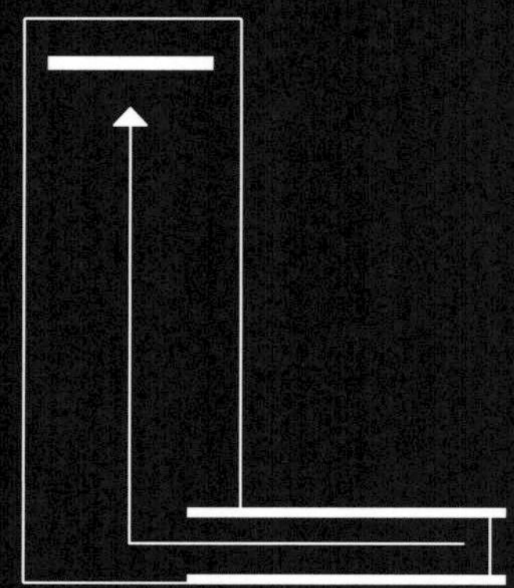

Reverse Approach

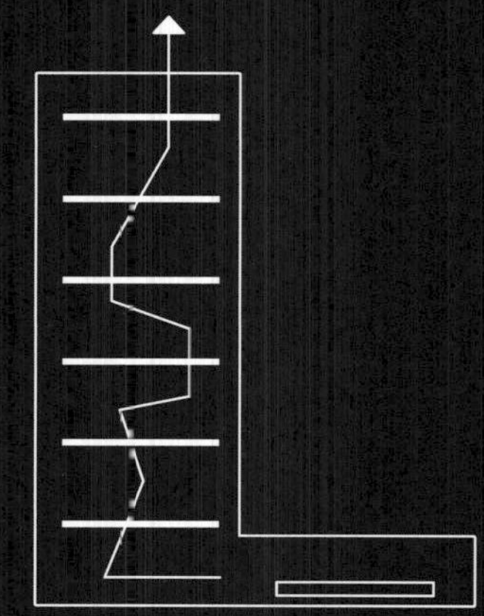

Linear Thresholds

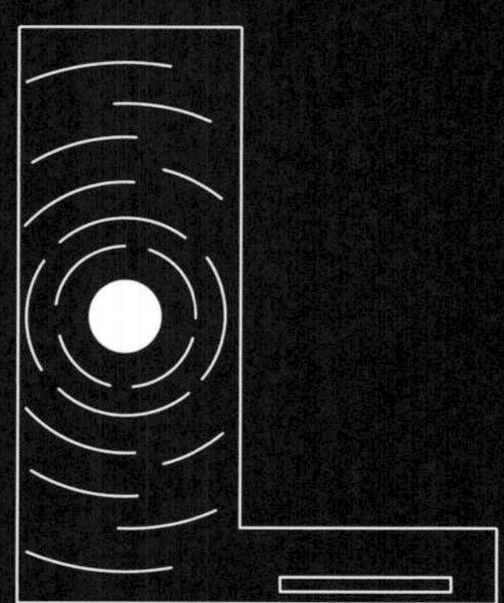

Inspirational Core

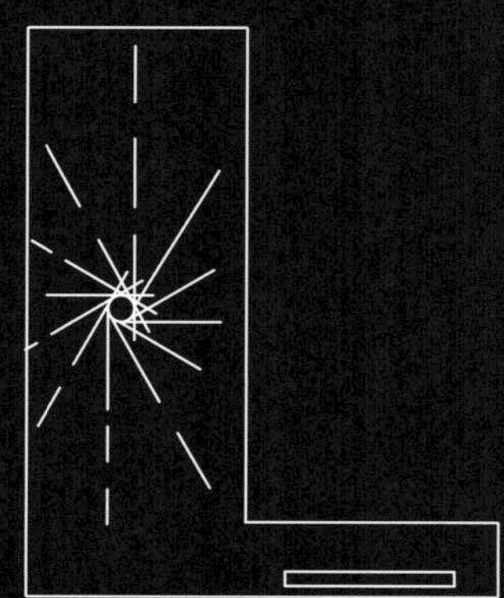

Radial Windmill

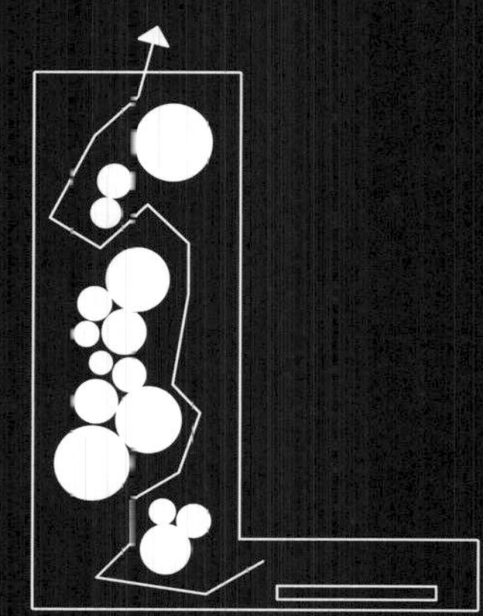

Tango Meander

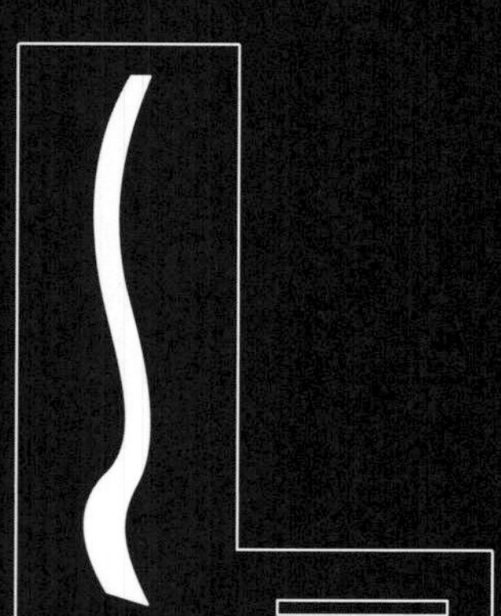

Organic Flow

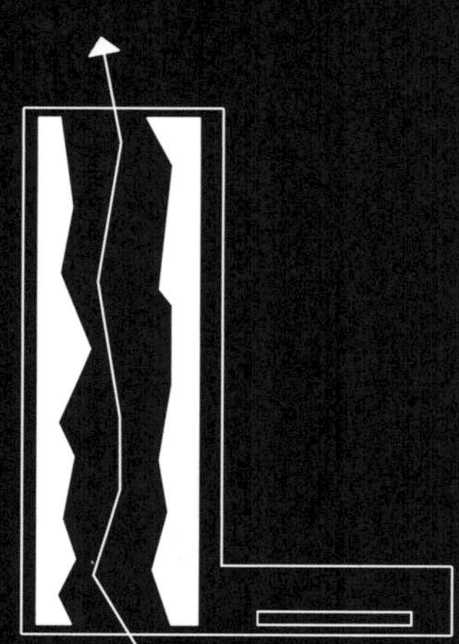

Plain Gorge

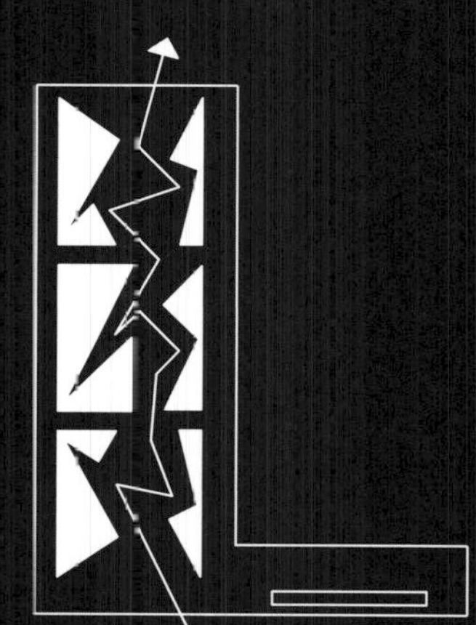

Fragmented Canyon

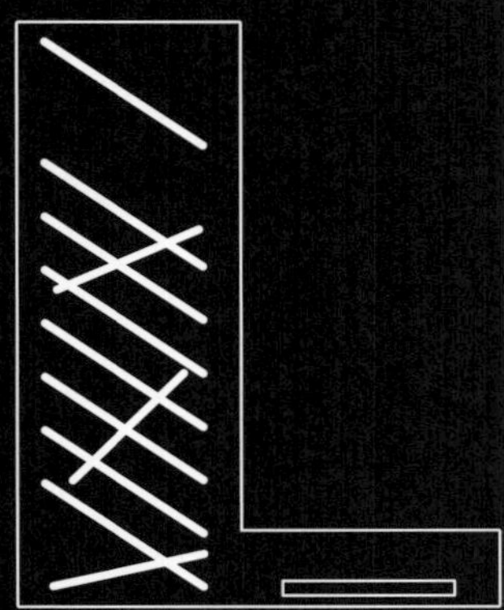

Rhythmic Layering

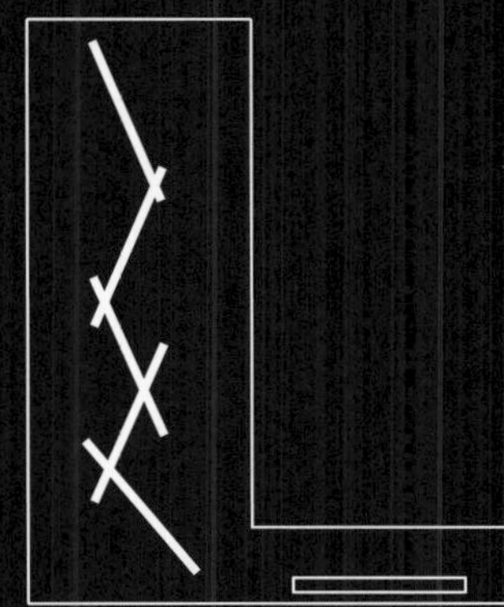

Interlocking Strands

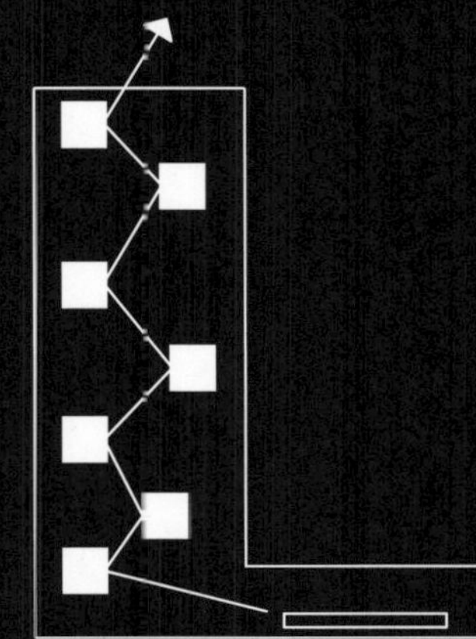

Point by Point

Linear Shifts

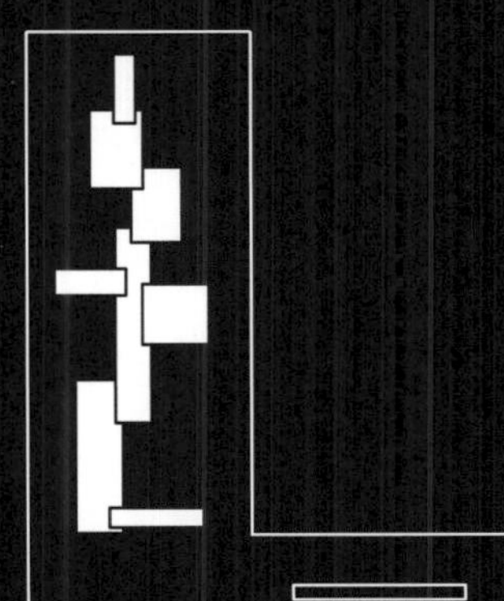

Intersection Themes

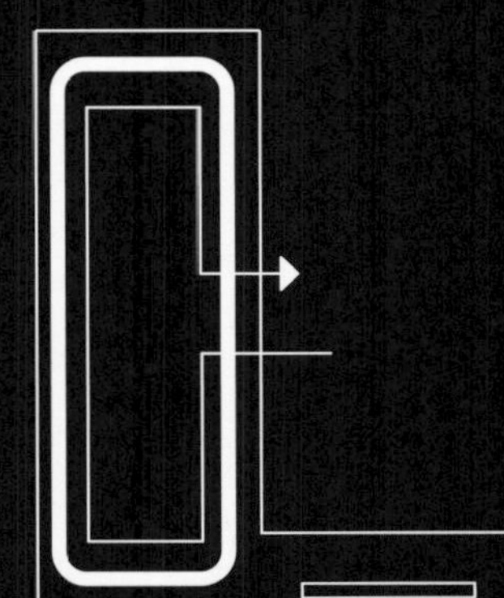

Perfect Tour

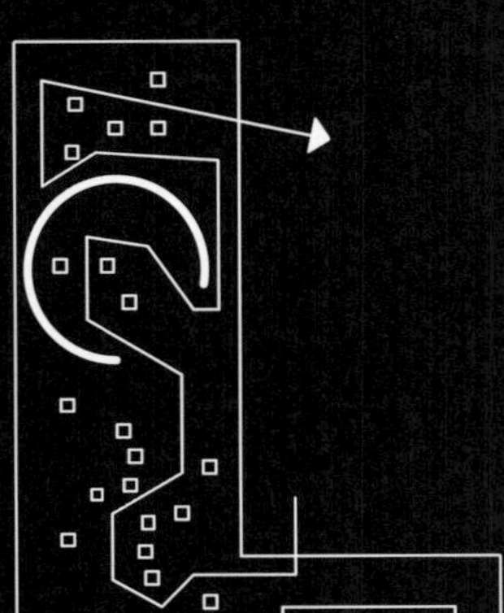

Contrasting Hybrid

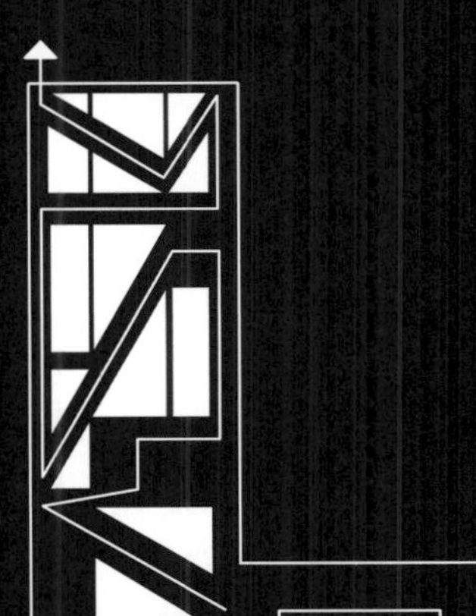

Polygonal Urbanity

What now?

VIESSMANN
Power
Power
weishaup

017

Into a new century
Plug & play ins Internet

019

018

FORUM
VIESSMANN

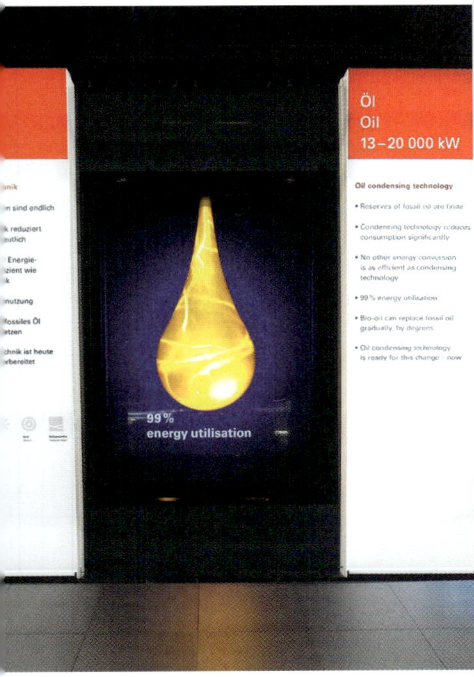

Öl
Oil
13–20 000 kW
Oil condensing technology
• Reserves of fossil oil are finite
• Condensing technology reduces consumption significantly
• No other energy conversion is as efficient as condensing technology
• 99 % energy utilisation
• Bio-oil can replace fossil oil gradually, by degrees
• Oil condensing technology is ready for this change – now
99 %
energy utilisation

Einfamilienhäuser

020

Blick in die Zukunft

from Atelier Markgraph connect to the company's forward-thinking ambitions and sought-after impacts. With its impressive six metres' height, *Viega Sphere*, a panoramic moving image theatre, is the site where Viega's multisensory imagination of the future comes to life.

A LITERAL PHYSICAL MANIFESTATION OF 'CIRCULAR DESIGN,' THE IMMERSIVE SCREEN ENVIRONMENT DISPLAYS VISUALISATIONS OF TOMORROW

designed by film director Shan Blume and Monomango, a Berlin-based production studio. Waterfall mists, ocean waves, tree foliage caressed by the wind, but also futuristic cities and infrastructure: with their depiction of natural and man-made worlds, the scenes projected (and scored) in the *Viega Sphere* celebrate phenomena and processes which tie users back to the very notion of Metabolism. Additionally, a large, technical-looking art piece adorns the centre's lobby; assembled from the company's manufactured products, this lifeline sculpture showcases flows of water, gases, oil and other vital liquids. Tubes and joints make for a fun mechanistic vision – a constructed tribute to industrial science and performance. Markgraph's spatial composition for Viega mixes the formal language of laboratories with that of sites of art and entertainment; the factory here meets the museum, and their encounter is forceful.

Markgraph's large-scale media installation for Mercedes-Benz at the 2017 Frankfurt Internationale Automobil Ausstellung consists of a multilevel, adaptable assembly of screen interfaces; in a space-transforming ballet, these screens can be hoisted up and down (flying out and in) the fair's large and open hall. Dozens of viewers are led to occupy different levels of this hall – they can observe the unfolding, mobility-themed media spectacle from the floor or mezzanine areas. The Atelier's conception and execution links back to old and new traditions of kinetic architecture, where design ambitions centre on the possible renewal of a physical environment. This is spatial regeneration at its most applied: an elaborate rigging system utilises chain lines, block pulleys, counterweights,

021 Immersive environments plunge visitors of the Viega Learning Centre into multisensory worlds of sounds, lights and monochrome hues.
022 The design of in-between passages is limited to black and white tints, making for a minimal, graphic experience of space. Here, words and sentences pop out of their dark canvas, replacing bodily sense-making with a more traditional form of cognition.
023 The large, spherical plan facilitates physical impressions of three-dimensionality: curved walls and moving images work in tandem to saturate one's feel (and vision).
024 A simple yet efficacious design decision: the highly polished and reflective floor surface doubles the lighting effects in the room.
025 Life-like cityscapes and natural landscapes are imagined and mapped onto various Viega spaces, which become lushly populated with buildings and trees.

WAS, WENN WIR STATT ROHRLEITUNGEN,
LEBENSADERN
INSTALLIEREN?
WHAT IF WE INSTALL
LIFELINES
INSTEAD OF PIPELINES?
DIGITALES BAUEN:
NOCH DIE ZUKUNFT
ODER BEREITS DER WEG DORTHIN?
DIGITAL BUILDING:
STILL THE FUTURE
OR ALREADY THE WAY THERE?
IST S
TR
SELB

viega world

SHANGHAI
2030
POPULATION
32.0Million
AREA
6340.5 km²
Average Temp.
16.5 °C
NEW YORK
2043
9.700.000.000
HELSINKI
POPULATION
0.9 Million

024

025

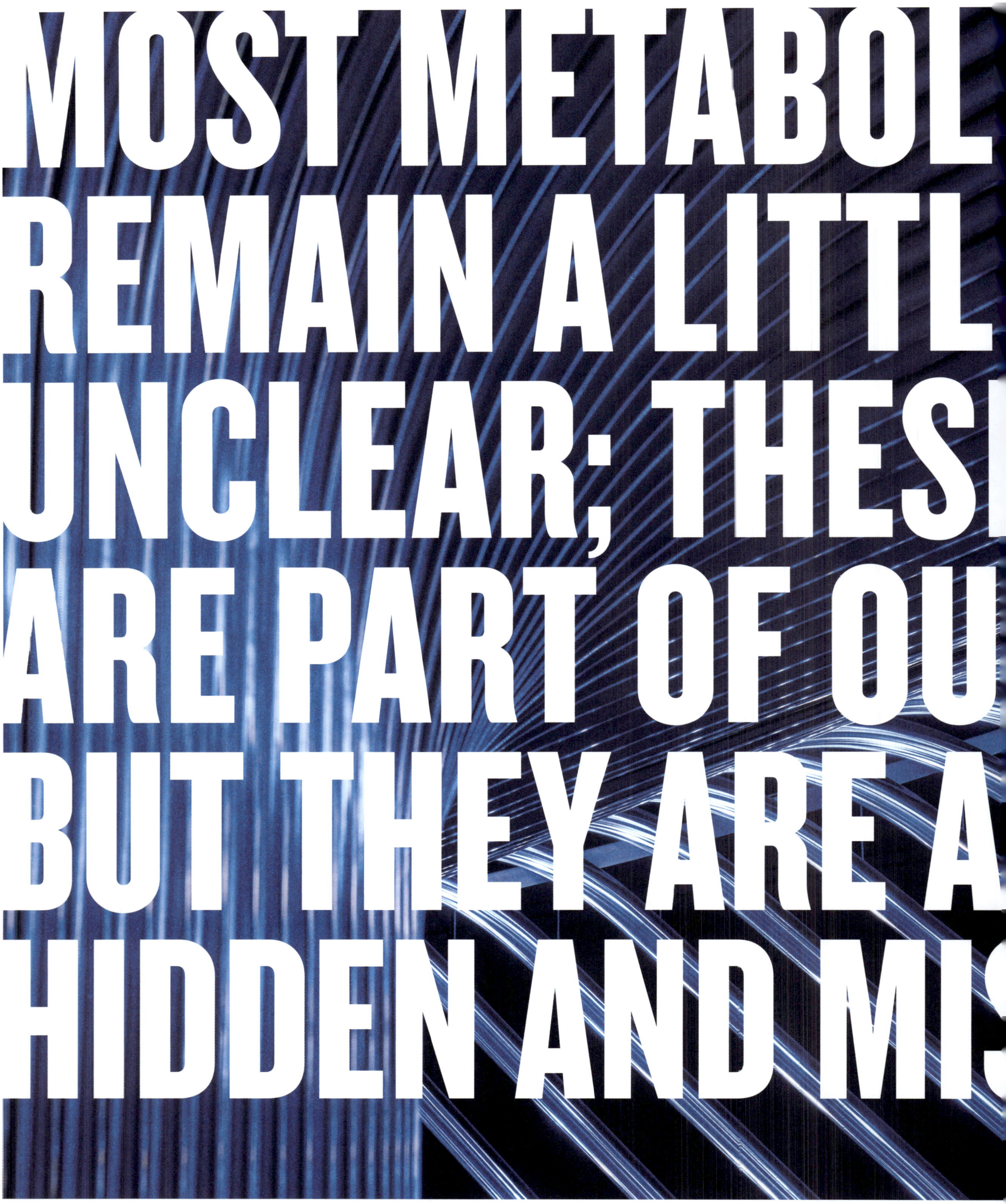

MOST METABOL
REMAIN A LITTL
UNCLEAR; THES
ARE PART OF OU
BUT THEY ARE A
HIDDEN AND MIS

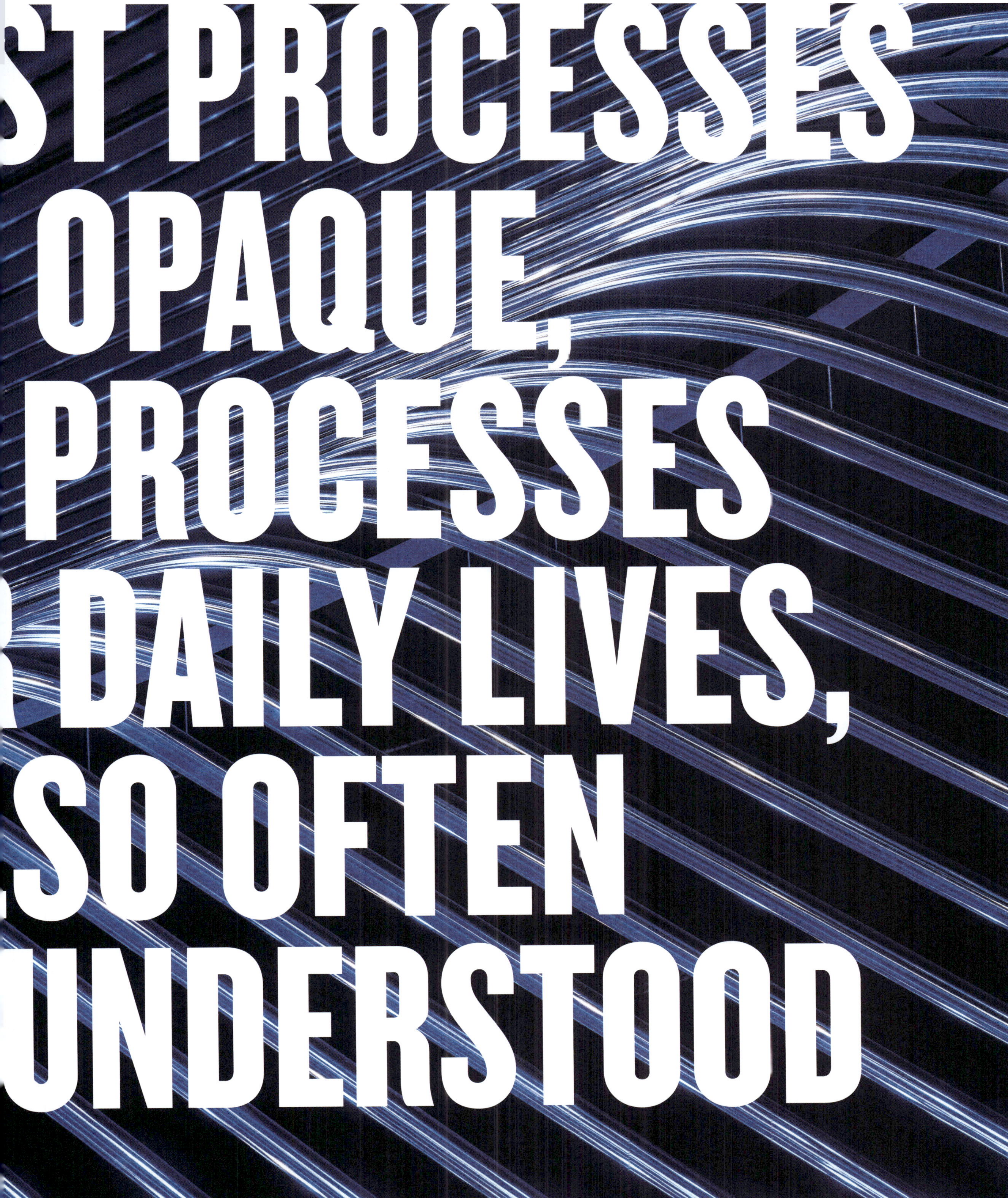

ST PROCESSES
OPAQUE,
PROCESSES
DAILY LIVES,
SO OFTEN
UNDERSTOOD

026 The booth design immediately recalls theatrical decors and mechanisms, in a fun nod to multiform spaces and changing modes of mobility.
027 A conceptual diagram shows the five vertical screens' placement in relation to the main horizontal one, as well as the many vantage points in the room.
028 Visitors can always catch a glimpse of the beautiful ceiling dome, which features technical rails filled with light beamers, cables and projectors. This strengthens the creative team's conceptual connection to the imagery of the stage.
029 The large assembly of screens is installed in a high and generous space, which can be observed from different mezzanine-like levels – or, to recuperate a theater analogy, from different 'balconies'.

and other related devices, enabling a technical crew to raise and lower screens in the IAA airspace. New, 'Metabolist' configurations symbolise the brand's dedication to mobility and its many forms. They remind visitors of theatre rigging and mechanical behaviour; of iterations of growth and renewal. The concept team knows well that mobile designs tend to be green in essence, as they can be repurposed, reused in different contexts and programmes – in the words of the modernist architect and kinetic thinker Cedric Price, this signals something like architecture's possible move from the curative to the preventive. As such, the coupling of physical, animated arrangements with the client's brand succeeds – the spatial impression is one of energy and futureproof opportunities, of transformative encounters and high-standard evolution.

The Greek word *metabolē* means 'to change' – many creatives and theorists are calling for a pressing change in present-day consumption behaviours and resources distribution, be it in architectural, cultural or socio-economic doings. As was shown with this chapter's project selection, Atelier Markgraph's Luminous Green insights have a ripple effect on its manner of conceiving of spatial design. Ultimately, Metabolism here arises as more than a figure of speech or a tool – it informs most aspects of Markgraph's production, situating it in the necessary realms of sustainability, renewal and environmentalism.

THE FUTURE IS NOW, AND IT'S OURS; LET'S MAKE SURE THAT WE BUILD (AND MEET) IT IN ROBUST, ADAPTIVE WAYS.

cars first?
Free imagination.

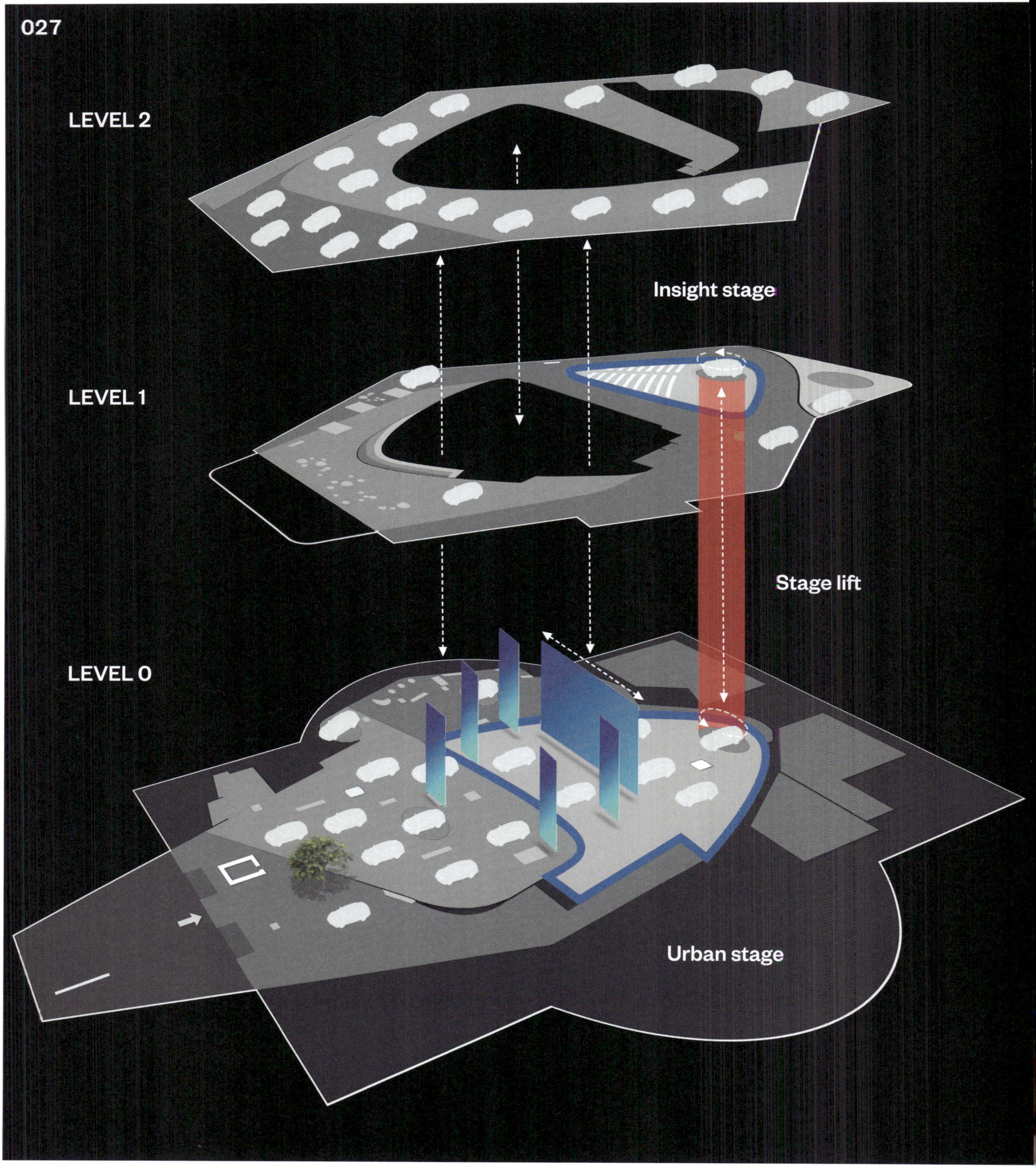
027
LEVEL 2
Insight stage
LEVEL 1
Stage lift
LEVEL 0
Urban stage

028

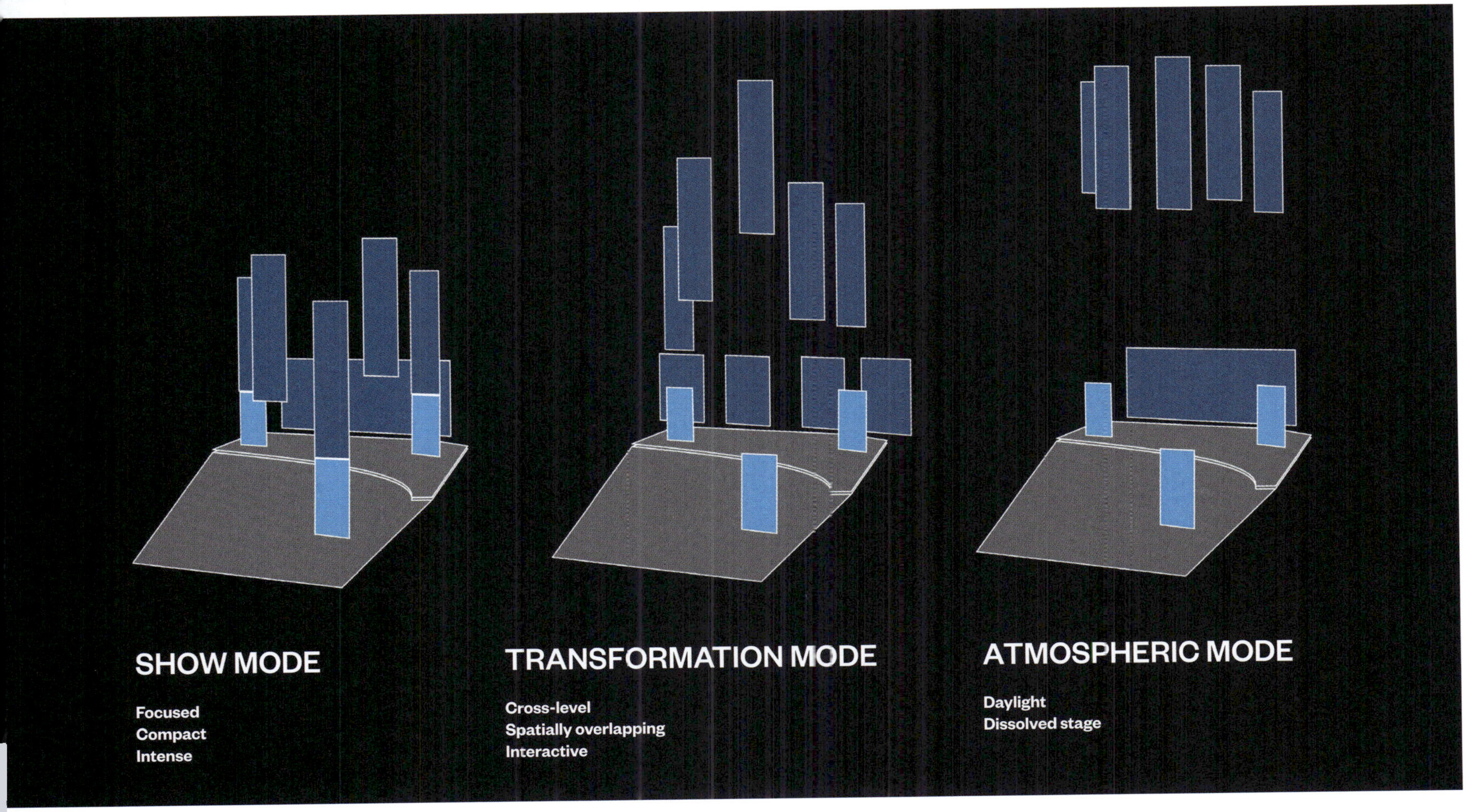
SHOW MODE
Focused
Compact
Intense
TRANSFORMATION MODE
Cross-level
Spatially overlapping
Interactive
ATMOSPHERIC MODE
Daylight
Dissolved stage

DAIMLER
cars
That's
us

029

ACKNOWLEDGEMENTS

Thank you to all our clients, collaboration and planning partners, many of whom we have had the pleasure of working with for a long time. We appreciate your trust and belief in our perspectives and recommendations.

Thank you to everyone who has helped us initiate, create, develop, plan, realise and implement our projects. We have personally acknowledged many of you. If we have inadvertently overlooked anyone, please accept our apologies. It has been an honour to have you all with us over the years and we look forward to our continued collaboration in the future. This includes our interdisciplinary team working closely with us in the studio, all our freelance experts, our collaborators who co-create as realisation partners and contribute their expertise and the photographers and filmmakers who document the often ephemeral.

Thank you to all those who reference and publish our work. Special thanks to the team at FRAME Publishers for providing us with this unique opportunity. Barbara, Erika, Noor, François and Robert, we appreciate your contributions. This is not merely a book by FRAME about AM, nor is it a book by AM published by FRAME. It stands as a stellar example of collaboration, jointly created by FRAME and AM. We also extend our gratitude to our internal team: Charlotte, Christina, Diana, Elisa, Sibylle, Martin, Joe and Uwe; as well as all those who were interviewed by Erika and François. This book thrives on numerous encounters – from Amsterdam in the Netherlands and Frankfurt in Germany, to Bergen in Norway and Montreal in Canada.

Thank you to the audiences, the visitors, the employees and all the people who have seen, benefited from and hopefully enjoyed our work. Our gratitude extends to the running staff, explainers and concierges. We would also like to thank all the individuals who make our work shine, such as the service and cleaning teams. A special mention goes to those who prepare and serve food and beverages at our productions.

Thank you to absolutely everyone who contributes to our productions, even if the tasks and performances might seem small or insignificant to the viewer. We value each and every one of you. Without your contributions, we would not be able to create, produce, maintain and run all these projects.

Finally, on the most personal level, we would like to express our gratitude to our families for their unwavering support, patience, and understanding. They have always stood by us, even when we were engrossed in creating a book as yet another extracurricular engagement.

Lars, Stefan & Tom

LEADERSHIP Our company has been owner-managed and independent since its founding in 1986. The management consists of Lars Uwe Bleher, Tom Schubert and Stefan Weil. In 2023, the management team was expanded to include a new executive level consisting of Sebastian Bausch, Christoph Diederichs, Antonia Eisert, Sarah Roßbach and Jennifer Ussner.

HISTORY Atelier Markgraph was founded in 1986 by Meinhard Hutschenreuther, Roland Lambrette and Rolf Engel in the Markgrafenstrasse in Frankfurt am Main – perhaps as the first agency for spatial communication. From 1990 to 2012, Christoph Meyer joined the founding trio as a partner and was significantly responsible for the further development and interdisciplinary orientation of the studio. Since the generation change in 2017, Lars Uwe Bleher and Stefan Weil have been the owners and, together with Tom Schubert, form the management team. From 2017 until 2021 Christian Neuber supported the Atelier as a partner.

CURRENT, FORMER & EXTENDED TEAM

A

arbara Ackermann – Jörg Ackermann – ami Alaeddin – Christoph Alker – Malik lpoguz – Björn Amend – Isabell Anhalt Arfst-Sönne Arfsten – Nadia Ayoub – artmut Ayrle

B

atharina Bahne – Tannaz Balazadehberenjian Elke Balger – Friedrich Bals – Boris Banozic Carolina Barros Fernandes da Silva – Elisa artat – Felix Barton – Benjamin Bauer – athrin Baumgartner – Sebastian Bausch Vanessa Beck – Rainer Bedding – Andreas ehl – Vincent Benard – David Berens – Pete ergens – Markus Bernatzky – Stefanie esler – Nicole Birlenbach – Lars Uwe Bleher Roland Blum – Shan Blume – Andreas oden – Denise Bohländer – Stephan Bolz – adleen Bommert – Stephanie Bonifer – Julia onnaire – Rahma Bouassam – Alexander Boz Frank Brammer – Jürgen Brandt – Valerie raun – Fabian Braunmiller – Wolfgang reuninger – Uta Brinksmeier – Mario rucculeri – Johannes Brückner – Gerd rünig – Laura Brunner – Lisa Budde – oe Burkmeyer – Barbara Bux

C

lena Caniova – Rüdiger Chmielus – Yoon-ung Choe – Pasu Chootai – Kim Angie icuttin – Clive Cobb – Jonathan Cook – ele Coors

D

nna Dageretzis – Sonja Dahbi – Claudia ahnelt – Jessica Day – Nasim Delkas – aphaël Demonthy – Janos Déri – Rolf Derrer Christoph Diederichs – Markus Dittrich – onja Donnert – Axel Dorner – Michel Dorus Marco dos Santos Vaz Dias Wicht – Manuel reesmann – Hans Drexler – Barbara Duchow Andrea Dung – Filip Dzaja

E

eter Eberhard – Stefan Ebling – Peter ckart – Barbara Eiden – Berit Eisenmann Antonia Eisert – Roland Eisert – Sandra llinger – Rolf Engel – Chris Engler – Markus nsel – Ben Erdmann – Marcel Eris – Alime rtürk – Anne-Helen Eßer – Katja Ewich

F

ulia Fadeicheva – Jürgen Fahlbusch – Maria eddersen – Rui Filipe – Alexandra Fischer Bastian Fischer – Hanna Fischer – Nina itzthum – Claudia Fortuni-Kummer – Markus ranz – Lucas Frenzel – Ole Freytag – Barbara risch – Olivier Fröhlich – Andreas Fuchs – ophia Fürbeck

G

orgelina Garcia Ayub – Anja Garcia iemsen – Günther Gebauhr – Andrea ehne – Christoph Geiger – Titus Georgi Stefan Geppert – Laura Gerritsen – hristian Gerster – Yvonne Gerster – Sanaz horbani – Angela Gläser – Mark Gläser – usanne Gocht – Anke Goeres – Alexander rabowsky – Thorsten Graf – Werner Graf Simone Gräf – Anita Grams – Don Grant Michaela Greiner – Joachim Grell – Lech rochola – Thomas Gross – Frank Gruner Wolfram Gruss – Marion Grünsteidl – hristiane Gumpert – Miriam Guter

H

Max Haacke – Sebastian Haase – Esther Hagenlocher – Kerstin Hahlbohm – Sebastian Hahn – Christoph Hahnemann – Katrin Hahnemann – Ali Haidari – Nicole Hanbaba – Alexander Hanowski – Heiko Härle – Daniel Hartard – Stefan Hartmann – Hermann Hartung – Joachim Hauser – Robin Heather – Christina Hecht – Peter Heilig – Jürgen Heinisch – Andreas Henkel – Bernhard Henrich – Stefanie Henrich – Eno Henze – Christian Hergarten – Karl-Heinz Herget – Agnes Herzberg – Johanno Hess – Birgit Hildebrandt – Christina Hilge – Henry Hilge – Michael Hilger – Jördis Hille – Bernd Hilpert – Carina Hinterkircher – Tine Hoefke – Petra Hoffmann – Reiner Hörner – André Hornischer – Elvis Hot – Antje Hottejan – Anne Hüart – Frank Hübner – Carlo Hutschenreuther – Meinhard Hutschenreuther

I

Thomas Ickenroth

J

Swen Jenzsch – Christoph Jia – Manuel Jörger – Birgit Joest – André Jouaux – Stefan Jung

K

Kerstin Kaczor – Michael Kadelbach – Lars Kaestner – Lois Kainhuber – Larissa Kalleitner – Jörg Kallmeyer – Ulrich Kapferer – Florian Käppler – Katharina Kauskopf – Holger Kautenburger – Thilo Kehrberger – Tobias Kehrberger – Benedikt Kestler – Peter Kiefer – Leon Kieven – Petra Kinne – Nina Kipp – Dorothea Kirstein – Louis Kitzinger – Rolf Klarmann – Heike Klasen – Hellen Kleine – Mirko Kleinlein – Tim Klinger – Sarah Klöpfer – Jürgen Kloster – André Knörig – Torsten Kohlbrei – Birgit Kolecki – Wolfgang Köllen – Uta König – Jacob Konrad – Katharina Körber – Alexander Korolkov – Julia Kracke – Marianne Kral – Angela Kratz – Alexander Kraus – Andrej Krause – Beate Krebsbach – Kim Krier – Frank Krugmann – Kristin Krugmann – Yvonne Krug-Prosek – Harald Kubiczak – Oliver Kuhlmann – Angelina Kuhnert – Mitali Kulkarni – Petra Kümmel – Nicolas Kunz – Ben Kunze – Daniela Kupetz – Piotr Kuroczinski – Carolin Kurrle – Clarissa Kurtz

L

Nicole La Croix – Mekong Lam – Roland Lambrette – Renate Lamprecht – Gernot Langeloth – Susanne Lämmer – Melanie Landro – Stefanie Larson – Alexander Leask – Eduard Lefter – Gisbert Lehle – Marco Lehmann – Ralph Lenhardt – Julian Lianarachchi – Victoria Liebrecht – Verena Linhard – Rebecca Littman-Smith – ZhenYu Liu – Christina Loeffler – Stephan Löper – Julia Löwe – Andreas Lorenschat – Manfred Lorenz – Werner Lorke – Katharina Lottner – Jiang Lu

M

Katja Maasch – Alexander Machytka – Cornelia Maier – Andreas Malsy – Holaku Mameghani – Karen Mandler – Silvia Manz – Roland Marloh – Leonie Martin – Denis März – Steffen Maubach – Verena Mauerer – Michael Mauler – Petra Mauntz – Christoph Mayer – Mathias Mayer – Alexandra Mehdi – Barbara Meder – Judith Mehrmann – Jan Meininghaus – Alexandra Meixner – Anne Metzen – Christoph Meyer – Frank Meyer – Tanja Meyer – Katsiaryna Mikhalenka – Charlotte Minkner – Natalija Miodragovic – Parviz Mir-Ali – Lydia Mokros – Joseph Möller – Gina Mönch – Michael Morris – Andrea Moseler – Theresa Muhl – Birgit Muhs – Aniruddha Mukherjee – Birgitta Müller – Franziska Müller – Peter Müller – Uwe Müller – Tim Münnich – Aylin Mutlu

N

Raphael Nagel – Nils Nahrwold – Stavros Nakos – Florian Nass – Svenja Mari Neeb – Jürgen Nemeth – Michael Neumann – Sascha Neumann – Anh Nguyen – Frank Nickerl – Conny Nientiet – Roger Nientiet – Clarissa Nießner – Birgit Nimtz – Angela Nitsch – Franziska Nori – Anthea Norman-Taylor – Christina Novak – Sebastian Nüßlein

O

Thomas Obmann – Sae-Zin Oh – Patrick Olivier – Osama Opre – Rosina Orendi – Anja Ott – Marie-Luise Ott – Anna-Kerstin Otto – Cornelius Otto

P

Stefan Pach – Kristina Pahl – Sabine Pahl – Nini Parlagaschwili – Sabina Pech – Egzon Peci – Sebastian Pein – Ralf Penkert – Clara Pesch – Martin Pesch – Kristine Petersdorf – Janine Petry – Johannes Petry – Rebecca Pfau – Benjamin Pfister – Tobias Pflug – Daniel Pistorius – Lena Catharina Pohl – Falk Prahl – Andrea Prazak – Andrea Preiss – Julian Preissinger – Beate Priolo – Maximilian Püchert

Q

Sebastian Quader

R

Sabine Raab – Claudia Radinger – Martina Rahner – Dirk Räppold – Dietmar Rauh – Parmida Razavi – Simone Rduch – Konrad Regel – Hajo Rehm – Jeanne Rehnig – Sabine Reibolt – Ines Reichle – Jürgen Reineke – Oliver Reitinger – Matthias Reitz – Isa Rekkab – Ronnie Renfro – Sabrina Renzel – Eva-Maria Reuß – Lorenzo Ricco – Claudia Riedl – Simone Rigamonti – Andreas Ritter – Romana Rokvić – Daniela Römgens – Petra Romini – Sarah Roßbach – Saschka Rosemann – Andreas Roos – Roberto Rossi – Claudine Roullet – Michel Rubner – Wolfgang Rühl – Andrea Ruhland – Jan-Philipp Rumpold – John Russo

S

Karim Sabano – Ulrike Sakhibov – Kismet Salahor – Niklas Sanders – Ina Sauter – Patrick Sauter – Dominik Schäfer – Aline Schaefer – Conny Schanz – Karim Scharabi – Bianca Schaurer-Spieß – Nikola Scheibe – Johannes Scherg – Ellen Scheuer – Wilfried Schiefer – Julia Schilling – Matthias Schilder – Elena Schindler – Gabi Schirrmacher – Lea Schliebusch – Alexander Schmidt – Madleine Schmidt – Michael Schmidt – Michel Schmidt – Miko Schmidt – Rafael Schmidt – Uwe Schmidt – Jens Schmidt-Mohan – Kerstin Schmidt-Ott – Katja Schmitt – Mareike Schmitt – Nikolaus Schmitt – Jan Schmelter – Stefan Schmotz – Florian Schneemann – Sibylle Schneider – Tina Schneyer – Ralf Schnürer – Peter Scholl – Ursula Schöndeling – Georg Schönwandt – Rudolf Schönwandt – Dorothee van Schoor – Chris Schott – Franz Schöttner – Ralph Schreck – Anja Schriever – Hannah-Vera Schröder – Lisa Schroth – Saskia Schubert – Tom Schubert – Andreas Schuler – Jürgen Schulz-Anker – Michael Schulze – Thomas Schulze – Stefan Schulze-Hausmann – Andrea Schwarz – Nora Schwarz – Sascha Schweinsberger – Heiko Schweizer – Martin Schwember – Mirella Sciortino – Aisha Scott – Ricarda Seel – Diana Seidenberg – Alina Seipel – Florian Seliger – Markus Sellner – Patrick Seuffert – Gregor Siber – Nina Siber – Andreas Sieberg – Christoph Siegl – Andreas Siemer – Anke Sierian – Anna Sieveking – Phillip Solga – Rita Somfalvy – Torsten Sorge – Eva Spangler – Willi Steinberg – Simon Steinbrecher – Marie Steinbrügge – Alexandra Steinert – Katharina Steinmeyer – Volker Stengele – Andreas Stephan – Christopher Stephan – Dominik Streib – Caroline Ströhle – Georg Stummer – Florian Stumpe – Oliver Stumpf – Bernd Stutter – David Suchy – Nils Suhr – Elena Sytko – Isabella Sztulman

T

Annette Täch – Ricardo Teixeira – Magdalena Teuber – K.P. Texter – Jochen Thamm – Renate Thomas – Madien Thorwarth – Melanie Thride – Agapi Tiffert – Cornelia Tödt – Damir Tomas – Irene Trampler – Han Tran – Carsten Trojan – Linda Tröppner – Thomas Tscherter – Philipp Tschida – Teresa Turber – Iris Türke – Julia Tyrakowska

U

Andreas Uhde – Marion Uhl – Jonathan Uhlemann – Frank Umland – Hansjörg Unrath – André Urban – Jennifer Ussner

V

Marc van der Meer – Xabela Vargas – Theresa Marie Victor – Leonardo Villani – Tobias Vogt – Kristina Voll – Claudia von der Bey – Nikolaus von Hanstein – Harriet von Plettenberg

W

Armin Waehlert – Kerstin Wagner – Marco Wagner – Stefan Wagner – Uwe Wagner – Meret Walter – Uli Walter – Daniela Walz – Oliver Wanke – Charlotte Wassermann – Jan Weber – Caroline Wegener – Annette Weidl – Stefan Weil – Vincent Weil – Kathleen Weinhold – Peter Weiss – Markus Weisbeck – Sophie Werner – Gerhard Westerath – Florian Wey-Lübeck – Bartek Wieczorek – Melina Wiedera – Christian Wierz – Dan Winge – Emma Wirth – Kathleen Wittkopp – Sandra Wittwer – Alexander Wladarsch – Sören Woelke – Monika Wolf – Anne Wolkodaw – Patrick Woodroffe – Patricia Wottrich – Benjamin Würkner – Sina Wüst

Y

Xianhua Yao

Z

Uli Zahn – Alexandra Zaree Parsi – Jürgen Zeller – Elisabeth Jelena Zickner – Raimund Ziemer – Dieter Ziermeier – Susanne Zilly – Claudia Zimmermann – Susanne Zimmermann

PROJECT INDEX

CHAPTER 1
THRESHOLDS
Interfaces as Encounters

Name of project: MOMEM
Location: Museum of Modern Electronic Music, Frankfurt am Main
Year: 2022
Pages: 20-31
Client: Friends of MOMEM e.V., Frankfurt am Main
Credits: concept and museum design, planning and realisation: Atelier Markgraph GmbH, Frankfurt am Main
Exhibition design: 'It's simple to tell what saved us from hell' Tobias Rehberger Studios, Street art MOMEM plaza: Philipp Alexander Schäfer, Frankfurt am Main
Digital Partner: Cosalux GmbH, Offenbach am Main
Lighting design: Stefan Zimmermann Light Solutions, Oberursel

Name of project: Ship of Ideas
Location: Riverbank Festival 2003, Frankfurt am Main
Year: 2003
Pages: 22, 29
Client: Tourismus+Congress GmbH, Frankfurt am Main
Credits: concept, design, planning and realisation: Atelier Markgraph GmbH, Frankfurt am Main
Software: MESO Digital Interiors GmbH, Frankfurt am Main
Event technology/lighting technology: PROCON Event Engineering GmbH, Frankfurt am Main
Video technology: XL-Video GmbH, Oststeinbek
Screen: Gerriets GmbH, Umkirch; PROCÉDÉS CHÉNEL INTERNATIONAL, Vanves, France
Ship owner: Karl Strack, Mainz

Name of project: ART|WHEEL
Location: Riverbank Festival 2005, Frankfurt am Main
Year: 2005
Pages: 22, 29
Client: Tourismus+Congress GmbH, Frankfurt am Main
Credits: concept, design, planning and realisation: Atelier Markgraph GmbH, Frankfurt am Main
Lighting technology: PROCON Event Engineering GmbH, Frankfurt am Main
Projection technique: XL-Video GmbH, Oststeinbek
Lighting design: Dietrich Körner, Cologne
Control technology: MESO Digital Interiors GmbH, Frankfurt am Main

Name of project: Ötztal 360
Location: Tourist Information Centre, Sölden, Austria
Year: 2021
Pages: 32-39
Client: Ötztal Tourismus, Sölden, Austria
Credits: concept and creation interaction software: Atelier Markgraph GmbH, Frankfurt am Main in cooperation with wirmachenbunt GmbH & Co. KG, Hamburg; Ötztal Tourismus, Sölden, Austria (footage)
Architects of building: Obermoser + Partner, Innsbruck
Construction exhibit: EM-Technik GmbH, Zirl, Austria
Lichting design: Miko Schmidt Four to One Lighting Design, Bonn

Name of project: Alles Neu! – 100 Years of Typography and New Graphics in Frankfurt am Main
Location: Museum Angewandte Kunst, Frankfurt am Main
Year: 2016
Pages: 40-43
Client: Museum für Angewandte Kunst, Frankfurt am Main
Credits: exhibition design: Atelier Markgraph GmbH, Frankfurt am Main
Curator: Klaus Klemp, Friedrich Friedl, Peter Zizka, Matthias Wagner K
Organisation and coordination assistance: Monika Wagener
Exhibition management: David Beikirch
Consultancy: Stefan Beuttler
Exhibition layout: Nadine Auth, Johannes Grehl, Florian Hundt, Peter Otterbein, Katrin Trost
Objects and wall labeling: Martincolor GmbH & Co. KG, Frankfurt am Main; Drechsler Medien, Geithain
Conservators: Sabine Maurischat, Christian Dressen
Museum technology: Marcel Bode, Tilo Kohl

Name of project: Beyond the Car – Mercedes-Benz at the Internationale Automobil-Ausstellung 2019
Location: Mercedes-Benz at the Internationale Automobil-Ausstellung 2019, Frankfurt am Main
Year: 2019
Pages: 44-51
Client: Daimler AG, Stuttgart
Credits: architecture and overall planning: jangled nerves GmbH, Stuttgart
me Convention: LIGANOVA GmbH, Stuttgart
Communication and staging: Atelier Markgraph GmbH, Frankfurt am Main
Lighting design and planning: TLD Planungsgruppe GmbH, Esslingen

Name of project: SkyArena – Overture of the 2006 World Cup in Frankfurt
Location: Frankfurt am Main
Year: 2006
Pages: 47, 52-57
Client: Tourismus+Congress GmbH, Frankfurt am Main
Credits: concept, design, planning and realisation: Atelier Markgraph GmbH, Frankfurt am Main
Graphic production: zinnecker-printstudio GmbH, Friedrichsdorf
Lighting design: Planquadrat GmbH, Kronberg
Construction: Nüssli GmbH, Hüttwilen
Façade coating: Marburger Dienstleistungen/ Special Climbing Unit, Marburg
Music composition: Parviz Mir-Ali
Music production: Meirelli O.S.T. GmbH, Frankfurt am Main

CHAPTER 2
SPECTRES
Fleeting, Poetic Encounters

Name of project: The New Potential of the IAA MOBILITY 2021
Location: Mercedes-Benz at the Internationale Automobil-Ausstellung MOBILITY 2021, Munich
Year: 2021
Pages: 62-73
Client: Mercedes-Benz AG, Stuttgart
Credits: architecture and overall planning: jangled nerves GmbH, Stuttgart
Communication and overall production: Atelier Markgraph GmbH, Frankfurt am Main
Lighting design and planning: TLD Planungsgruppe GmbH, Esslingen
Artwork: *Earthtime 1.26 Munich*, Janet Echelman

Name of project: Revenge. History and Fantasy
Location: Jüdisches Museum Frankfurt, Frankfurt am Main
Year: 2022
Pages: 74-82
Client: Jüdisches Museum Frankfurt, Frankfurt am Main
Credits: exhibition design: Atelier Markgraph GmbH, Frankfurt am Main
Lighting design: Stephan Zimmermann Lightsolutions, Oberursel
Media technology: Satis&Fy AG, Karben
Exhibition construction and graphic production: Messegrafik & Messebau Schreiber e.K., Schmitten
Installation: Victoria Hanna in cooperation with Atelier Markgraph GmbH, Frankfurt am Main
Three-channel video installation: Daniel Laufer

Name of project: Sound of Squares – Mannheim's 400th Anniversary
Location: Mannheim, Berlin, Cologne, Munich
Year: 2007
Pages: 82-91
Client: Stadtmarketing Mannheim GmbH, Mannheim
Credits: concept, design, planning and realisation: Atelier Markgraph GmbH, Frankfurt am Main
Software development and programming "Klanglabor": MESO Digital Interiors GmbH, Frankfurt am Main
Music "Pulse of the City": Chris Oz, Mannheim

Name of project: LAB.01 – Interfaces. Interaction. Exhibition & Tour EXPO 2000
Location Berlin, Cologne, Hamburg, Warsaw, Poland; Dresden, Barcelona, Spain; Hanover
Year: 1999-2000
Pages: 85
Client: DaimlerChrysler AG, Stuttgart
Credits: concept, design, planning and realisation: Atelier Markgraph GmbH, Frankfurt am Main
Construction: Ernst F. Ambrosius & Sohn GmbH, Frankfurt am Main
Sound design: Roger Cobernus, Can Oral
Photography/key visuals: Sandra Mann, Daniel Wöller, wemove digital solution GmbH, Frankfurt am Main, ART+COM Studio GmbH, Berlin
Interactive hands-on exhibits: unit-design GmbH, Frankfurt am Main in cooperation with Atelier Markgraph GmbH, Frankfurt am Main

Name of project: House of Play – An Interactive Pop-Up Parcours for Magnum
Location: Berlin and Vienna, Austria
Year: 2019
Pages: 90-97
Client: Unilever DACH, Hamburg
Credits: idea and communication concept: COR Berlin Kommunikation GmbH, Berlin
Design, scenography and implementation: Atelier Markgraph GmbH, Frankfurt am Main

CHAPTER 3
PATTERNS
(Subject-in-the) Field Encounters

Name of project: ZDF Sport – Modular TV Set Design
Location: ZDF Zweites Deutsches Fernsehen, Mainz
Year: 2017
Pages: 102-111
Client: ZDF Zweites Deutsches Fernsehen, Mainz
Credits: concept, design, planning and realisation: Atelier Markgraph GmbH, Frankfurt am Main
Set construction: Studio Hamburg Atelierbetriebs GmbH, Hamburg
On Air Design: Alpenblick GmbH, Munich

Name of project: MINISCHIRN – Art Education as an Adventure Parcours
Location: SCHIRN KUNSTHALLE FRANKFURT, Frankfurt am Main
Year: 2014
Pages: 109,112-119
Client: SCHIRN KUNSTHALLE FRANKFURT, Frankfurt am Main
Credits: concept, design, planning and realisation: Atelier Markgraph GmbH, Frankfurt am Main
Graphic design: christian bitenc graphic design & illustration, Frankfurt am Main
Exhibit construction and media: Expotec Pro GmbH, Mainz
Lighting design: Stephan Zimmermann Lightsolutions, Oberursel
Exhibition construction: ET GLOBAL GmbH, Frankfurt am Main

Name of project: Finanz Informatik Convention – Swarm Intelligence in Action

cation: Frankfurt am Main
ar: 2018
ges: 120-127
ent: Finanz Informatik GmbH
Co. KG, Münster
edits: concept, design, planning and
alisation: Atelier Markgraph GmbH,
ankfurt am Main
ommunication and graphic design:
ierarbeit GmbH, Bielefeld
otion Design: APPARAT, Hamburg
hibition construction: Display International
hwendinger GmbH & Co. KG, Würselen
edia technology: AV-X GmbH, Oststeinbek
ghting, rig, sound: BELA GmbH, Neufahrn

ame of project: Constellations –
Celebration for the New Old Town of
ankfurt
cation: Frankfurt am Main
ar: 2018
ges: 128-136
ient: Tourismus+Congress GmbH,
ankfurt am Main
edits: concept, design, planning and
alisation: Atelier Markgraph GmbH,
ankfurt am Main
anning and realisation partners: Bright!
tudios, Maintal; SKYMAGIC, Singapore,
hina
ound design: Hoerfeld, Offenbach am Main

ame of project: EQ Teaser – Interactive
isual Interface
ocation: Mondial Paris Motor Show, Paris;
ternationale Automobil-Ausstellung,
rankfurt am Main; Internationale Automobil-
usstellung MOBILITY, Munich; at the
oadshow in Festival Format: Rome, Italy;
erlin, Germany; Bern, Switzerland
ear: continuous
ages: 136-143
lient: Mercedes-Benz AG, Stuttgart
redits: concept, design, planning and
ealisation: Atelier Markgraph GmbH,
rankfurt am Main
onstruction: Das Schauwerk GmbH,
reiberg am Neckar
oftware: wirmachenbunt
mbH & Co. KG, Hamburg

ame of project: MYTHOS 6 – A Look
nto the Future on the Way to an Emissions-
ree Mobility
ocation: Mercedes-Benz Museum
mbH, Stuttgart
ear: 2011
ages: 140-141
lient: Mercedes-Benz Museum GmbH,
tuttgart
redits: concept, design, planning and
ealisation: Atelier Markgraph GmbH,
rankfurt am Main
ound design: Klangerfinder GmbH
Co KG, Stuttgart
nitial scenography of the entire museum:
G Merz Architekten/Museumsgestalter,
tuttgart/Berlin
rchitects of building: UNStudio, Amsterdam

CHAPTER 4
CONVIVIALITIES
Friendly Encounters

ame of project: Margarete Restaurant
ocation: Frankfurt am Main
Year: 2012
Pages: 148-155
Client: Gastronomie Betriebsgesellschaft
Schöbel & Horn mbH
Credits: concept, naming, interior design:
Atelier Markgraph GmbH, Frankfurt am Main
Vintage furniture: Frank Landau, Frankfurt
am Main
Lighting design: Serien Raumleuchten
GmbH, Rodgau
Brand identity: Atelier Populaire,
Frankfurt am Main

Name of project: Networking Toolkit –
Wearable Tool for Communication and
Interactive User Experiences
Location: Amsterdam, Netherlands
Year: 2019
Pages: 153, 156-159
Client: Daimler AG, Stuttgart
Credits: concept, design, planning and
realisation: Atelier Markgraph GmbH,
Frankfurt am Main

Name of project: Atelier Markgraph Office –
New Work Concept – Atelier 2.0
Location: Atelier Markgraph GmbH,
Frankfurt am Main
Year: 2023
Pages: 159-171
Credits: concept, design, planning and
realisation: Atelier Markgraph GmbH,
Frankfurt am Main
Idea workshop and masterplanning:
Vitra Workplace Consultants, Weil
am Rhein

Name of project: DFB-Campus –
Brand Space and Guidance System
Location: Frankfurt am Main
Year: 2020-2023
Pages: 172-183
Client: DFB GmbH & Co. KG, Frankfurt
am Main
Credits: concept, design, planning and
realisation: Atelier Markgraph GmbH,
Frankfurt am Main
Signage: Atelier Markgraph GmbH,
Frankfurt am Main
Architecture: kadawittfeldarchitektur,
Aachen
Exhibition construction: Metron Eging
GmbH, Eging am See
Graphic production: Eicher Werkstätten
GmbH & Co. KG, Kernen im Remstal; Leko
Grafik Produktion, Schorndorf; Schreiner
Coburg GmbH, Coburg; Stadelmayer
Werbung GmbH, Kirchheim unter Teck

CHAPTER 5
MIGRATIONS
Mobile Encounters

Name of project: AM CI Relaunch –
Voice-Driven, Reactive Brand Identity
Location: Frankfurt am Main
Year: 2017
Pages: 188-195
Credits: brand identity, custom typeface,
typographic system: SchultzSchultz GmbH,
Frankfurt am Main

Name of project: Athens – Triumph of Imagery
Location: Liebieghaus Skulturensammlung,
Frankfurt am Main
Year: 2016
Pages: 196-208
Client: Städel Museum/Städelsches
Kunstinstitut, Frankfurt am Main
Credits: concept, design, planning and
realisation: Atelier Markgraph GmbH,
Frankfurt am Main

Name of project: Roadshow in Festival
Format – E-Mobility Experienced First-Hand
Location: Rome, Italy; Berlin, Germany; Bern,
Switzerland; Paris, France
Year: continuous
Pages: 208-217
Client: Daimler AG, Stuttgart
Credits: project coordination, lectures
& talks, operations: LIGANOVA GmbH,
Stuttgart
Concept, design, planning and realisation:
Atelier Markgraph GmbH, Frankfurt am Main

Name of project: Union Investment –
Financial Investment Traveling Exhibition
Location: Frankfurt am Main
Year: 2018
Pages: 215,218-225
Client: Union Investment Privatfonds
GmbH, Frankfurt am Main
Credits: concept, design, planning and
realisation: Atelier Markgraph GmbH,
Frankfurt am Main
Programming: MESO Digital Services
GmbH, Frankfurt am Main
Furniture and exhibit construction:
MKT AG, Olching

Name of project: Strategic and Spatial
Conceptualisation of the Mercedes-Benz
Brand
Year: continuous
Pages: 225-231
Client: Mercedes-Benz AG, Stuttgart
Credits: concept, design, planning and
realisation: Atelier Markgraph GmbH,
Frankfurt am Main

CHAPTER 6
PLASTICITIES
Tectonic Encounters

Name of project: What's Your Utopia? –
Trend Space at the Heimtextil
Location: Frankfurt am Main
Year: 2019
Pages: 236-344
Client: Messe Frankfurt Exhibition GmbH,
Frankfurt am Main
Credits: concept, design, planning and
realisation: Atelier Markgraph GmbH,
Frankfurt am Main
Trend council: Franklin Till Studio, London,
United Kingdom; SPOT Trends & Business
ApS, Silkeborg, Denmark; Stijlinstituut
Amsterdam, Amsterdam, Netherlands
Stand construction: Messe Frankfurt
Exhibition, Frankfurt am Main

Name of project: Built Excellence as a
Statement of Corporate Architecture –
Investa at the Expo Real in Munich
Location: Munich
Year: 2017
Pages: 244-249, 251
Client: Investa Holding GmbH, Eschborn
Credits: concept, design, planning and
realisation: Atelier Markgraph GmbH,
Frankfurt am Main
Exhibition construction: mac. brand spaces
GmbH, Langenlonsheim
Lighting design: BELA GmbH, Neufarn

Name of project: Cultural Landscapes –
Pitch Project for the Milan World Expo 2015
Year: 2013
Pages: 250-255, 257
Client: Bundesministerium für Wirtschaft/
Messe Frankfurt Exhibition GmbH,
Frankfurt am Main
Credits: bidding consortium: Atelier
Markgraph GmbH, Frankfurt am Main; Werner
Sobek AG, Stuttgart
Overall concept, architecture:
haascookzemmrich STUDIO2050, Stuttgart
Overall concept, exhibition and experience:
Atelier Markgraph GmbH, Frankfurt am Main
Media concept main act: ART+COM Studios
Engineering and sustainability: Werner
Sobek AG, Stuttgart; Werner Sobek Green
Technologies GmbH, Stuttgart
Landscape architecture: Bureau Baubotanik,
Stuttgart
People Flow Planning: Robert LaMarre,
Lord Cultural Resources

Name of project: Moments of Savour –
WMF at the Ambiente
Location: Frankfurt am Main
Year: 2015
Pages: 256-261, 263
Client: WMF Group GmbH, Geislingen/Steige
Credits: concept, design, planning and
realisation: Atelier Markgraph GmbH,
Frankfurt am Main
Graphic, lighting, media, trade fair
construction: Raumtechnik Messebau & Event
Services GmbH, Ostfildern

Name of project: Beyond the Car –
Mercedes-Benz Experience at the
Internationale Automobil-Ausstellung 2019
Location: Frankfurt am Main
Year: 2019
Pages: 262-271
Client: Client: Daimler AG, Stuttgart
Credits: architecture and overall planning:
jangled nerves GmbH, Stuttgart
me Convention: LIGANOVA GmbH, Stuttgart
Communication and staging: Atelier
Markgraph GmbH, Frankfurt am Main
Lighting design and planning: TLD
Planungsgruppe GmbH, Esslingen

CHAPTER 7
METABOLISMS
Processes as Encounters

Name of project: A Declaration of Love
for Organic Food – A Museum in the
Rapunzel World
Location: Legau
Year: 2022
Pages: 276-283
Client: Rapunzel Naturkost GmbH, Legau
Credits: architecture visitor centre:
haascookzemmrich STUDIO2050,
Stuttgart
Museum concept, design, planning, realisation:
Atelier Markgraph GmbH, Frankfurt am Main
Exhibition construction: Möslang Sitzmöbel
e. K., Leutkirch
Tree sculpture: Allgäugast GmbH
Marble run: Rotes Pferd GmbH, Berlin
Decorations, exhibit construction:

Das Schauwerk GmbH & Co KG, Freiberg am Neckar
Lighting design: BELZER HOLMES und PARTNER LICHT-DESIGN, Stuttgart
Graphic production: Eicher Werkstätten GmbH & Co. KG, Kernen im Remstal
Conception and creation of interactive software: Atelier Markgraph GmbH, Frankfurt am Main in cooperation with wirmachenbunt GmbH & Co. KG, Hamburg

Name of project: Garden Delight – Historisches Museum Frankfurt am Main
Location: Frankfurt am Main
Year: 2021
Pages: 279, 284-288
Client: Historisches Museum Frankfurt, Frankfurt am Main
Credits: creative direction, exhibition design, graphic design, illustrations and animations: Atelier Markgraph GmbH, Frankfurt am Main
Exhibition graphics, stand construction: Messegrafik & Messebau Schreiber e.K., Schmitten
Graphic production and assembly: Plot.com GmbH, Erlensee
Lighting design: Stephan Zimmermann Lightsolutions, Oberursel
Media technology: AV Kommunikationstechnik GmbH, Eichen

Name of project: Environment, Climate & You – Historisches Museum Frankfurt am Main
Location: Frankfurt am Main
Year: 2021
Pages: 279, 285, 289
Client: Junges Museum, Frankfurt am Main
Credits: creative direction, exhibition design, graphic design, illustrations and animations: Atelier Markgraph GmbH, Frankfurt am Main
Exhibition construction: Woodworks, Frankfurt am Main
Graphic production: Plot.com GmbH, Erlensee

Name of project: Energy Transitions – Viessmann at the ISH Frankfurt 2023
Location: Frankfurt am Main
Year: 2023
Pages: 290-297
Client: Viessmann Climate Solutions SE, Allendorf
Credits: overall concept, design and dramaturgy of the production: Atelier Markgraph GmbH, Frankfurt am Main
Design, production, programming and realisation of the staging: NSYNK Gesellschaft für Kunst und Technik mbH, Frankfurt am Main
Motion design, key visuals: 27 Kilometer Entertainment GmbH, Hamburg
Sound concept and production: Sound Innovation Lab, Berlin

Name of project: Partnership Lane – Viessmann at the ISH Frankfurt 2019
Location: Frankfurt am Main
Year: 2019
Pages: 285, 290-297
Client: Viessmann GmbH & Co KG, Allendorf (Eder)
Credits: concept, planning, design and realisation: Atelier Markgraph GmbH, Frankfurt am Main
AR presentation concept, realtime media design, realisation: NSYNK Gesellschaft für Kunst und Technik mbH, Frankfurt am Main
Media design: UNFOLD Design & Motion Studio, Hamburg
AV media and light: AV-X, Oststeinbek; Bela, Neufahrn bei Freising
Graphic production: catdesign, Kleve
Sound design: kling klang klong, Berlin
Exhibition construction: Metron Vilshofen GmbH Vilshofen an der Donau

Name of project: Central Forum – Viessmann at the ISH Frankfurt 2017
Location: Frankfurt am Main
Year: 2017
Pages: 285, 290-297
Client: Viessmann GmbH & Co KG, Allendorf (Eder)
Credits: concept, design and implementation: Atelier Markgraph GmbH, Frankfurt am Main
Media feeds: NSYNK Gesellschaft für Kunst und Technik mbH, Frankfurt am Main
Booth construction: mac. brand spaces GmbH, Langenlonsheim
Decoration: Das Schauwerk GmbH & Co KG, Freiberg am Neckar
Digital and post production: ACHT FRANKFURT, Frankfurt am Main

Name of project: Energy Towers – Viessmann at the ISH Frankfurt 2015
Location: Frankfurt am Main
Year: 2015
Pages: 285, 290-297
Client: Viessmann GmbH & Co KG, Allendorf (Eder)
Credits: concept, design and realisation: Atelier Markgraph GmbH, Frankfurt am Main
Media production: NSYNK Gesellschaft für Kunst und Technik mbH, Frankfurt am Main
Construction: mac. brand spaces GmbH, Langenlonsheim
Sound: kling klang klong GmbH & Co. KG, Berlin
Media: Neumann&Müller GmbH & Co. KG, Essligen am Neckar
Graphic design: apfel,hübsch design studio, Berlin
Graphic production: Leko Grafik Produktion, Schorndorf

Name of project: Lane of Innovation – Viessmann at the ISH Frankfurt 2013
Location: Frankfurt am Main
Year: 2013
Pages: 285, 290-297
Client: Viessmann GmbH & Co KG, Allendorf (Eder)
Credits: concept, design and realisation: Atelier Markgraph GmbH, Frankfurt am Main
Graphic: Atelier Markgraph GmbH, Frankfurt am Main
Graphic production: Leko Grafik Produktion, Schorndorf
Media design: Atelier Markgraph, Frankfurt am Main; XL-Video GmbH, Oststeinbek and ICT AG, Kohlberg
Lighting design: Rock-Service Deutschland, Salzgitter

Name of project: Medial Dioramas – Viessmann at the ISH Frankfurt 2011
Location: Frankfurt am Main
Year: 2011
Pages: 285, 290-297
Client: Viessmann GmbH & Co KG, Allendorf (Eder)
Credits: concept, design and realisation: Atelier Markgraph GmbH, Frankfurt am Main
Lighting design: PROCON Event Engineering, Berlin Booth construction: mac messe- und ausstellungscenter Service GmbH, Langenlonsheim

Name of project: Hanging Cities – Viessmann at the ISH Frankfurt 2009
Location: Frankfurt am Main
Year: 2009
Pages: 285, 290-297
Client: Viessmann GmbH & Co KG, Allendorf (Eder)
Credits: concept, design and realisation: Atelier Markgraph GmbH, Frankfurt am Main
Booth construction: mac. brand spaces GmbH, Langenlonsheim
Light technology: PROCON Event Engineering GmbH, Hamburg
Media technology: XL-Video GmbH, München
Graphic production: Stadelmayer Werbung GmbH, Kirchheim unter Teck
Audio engineering: PROCON Event Engineering GmbH, Frankfurt am Main
Motion graphics: Grosse 8 GmbH & Co. KG, Köln
Lighting design: SfS Project, Aschaffenburg
Music/ambient sound: Floridan Studios GmbH, Stuttgart

Name of project: Energy Shelf – Viessmann at the ISH Frankfurt 2007
Location: Frankfurt am Main
Year: 2007
Pages: 285, 290-297
Client: Viessmann GmbH & Co KG, Allendorf (Eder)
Credits: concept, design and realisation: Atelier Markgraph GmbH, Frankfurt am Main
Booth construction: mac. brand spaces GmbH, Langenlonsheim
Graphic production: zinnecker-printstudio GmbH, Friedrichsdorf
Staging construction: Kubix GmbH, Berlin
Lighting design: Andreas Fuchs Lichtdesign, Berlin; PROCON Event Engineering GmbH, Berlin
Motion graphics: Grosse 8 GmbH & Co. KG, Köln

Name of project: Viega Sphere – Multimedia Knowledge Transfer in 360°-Degree Space
Location: Ennest
Year: 2013
Pages: 290, 298-307
Client: Viega GmbH & Co. KG, Attendorn
Credits: brand consultancy: Kai Röffen, think, Düsseldorf; Jasna Bilen, BilenBuidingBrands, Hamburg
Concept, design, planning, realisation, creative supervision of the entire project, general contractor for communication measures: Atelier Markgraph GmbH, Frankfurt am Main
Visualisation: MZ motion design GmbH, Stuttgart
Sound design: Klangerfinder GmbH & Co KG, Stuttgart
Video, audio and lighting technology Viega Sphere: Bewunder GmbH, Berlin
Film production: Monomango GmbH, Berlin
Directed by: Shan Blume, Berlin

Name of project: A Dialogue Platform – Mercedes-Benz at the Internationale Automobil-Ausstellung 2017
Location: Frankfurt am Main
Year: 2017
Pages: 299, 308-313
Client: Daimler AG, Stuttgart
Credits: architecture and overall planning: jangled nerves GmbH, Stuttgart
me Convention: LIGANOVA GmbH, Stuttgart
Communication: Atelier Markgraph GmbH, Frankfurt am Main
Lighting design and planning: TLD Planungsgruppe GmbH, Esslingen

IMAGE CREDITS

PHOTOGRAPHY

ristof Lemp, Darmstadt
ages: 21, 24-25, 26-27, 28, 30-31, 41,
2-43, 44-45, 50, 51, 67, 68-69, 74, 76-77,
3, 79, 80-81, 90, 92-93, 95, 96-97, 112-
13, 115, 118-119, 120-121, 122, 124,
25, 126, 127, 130-131, 132, 133, 134-
35, 137, 139, 142, 163, 164, 168-169,
72, 174, 175, 176-177, 181, 182-183,
88-189, 193, 194, 196-197, 198, 200,
01, 202-203, 204-205, 206-207, 212,
13, 214, 216-217, 219, 220-221, 222,
23, 236, 238-239, 241, 242, 243, 256,
58-259, 261, 264-265, 268, 269, 270,
84, 286-287, 288, 289, 292-293, 296-
97, 298, 300, 301, 302-303, 306-307,
09, 312-313, backsticker on cover

xl Jansen, Berlin
age: 9

hilip Koespell, Berlin
age: 24

adine Fraczkowski, Berlin
age: 31

ndreas Keller, Altdorf
ages: 32-33, 36-37, 38-39, 48-49,
0-71, 72-73, 142, 143, 230-231,
62, 266-267, 269, backsticker on cover

Verner Elmer, Längenfeld
ages: 38-39

pa Picture-Alliance GmbH
age: 53

alph Larmann, Hadamar
ages: 54-55, 56-57, 84, 88-89, 129,
34-135, 296-297

ina Siber, Frankfurt am Main
ages: 9, 56-57, 160-161

opterbrothers, Stuttgart
angled nerves, Stuttgart
ages: 64-65

icole Simon, Vierheim
ages: 83, 88-89

as aktuelle sportstudio
ZDF/Ralph Orlowski
ages: 108 (Sven Voss standing in the
niddle), 110-111

Schirn Kunsthalle Frankfurt am Main,
hoto: Norbert Miguletz, Frankfurt am Main
ages: 118-119

rank Baudy, Mühlheim an der Ruhr
ages: 134-135

rigida Gonzales, Stuttgart
ages: 140-141

Peter Unsinn, Frankfurt am Main
pages: 149, 151, 154, 155

wirestock on Freepik
page: 260

SCHMOTT Studios, Frankfurt am Main
pages: 164, 165, 166-167, 168-169

Chris Gerster for Atelier Markgraph,
Frankfurt am Main
pages: 209, 216-217, 277, 278, 280-281,
282-283

Mercedes-Benz AG, Stuttgart
page: 229

Mercedes-Benz AG, China
pages: 230-231

Pixabay
pages: 252-253

Jörg Hempel Photodesign, Aachen
pages: 291, 296-297

Dieter Schwer, Frankfurt am Main
pages: 296-297

Lars Uwe Bleher for Atelier Markgraph,
Frankfurt am Main
pages: 34, 106-107, 227, 297

Stefan Weil for Atelier Markgraph,
Frankfurt am Main
pages: 150, 152, 155, backsticker on cover

Atelier Markgraph, Frankfurt am Main
page: backsticker on cover

VISUALISATIONS

Atelier Markgraph, Frankfurt am Main
pages: 30, 118, 156, 192, 210-211, 216,
260, 270, 312-313

Monomango GmbH, Berlin for Atelier
Markgraph, Frankfurt am Main
pages: 46, 304-305

Hajo Rehm for Atelier Markgraph, Frankfurt
am Main
page: 62

Sebastian Nüßlein for Atelier Markgraph,
Frankfurt am Main
pages: 102-103, 106-107

Julian Lianarachchi for Atelier Markgraph,
Frankfurt am Main
page: 230

Michel Dorus for Atelier Markgraph,
Frankfurt am Main
pages: 170-171

Schulzschulz GmbH, Frankfurt am Main
page: 191

Karim Sabano for Atelier Markgraph,
Frankfurt am Main
page: 229

Werner Sobek Green Technologies GmbH,
Stuttgart
page: 250

haascookzemmrich STUDIO2050, Stuttgart
with MISS3 s.r.o., Brno
pages: 250, 252-253, 254-255

Bureau Baubotanik, Stuttgart
pages: 252-253

DRAWINGS

Lars Uwe Bleher for Atelier Markgraph,
Frankfurt am Main
pages: 18-19, 34, 60-61, 88, 100-101,
146-147, 186-187, 234-235, 274-275

Bartek Wieczorek for Atelier Markgraph,
Frankfurt am Main
pages: 46, 67, 70-71,

Atelier Markgraph, Frankfurt am Main
pages: 56, 191

Stefan Pach for Atelier Markgraph,
Frankfurt am Main
pages: 105, 278

Martin Schwember for Atelier Markgraph,
Frankfurt am Main
page: 122

Christoph Geiger for Atelier Markgraph,
Frankfurt am Main
page: 226

Karim Sabano for Atelier Markgraph,
Frankfurt am Main
pages: 230-231

Mercedes-Benz AG, Stuttgart
pages: 230-231

Sarah Klöpfer for Atelier Markgraph,
Frankfurt am Main
pages: 294-295

ARCHIVAL MATERIALS

Atelier Markgraph, Frankfurt am Main
poster design
page: 31

Atelier Markgraph, Frankfurt am Main
pages: 116-117

Uwe Schmidt, Frankfurt am Main
page: 231

All photographs, visualisations, drawings and archival material shown in this book are listed with page numbers and their owners. Every effort has been made to identify the copyright holders. Errors or omissions will be corrected in subsequent editions. The naming of copyright is based on the information and research available at the time of publication. It is not the intention of the authors or the publisher to make an incorrect attribution.

COLOPHON

ENCOUNTERS BY DESIGN
Strategies for Spatial Stories

Publisher
FRAME

Managing Editor
François-Luc Giraldeau

Editor
Noor Al Qayem

Texts
Erika Brandl Mouton

With Introduction by François-Luc Giraldeau and Noor Al Qayem

Graphic Design
Barbara Iwanicka

Printing
IPP Printers

Lithography
Design & Prepress Studio, Amsterdam

TRADE DISTRIBUTION USA AND CANADA
ACC Art Books
6 West 18th Street, Suite 4BNYC, NY 10011E
ussales@accartbooks.com
T +1 212 645 1111
F +1 716 242 4811
Books are billed and shipped by
The National Book Network

TRADE DISTRIBUTION BENELUX
Frame Publishers
Zeeburgerkade 1198
1019 VK Amsterdam
the Netherlands
distribution@frameweb.com
frameweb.com

TRADE DISTRIBUTION REST OF WORLD
Thames & Hudson Ltd
181A High Holborn London WC1V 7QX
United Kingdom
T +44 20 7845 5000
F +44 20 7845 5050

ISBN: 978-94-92311-59-7

The Koninklijke Bibliotheek lists this publication in the Nederlandse Bibliografie: detailed bibliographic information is available on the internet at http://picarta.pica.nl

Printed on acid-free paper produced from chlorine-free pulp. TCF ∞

Printed in Poland

987654321